THE TELEVISION SERIES

Alan Clarke

Manchester University Press

THE
TELEVISION
SERIES

series editors

SARAH CARDWELL
JONATHAN BIGNELL

already published

Terry Nation JONATHAN BIGNELL AND ANDREW O'DAY
Andrew Davis SARAH CARDWELL
Jimmy Perry and David Croft SIMON MORGAN-RUSSELL

DAVE ROLINSON

Alan Clarke

Manchester University Press

MANCHESTER AND NEW YORK

distributed exclusively in the USA by Palgrave

Published by Manchester University Press
Oxford Road, Manchester M13 9NR, UK
and Room 400, 175 Fifth Avenue, New York, NY 10010, USA
www.manchesteruniversitypress.co.uk

Distributed exclusively in the USA by
Palgrave, 175 Fifth Avenue, New York, NY 10010, USA

Distributed exclusively in Canada by
UBC Press, University of British Columbia, 2029 West Mall,
Vancouver, BC, Canada V6T 1Z2

British Library Cataloguing-in-Publication Data
A catalogue record for this book is available from the British Library

Library of Congress Cataloging-in-Publication Data applied for

ISBN 0 7190 6830 4 *hardback*
EAN 978 0 7190 6830 0

First published 2005

14 13 12 11 10 09 08 07 06 05   10 9 8 7 6 5 4 3 2 1

Typeset in Scala with Meta display
by Koinonia, Manchester
Printed in Great Britain
by Bell & Bain, Glasgow

FOR ME MAM

Contents

General editors' preface

Television is part of our everyday experience, and is one of the most significant aspects of our cultural lives today. Yet its practitioners and its artistic and cultural achievements remain relatively unacknowledged. The books in this series aim to remedy this by addressing the work of major television writers and creators. Each volume provides an authoritative and accessible guide to a particular practitioner's body of work, and assesses his or her contribution to television over the years. Many of the volumes draw on original sources, such as specially conducted interviews and archive material, and all of them list relevant bibliographic sources and further reading and viewing. The author of each book makes a case for the importance of the work considered therein, and the series includes books on neglected or overlooked practitioners alongside well-known ones.

In comparison with some related disciplines, Television Studies scholarship is still relatively young, and the series aims to contribute to establishing the subject as a vigorous and evolving field. This series provides resources for critical thinking about television. While maintaining a clear focus on the writers, on the creators and on the programmes themselves, the books in this series also take account of key critical concepts and theories in Television Studies. Each book is written from a particular critical or theoretical perspective, with reference to pertinent issues, and the approaches included in the series are varied and sometimes dissenting. Each author explicitly outlines the reasons for his or her particular focus, methodology or perspective. Readers are invited to think critically about the subject matter and approach covered in each book.

Although the series is addressed primarily to students and scholars of television, the books will also appeal to the many people who are interested in how television programmes have been commissioned, made and enjoyed. Since television has been so much a part of personal and public life in the twentieth and twenty-first centuries, we hope that the series will engage with, and sometimes challenge, a broad and diverse readership.

Sarah Cardwell
Jonathan Bignell

Acknowledgements

When I first discovered Clarke's work, I was a teenager growing up on a Hull council estate. When I finished this book, I was a university lecturer. So, I would like to thank first of all Neil Sinyard at the University of Hull. Had he not supported me when poverty threatened my original Ph.D. on Clarke, this book would never have been written. The support of Helen Baron was also crucial. Thanks to editors of fanzines who recognised my ability before I went anywhere near a university. For opening my eyes to the possibilities of television drama, and for my writing apprenticeship, respect is due to the erudite Colin Brockhurst, John Connors, Tim Worthington and many others.

I warmly thank Richard Kelly for his exhaustive interview efforts, which provided invaluable support for my research, particularly when finances restricted my own interviews and prevented me from giving in to my inner stalker. Some gaps remained, and for filling those I thank the following, for interviews or shared research: Nick Cooper, Simon Coward, Ann Edmonds at Granada Media, Arthur Ellis, Carla Field of the Questors Theatre in Ealing for archive material and an interview on 6 February 2003, Katy Limmer, Shane Murphy, Derek Paget, Chris Perry, Brian Rigby for French translation, Maire Steadman for archive material and research at the Royal Shakespeare Company, David M. Thompson for an interview at BBC Films on 7 November 2002, John E. Twomey – Professor Emeritus at the Ryerson Institute in Toronto – for archive material, Malcolm Watson, Colin Welland for a telephone interview with Ian Greaves on 19 January 2003, Frangcon Whelan, and Peter Whelan for an interview on 6 February 2003. Furthermore, thanks to the staffs of the Brynmor Jones library at the University of Hull, Hull Central Library, the Colindale newspaper library, the BBC's Written Archives Centre (particularly Erin O'Neill) and the library and viewing services of the British Film Institute. It is also my pleasure to acknowledge the vital contribution made by Ian Greaves, for advice, encouragement and comments on drafts, as well as his practical help with research, particularly in the ITV sections of the appendix.

A note on the lack of illustrations in this book: this was purely my decision. As well as being often prohibitively expensive to use, library photographs are posed for photographers and do not represent a director's work. Although some authors get around this by using screen grabs, it is my opinion that the picture quality tends to be so poor as to do a disservice to the director's work. Hopefully this book will help trigger a release of some of these productions so that they can be seen as they were intended.

On a personal level, thanks for keeping me sane go to my family: me dad and Margo; Bryan, Kerry and my precious nieces Amber and Chloe; Donna and Stuart; Steve, Gary and Daniel; and Kelly. I am delighted to dedicate this book to me mam, who is the strongest, funniest and most loving human being I have ever met, and as much our best friend as our mam. Finally, I give my thanks and my love to Karen and Emily. Karen's practical advice, and their mutual tolerance, patience and laughter were invaluable, helping me to finish the book as well as giving me a reason for breathing in and out.

Introduction

This book, a critical study of the work of Alan Clarke, is the first Television Series title about a director. It combines a broadly chronological study of Clarke's dominant themes and approaches with an awareness of various contexts: the institutional contexts in which he worked, critical debates on television form, and the methodological problems which arise when attributing authorship to a television director.

Chapter 1 covers Clarke's background, his early theatre work, and several television plays from his first, *Shelter* (1967), through to case studies of the drama-documentary *To Encourage the Others* (1972) and the fantasy *Penda's Fen* (1974). This chapter illustrates that his work in this period is more distinctive than its institutional and technological restrictions would suggest. Chapter 2 traces his emerging personal vision in various plays from the 1970s, sparse studies of institutionalisation and incarceration such as *Sovereign's Company* (1970), *A Life Is For Ever* (1972) and *Scum* (1977, 1979). The banning of the last was a turning point in his career; the chapter focuses on this and contextualises it within debates on drama-documentary and academic writing on ideologically progressive form. Chapter 3 covers his work in the 1980s, discussing the stylistic and narrative strategies of vibrant pieces such as *Made in Britain* (1983) and his Northern Ireland experiments *Contact* (1985) and *Elephant* (1989), which mark him out as a true auteur director.

Clarke was, as W. Stephen Gilbert (1990) argued upon the director's untimely death from cancer at the age of fifty-four, 'an unswerving champion of the individual voice and the nonconformist vision'. He gave a voice to those on the margins of society, whether empathising with victims of neglect and poverty in *Horace* (1972), *Diane* (1975) and *Road* (1987) or unflinchingly exploring the racism of Tim Roth's neo-Nazi Trevor in *Made in Britain* and the hooliganism of Gary Oldman's Bex in *The Firm* (1989). Individuals often come into contact with institutions, and are either initiated into them or broken, rehabilitated or cut adrift, rendered compliant or silenced. They face a struggle to articulate themselves in their own language, resulting in Trevor's verbal pyrotechnics, or the heartbreaking search for articulacy in *Road*. Voices are not simply the means by which their identity is expressed; they are synonymous with that identity, and the struggle of characters to be heard by a society that does not want to listen constitutes a struggle to exist. As I argue of *The Love-Girl and the Innocent* (1973), Clarke explores landscapes of private histories silenced by public narratives. He portrays characters resisting the 'discourses' of the state, whilst simultaneously avoiding imposing a discourse upon them himself, by refusing narrative embellishment or inappropriate stylistics. David Leland, who acted and wrote for Clarke, argued in the 1991 documentary *Director – Alan Clarke* (subsequently referred to as *Director*) that Clarke 'brought compassion, humour and understanding to situations where other film-makers might simply expect us to hate' and 'worked obsessively to find a visual style for each of his productions so as to allow the viewer unimpeded access to the heart of the material'. If Clarke's style were an anonymous, selfless articulation of these voices, it would be commendable enough, but Clarke also developed a distinctive voice, a 'nonconformist vision', of his own.

Clarke is reductively associated with the visceral social realism of the bruising Borstal study *Scum*, if only because of its notoriety. The struggle with institutions that the ban triggered invites biographical comparisons; as Howard Schuman (1998: 18) argued, it was difficult to 'disentangle the man and the artist: to paraphrase *Made in Britain*, Clarke was in it for life'. For those who worked with him, Clarke was, like Carlin in *Scum*, 'his own man, not one of the shadows of this world' (Minton 1979: 14). For the patronised dissident Yuri in *Nina* (1978), read Clarke after the suppression of *Scum*. For Trevor hurling a paving stone through a Job Centre window, read Clarke at his most nihilistic, disrobing at punk gigs or ending drunken nights with the attentions of the police, casualty units, attractive young women and/or bans from BBC facilities (see Kelly 1998). However, Clarke's off-screen legend should not obscure his work. David Hare told the 2000 documentary *Alan Clarke: 'His Own Man'* (subsequently referred to as *Own Man*) that, beneath Clarke's 'scruffy, apparently undisciplined' manner, 'hours and hours of thought had gone in, mostly at night, where he'd been working on the script in bed at three o'clock in the morning'. Hare added that 'the thing that people miss about him' was that 'he's a poet ... He wasn't in the slightest interested in brutality or violence in itself. He was interested in the poetry of the pain of people who are victims'.

Although he genially defined his approach to Mike Hutchinson (1987) as 'realism – gritty realism, the real world, how thing are. That's me', Clarke also rejected the stereotype of a 'drama-doc, hard-hitting, controversial warrior', arguing that he was 'a journalist, a messenger' (Nightingale 1981). He was far from just a dour social realist, bringing a masterful surety of tone to a wide variety of work, including the mythic *Penda's Fen* and the disorienting studio conceptualisation of *Psy-Warriors* (1981) and *Stars of the Roller State Disco* (1984). Unlike Richard Kelly's *Alan Clarke*, an excellent collection of interviews with his collaborators, I place more emphasis on the work than on the man. I regret the relative lack of Clarke's legendary humour, although his voice comes across in archival interviews, plus a piece he wrote in the 1960s which is reproduced in Chapter 1. However, this is a book which attempts the long overdue task of testifying to the intelligence and seriousness of Clarke's work. His distinctive and profoundly ideological explorations of style and form made him one of television's greatest innovators.

Indeed, it remains a vicious irony that a body of work concerned with ignored voices has itself been largely ignored. Although he won several awards in Europe, he was neglected in Britain during his lifetime, as Mark Shivas, producer of several of his plays, lamented: 'Why did *Sight & Sound* never write about him? ... had he been called Clarkovsky rather than plain old Alan Clarke, he would have had an international reputation' (Kelly 1998: 225–6). As we shall see, some critics did pick up on his signatures; for instance, the ever-diligent W. Stephen Gilbert (1981) said of *Psy-Warriors* that 'Clarke has become the medium's most confident drama director and the confidence is well-founded'. However, most attention has been posthumous. BAFTA partly atoned for their neglect by naming their Outstanding Creative Contribution to Television award after him. Tribute seasons followed in film festivals around the world and on BBC2 in 1991, my own moment of conversion. Key polemics followed from David Thomson (1993, 1995, 2002) – particularly in his *Biographical Dictionary of Film*, in which several sacred cows fared rather less well – and Richard Kelly, whose book, and programming of a two-month retrospective at the National Film Theatre, persuasively demonstrated that Clarke was 'the most important British film-maker to have emerged in the last thirty years' (Kelly 1998: xvii, 2002a, 2002b). Where these seasons and tributes led, others followed (see, as well as others cited here, Clifford 1991, Truss 1991, Taubin 1994, Preziosi 1995, Cornell *et al.* 1996, Hattenstone 1998, Barrett 2002). Many film-makers have cited his influence, from those who worked with him – among them Roth, Oldman and Danny Boyle, the latter of whom described him as 'a visionary ... one of the most gifted, innovative and radical British film-makers' (*Own Man*) – to Paul Greengrass (2002), who remarked upon 'unquestionably the finest body of work created by a British director'. After Harmony Korine and Chloe Sevigny mentioned him, one critic argued that Clarke was the 'father of NYC cool' (Venner 2001), whilst the Dogme manifesto has resulted in some recognisably Clarke-like productions. Most recently, Gus Van Sant's *Elephant* (2003), an acknowledged homage to Clarke's 1989 production of the same name, attracted widespread interest in Clarke, including a piece in *Cahiers du cinéma* (Tessé 2003).

This book explores Clarke's work for the 'unmistakable individuality and authenticity' which, as Mark Shivas (1990) argued, made him 'a real auteur in a way that very few British directors are'. However, I also acknowledge the restrictions which exist in the application of this terminology to a television director. Television Studies approaches tend to emphasise the medium's collaborative nature, placing the central 'authority' figure within networks of multiple authorship. Although John Cook (1998: 4) qualified this by arguing that this complexity 'can be seen to resolve itself into a clear hierarchical system of creative power relations', in this hierarchy 'the writer was privileged' and the director was often 'relegated to the secondary role of interpreter ... of the writer's ideas'. Discussing Clarke, Howard Schuman (1998: 18) noted that, because 'television prided itself on being a writers' medium', directors were 'often regarded as little more than opinionated camera movers' and were excluded from 'Auteurist critical approaches'. For instance, promoting a collaboration with Clarke, Douglas Livingstone stressed to Myles Palmer (1970) that 'A bad director is the bloke who is out to show how good a director he is. A good one is a bloke who does the play.' This idea is explored through the plays covered in Chapter 1, in which, with a respect for the script inherited from his time in the theatre, Clarke was, according to collaborators David Hare and Stella Richman respectively, 'basically pro-screenplay ... he never changed a word' (*Own Man*). As late as 1987, Clarke told Mike Hutchinson that 'I'm not an author, but I am a writer's director. I feel strongly about what my writers feel strongly about.' Although his subsequent imposition of his personal vision over his writers undermines this claim, I locate his 'signatures' alongside the contributions made by his collaborators.

When critics describe single-play strands such as *The Wednesday Play* (1964–70) and its successor *Play for Today* (1970–84) as television's cutting edge, 'a special place for the expression of the individual, dissident or questioning voice' (Cook 1998: 6), it tends to be as a forum for writers. However, Clarke also grasped the opportunity to become one of single drama's most 'individual' and 'dissident' voices, thriving within the single-play remit, which encouraged aesthetic experimenta-tion and political radicalism, broadcast to mass audiences. David Hare argued that 'As long as some bastard of a Director General didn't come along and actually ban your film ... there was this freedom to say what you wanted, and the rare excitement of knowing that it was being talked about by people all over the country' (*Own Man*). After the struggles of Ken Loach and Tony Garnett to get film cameras out on the streets for productions such as *Cathy Come Home* (1966), play strands featured small numbers of prized slots for plays shot entirely on 16mm film, which acted as a training ground for a generation of directors, many of whom moved into the cinema, such as Michael Apted, Stephen Frears, Roland Joffé, Mike Leigh, Ken Loach and Ridley Scott. Add to this list those directors who maintained distinctive careers within television, from the early pioneers Rudolph Cartier and George More O'Ferrall to such fascinating figures as Philip Saville and Charles Jarrott, and it becomes clear that a study of television direction is long overdue. As this book demonstrates, Clarke remained loyal to television, which provided, according to David Thomson (1995: 132), 'the last great example of the studio system'. Similarly, Andrew Clifford (1991) placed Clarke within 'that great (and critically neglected) flowering of talent in British television drama', paralleling this 'studio system' with the American system which produced Martin Scorsese and Francis Ford Coppola. Here, Clarke could 'learn, make mistakes, do new things without his career resting on each new play'. According to David Hare, Clarke was aware of the benefits, sharing 'that analogy between Hollywood in the 1930s and 1940s and the BBC'. Clarke is quoted as saying that 'This is a place where you can do a lot of work, and because of that you can do a lot of *different* work, you can push your luck' (Kelly 1998: 67). He benefited from rewarding collaborations with producers such as David Rose and Margaret Matheson, who were given a degree of autonomy within that system.

Another of his producers, Kenith Trodd (1983: 53), argued that these play strands constituted 'the most healthy, thriving and varied incidence of fiction film-making in British movie history', which in terms of 'overall quality, audience pleasure, the development of talented artists and technicians, and the honest reflection of contemporary life and crises', towered over many feature films of the time. It is a mark of their relative cultural value that even the cinema's most ordinary output from the period is commercially available today whilst critically acclaimed television plays, which were often seen by a far greater audience, are not. This lack of permanence is a further reason for the neglect of

Clarke's plays: many were repeated once at the most, and then banished to the archives. At the time of writing only four of around sixty productions are commercially available in Britain (and two of those are cinema films), although in late 2004 Blue Underground issued several previously unreleased plays on their Alan Clarke box set, the 'first DVD box-set devoted to a British director other than Alfred Hitchcock' (Lucas 2004). Although it denied him respect amongst film critics, Clarke's devotion to television resulted in a wide variety of work. He stressed to Jennifer Selway (1979) that he 'never wanted to use television as a stepping-stone into feature films', which were 'after all no more than a saleable commodity'. Indeed, his three cinema films – the remake of *Scum, Billy the Kid and the Green Baize Vampire* (1986) and *Rita, Sue and Bob Too* (1987) – are among his weakest work.

This book attends to another of the reasons for the lack of critical respect afforded to television directors: the specificity of television. Although my approaches to some of Clarke's filmed work demonstrate a fluid interplay between Television and Film Studies approaches, I also devote much space to those productions which require a different methodology: television plays recorded in multi-camera studios and on Outside Broadcast. By doing so, I attend to Clarke's experiences and skills as a director, and also attend to issues of aesthetics. The lack of writing on television directors is all the more surprising since they played a crucial part in establishing the visual, spatial and performative criteria of the televisual (see Jacobs 2000 on the aesthetics of early television drama). My approach also serves to counter technological essentialism, because this book is not structured simply to reflect the way in which television drama is often seen to develop 'from a static, theatrical, visual style to a mobile, cinematic one', implicit in which is a belief that television drama, particularly in its early days, 'did not develop its own aesthetic' (Jacobs 2000: 1). The studio play was 'not simply a stage, through which television had, inevitably to pass before arriving at its true destiny (film)' (Bignell *et al.* 2000: 38). Indeed, Clarke seized the technology's possibility of a '"poetic" and metaphoric approach to social reality', which allowed 'some of the experiments and discoveries of contemporary, anti-naturalist theatre to be shared with a television audience'. The section on *To Encourage the Others* proposes a visual analysis distinct from the stereotype of studio plays as compromises rooted in television's early theatrical heritage. It was this kind of drama that Troy Kennedy Martin (1964: 24–5) attacked, in his much-quoted 'battle for a televisual form', as a 'makeshift bastard born of the theatre and photographed with film techniques'. Because 'naturalism evolved from a theatre of dialogue', directors were 'forced into photographing faces talking and faces reacting', forced to 'retreat into the neutrality of the two- and three-shot'. He advocated a new form of drama which would 'free the structure from natural time' and 'exploit the total and absolute objectivity of the television camera'. Lez Cooke (2003: 66) observed that the form suggested by Kennedy Martin 'inflamed writers' precisely because it gave 'more responsibility to the director, with its emphasis on a new form of "visual storytelling"'. John McGrath (1977: 100), whose own *The Cheviot, the Stag and the Black, Black Oil* (1974) remains the greatest example of Brechtian practice in television, justifiably bemoaned the lack of a response to this polemic by other practitioners. However, there is in Clarke's 1980s work precisely the kind of Brechtian rigour called for by Kennedy Martin in the 1960s and, as I articulate in Chapter 2, the intellectual Left in the 1970s.

In its alliance of form and style for ideological purposes, Clarke's 1980s work forms an aesthetically and politically radical response to Thatcherism, and in its sparse formalism and narrative minimalism marks his confirmation as an auteur. As David Hare argued, 'It's only in the later years, it's only with the experiments ... particularly with *Elephant*, that he becomes what you might call an auteur, in the sense of only thinking of the script as a beginning' (*Own Man*). However, the book's chronological structure should not imply that the development of Clarke's distinguishable personality was the result of television drama's convergence with cinema during the same period. Although Hare argued elsewhere that the use of film freed directors from 'the depressing grammar of so much British television – the master-shot, the two-shot and the close-up' (Petley 1985: 72), it did little to improve the critical reputation of television directors. Penelope Houston (1984: 115) wrote of Channel Four's cinema output that 'the movie movie, as opposed to the TV movie, enjoys not only a wider vitality, but the power to probe more deeply'. (Presumably this does not extend to other 'television films' such as Rainer Werner Fassbinder's thirteen-episode *Berlin Alexanderplatz* (1980) or Bernardo Bertolucci's *Strategia del ragno* (*The Spider's Stratagem*, 1970).) Such statements are undermined by the fact that, as Robert Chilcott (2001: 57) argued, 'Clarke made no concessions to the medium he worked on'.

This book attempts to stimulate debate on the future use of director-centred auteur theory in Television Studies. I place Clarke in his institutional, theoretical and social contexts, although I occasionally allow the importance of establishing the hitherto neglected 'authority' of a television director to override the questioning of terminological usage which a similar study of a cinema director might employ (for instance, in phrases like 'Clarke cuts to a reverse-shot', I may elide the distinction in auteur-structuralism between Clarke the person and 'Clarke' the organising structure). But this is not to imply that the book's defining focus is on unearthing 'neglected' directors in industrial structures, as if Television Studies can recreate the pioneer spirit of early auteur theory in Film Studies. Instead, my interest in histories and aesthetics is predicated upon an ideological analysis. Clarke reflects the ways in which his characters are engulfed by dominant discourses through formal strategies with which he queries the dominant discourses of state and media. He addresses, to borrow from David Leland's notes on *Made in Britain*, the 'gulf' between people's 'experiences and the way the media tells their story, or fails to tell their story at all', which leaves behind 'an awareness that everything we see on television is political and that there is no such thing as an impartial, balanced point of view' (1986: 11). His restless experimentation with the signifying practices of film becomes his own defining voice, involving, as David Thomson (1993: 80) observed, a 'great formal interest in film as a way of seeing or presenting'. Clarke was 'always on the urgent beat of news stories', but also 'forever testing out his own savage stylistics'. By Chapter 3, there is a tension between authorship and ideology which is indebted to Michel Foucault's writing on authors as 'initiators of discursive practice'. Although crucially stressing that 'the subject should not be entirely abandoned', he proposed that critics should 'seize its functions, its intervention in discourse, and its system of dependencies', replacing typical questions such as 'Who is the real author?' and 'What has he revealed of his most profound self in his language?' with: 'Under what conditions and through what forms can an entity like the subject appear in the order of discourse ... what are the modes of existence of this discourse?' and 'Where does it come from; how is it circulated; who controls it?' For the director, as for his characters, the question persists: 'What placements are determined for possible subjects?' (Foucault 1981: 290)

The book's chronological structure also ensures that I maintain a sense of Clarke's practical experience in moving between often very different productions, making the work, in order to smooth the epistemological gap between practitioners and critics. To reflect the ways in which Clarke portrays the imposition of discursive strategies, and avoids imposing discursive strategies of his own, I aim to avoid imposing my own discursive strategies upon his work. The analytical tools and elements of theory which I use are offered in support of that work; for instance, my discussion of drama-documentary and progressive form is centred on its consequences for Clarke's style. In my Conclusion, I will acknowledge any points at which this balance fails. However, the book does have one unifying aim: to explore Clarke's work in terms of the politics of form, demonstrating the ways in which his work explores ideology through experimentation with narrative and the representational apparatus of television and film, and how he developed a politicised aesthetic, a brilliant marriage of form and content. In other words, a voice.

The director in television's 'studio system'

In this chapter I explore Alan Clarke's personal and professional origins, and his emergence as a director in a writer's medium. I begin with a sketch of his background and early theatre work, comparing these with the backgrounds of others of his generation in order to establish the social contexts which shaped Clarke's thematic concerns and the television landscape around him. I then trace his developing technique by looking at several of the plays which he made for ITV in the 1960s and the BBC in the early 1970s. The chapter's focus is on questioning the extent to which the distinctiveness of Clarke's work is restricted by the institutional expectation that directors 'serve' the scripts of a variety of writers.

Edward Buscombe (1973: 76) summarised François Truffaut's distinction between the kind of director labelled a metteur-en-scène and the kind labelled an auteur: 'Instead of merely transferring someone else's work faithfully and self-effacingly, the auteur transforms the material into an expression of his own personality.' Although it is testament to Clarke's versatility that producer Stella Richman felt she 'could put Alan with anybody' (Kelly 1998: 24–5), the fact that Clarke did not originate his projects during this period places him closer to the definition of a metteur-en-scène than that of an auteur. Discussing their collaboration on *Penda's Fen*, David Rudkin felt that Clarke was 'not an auteur in the classical, Godardian sense' of generating his projects 'regardless of who's written the screenplay' (Kelly 1998: 73). However, addressing the absence of a language with which to analyse television direction by appropriating auteur theory creates more problems than it solves. Employing a tool of film criticism – particularly one which has been so fiercely contested – undermines the specificity of television drama. The need for criticism to engage with the televisual informs a section on *To Encourage the Others*, in which I explore the distinctive use which Clarke makes of the purportedly restrictive multi-camera set-up of the television studio.

Equally, it would be an oversimplification to argue that Clarke self-effacingly transfers other people's material. His work in this period features emerging signs of thematic and stylistic continuities, including a concern with the representative capacity of form in the telling of his protagonists' stories. Drawing attention to such factors is not to detract from Clarke's working experience by implying that these plays are only relevant as the start of an auteurist narrative imposed upon them. His collaborations with writers often result in distinctive and complex material. At the end of this chapter I discuss arguably the ultimate example of this, *Penda's Fen*, which has been described by W. Stephen Gilbert (1990) as 'one of the most remarkable achievements in all television drama'.

'Kick hell out of sacred cows': the early days

It seems appropriate that a man who dedicated his prodigious talent to television shares such biographical links with the medium's development. Alan John Clarke was born in Seacombe on 28 October 1935, within an eighteen-month period which saw not only the births of other crucial practitioners (among them Tony Garnett, Trevor Griffiths, Ken Loach, Dennis Potter, Kenith Trodd and Peter Watkins) but also the beginning of the BBC's television service. Many of this generation shared attitudes towards society and television formed by common experiences. Clarke was one of several to come from a working-class background and go through the grammar school system (he gained a scholarship to Wallasey Grammar School after passing his Eleven Plus in 1947). The product of Butler's 1944 Education Act, the Eleven Plus offered opportunity for advancement – Tony Garnett (2000: 12) recalled that this was 'the first working-class generation to attend university in any numbers' – but selection also constituted a divisive siphoning-off of the most intelligent working-class children from their peers, described by Kenith Trodd as 'the first sheep-and-goats separation' (Carpenter 1998: 49). Their subsequent alienation from their backgrounds also fostered class consciousness; talking to Paul Bream (1972: 40), Garnett also described Butler's Act as 'sophisticated and wicked' legislation, an 'underestimated piece of class villainy' which 'put the silver spoon in my mouth'. Its effects were documented in *The Uses of Literacy*, in which Richard Hoggart explored the 'sense of loss' faced by 'the uprooted and the anxious'. Hoggart's description of that generation echoes so many of the alienated individuals in Clarke's work: 'Almost every working-class boy who goes through the process of further education by scholarships finds himself chafing against his environment during adolescence. He is at the friction point of two cultures' (Hoggart 1957: 242). It is not easy to describe Clarke as 'anxious', as he thrived at grammar school, even winning a prize for Latin (Kelly 1998: 5), and his university education in Canada was very different to the Oxbridge experiences of many of his television contemporaries.

However, as Howard Schuman stated, Clarke 'wasn't someone who came from a working-class background and found success, a comfortable middle-class lifestyle, and left his previous life behind. It was always with him' (*Own Man*). Perhaps 'Scruff' Clarke's legendarily colourful leisure pursuits and at times pathologically dirty living conditions in London could be seen as an expression of discontent – after visiting Clarke's family in Leasowe, collaborator Jehane Markham wondered if his 'annihilation of domesticity' was related to 'where he came from' (Kelly 1998: 85). Although not the type to publicly express feelings of living 'between two rivers' like Potter, he kept in only sporadic contact with his family. His work often portrays the problematic relationship between origins and belonging. Sometimes this appears as social and familial awkwardness, as in Edna O'Brien's *Which of These Two Ladies Is He Married To?* (1967), in which an Irish mother visits her socially mobile daughter and her outwardly successful friends in London. But when such questions of identity are raised, they are more often focused around nationality, as in *Penda's Fen* and *Made in Britain*, or masculinity, which complicates the public and grammar school undercurrents of *Sovereign's Company* and the territorial marking of *The Firm*.

This generation seized the importance of television as, in Stephen Frears's phrase, a 'tremendously new democratic, populist medium' (*Own Man*). They made the 'politically motivated' decision to enter television, according to Tony Garnett (2000: 12), 'to show the Britain *we* knew, to incite, to express our anger'. Television had the power, Dennis Potter (1994: 55) felt, to 'slice through all the tedious hierarchies of the printed word and help to emancipate us from many of the stifling tyrannies of class and status and gutter-press ignorance'. Like Potter, Clarke embraced the medium's potential to directly address large audiences, but also to reflect them in such a way as to draw attention to those very 'hierarchies' through which they were usually presented. Potter's commitment to non-naturalism to achieve this was matched by Clarke's distinctive approach to realist form. Raymond Williams (1977a: 63) argued that realist innovations often involve a 'movement towards social extension', and, according to Frears, Clarke was attracted to the medium because 'one of the things that television told was the history of ordinary working-class people in England' (*Own Man*). The idea that 'the lives of working-class people should be afforded on television the same depth and passion which is usually given to middle-class subjects' was Clarke's 'governing conviction' according to David Hare (1990); therefore, Clarke may have shared the view of his collaborator Colin Welland, that his 'responsibility lies in reaching those people I supposedly left behind or moved away from' (Burn 1970).

Another experience shared by Clarke's generation which became a recurring feature in his work was the encroachment of institutions upon individuals. This manifested itself in wartime collectivism, the development of the Welfare State and particularly in National Service. Much of Clarke's work portrays the military in negative terms, unsurprisingly given that his grandfather was killed on Armistice Day in the First World War, and his father returned in some distress from the Second (Kelly 1998: 1–3). However, as Richard Kelly's interviewees recall, Clarke handled army life after his call-up in 1954 with the same combination of raucous bad behaviour and professional advancement which characterised his career in that other institution, the BBC. After National Service and an attempt at an office job in Liverpool, Clarke moved to Canada with friends in 1957. The Questors Theatre's newsletter *Questopics* later summarised his 'masterfully improvised' career: 'furniture remover, income tax assessor, miner, railway brakesman and chain-ganger, baker's assistant, dance M.C. and a disc jockey at a skating rink' (Anonymous 1968). In 1958, after hearing about it while in hospital recovering from an injury sustained working in a gold mine (Kelly 1998: 6), he enrolled on a three-year course in Radio and Television Arts at the Ryerson Institute of Technology in Toronto. This pioneering course gave Clarke 'training in broadcast methods' in both radio – with Canada's educational radio station, CJRT-FM – and television. Ryerson's 1960–61 calendar explained that classroom theory became 'a practical reality through closed-circuit productions of which several are taped and kinescoped during the year for further telecasting by co-operating private television stations'. Alongside this training, students acquired 'a sound knowledge of the world around us based on a broad understanding of the humanities and the social sciences', including modules on the history and application of music, the phonetics of modern languages, writing for television and acting for radio, television and the stage. Away from class, he played for the Ryerson Zebras Soccer team, and was one of their most promising rookies in the 1958–59 season, in which they were the champions of the Intermediate Ontario–Quebec conference (Ryerson). In his vacations, he trained as an actor in 'method' schools, and worked in a theatre-in-the-round in Buffalo, New York, playing a eunuch (surely one of the least appropriate pieces of casting the world has ever known) in *The Desert Song* (Anonymous 1968). Active in student theatre, he took part in musicals mounted by the Ryerson Opera Workshop, playing the sheriff in *Finian's Rainbow* in 1960 and the sorcerer in *The Boys From Syracuse* in 1961 (Ryerson). In his third year, he began directing student plays; then-girlfriend and future wife Jane Harris recalled that he started with Jean-Paul Sartre's *No Exit*, which failed to win a competition at Midwestern University arguably because of a characteristic stillness (Kelly 1998: 9).

After producing a couple of educational films, Clarke returned to Britain, gaining work as an Assistant Floor Manager at ATV, and then, after experiences in Europe, Associated Rediffusion. He worked on a variety of productions, including the pop music programme *Ready Steady Go* (1963–66) and Joe Orton's *The Erpingham Camp* (1965). Meanwhile, he directed plays at the amateur Questors Theatre in Ealing. As at the BBC, in spite of somewhat *louche* extra-curricular activities, he saw the value of an institution in which he could develop his skills. He sat on the Plays and Productions Committee, and befriended Alfred Emmet, who had founded the theatre with the belief that 'any theatre which does not actively encourage young people is failing in its duty' (Bowley 1991). As *Questopics* noted, Clarke even left ATV after eight months to work as an invoice clerk in Sainsbury's to keep his evenings free for Questors. He directed the following productions: in 1962, *Krapp's Last Tape* by Samuel Beckett as an audition piece and *Traveller Without Luggage* by Jean Anouilh (September); in 1963, *Long Day's Journey into Night* by Eugene O'Neill (March) and *One Leg Over the Wrong Wall* by Alfred Berwel (June); in 1964, *Neighbours* by James Saunders and *No Quarter* by Barry Bermange as a double bill (October); in January 1965 he toured Berlin with *Neighbours* and *No Quarter*, and directed *Neighbours* in Paris. In June that year, he staged *How I Assumed the Role of the Popular Dandy: For Purposes of Seduction and Other Base Matters* by Derek Marlowe. In 1966, he directed *Hecabe* by Euripides (January) and *Macbeth* by William Shakespeare (November). Finally, in 1967, he staged *The Maids* by Jean Genet, ostensibly as an audition for television.

It is important to dwell on Clarke's work at Questors, because Clarke himself argued that he developed as a director in his time there. On *Traveller Without Luggage* he learned 'to put the rule-book in the background' of his mind, after he had 'translated mechanically a proscenium arch production into the round', whilst on *Long Day's Journey into Night* he 'learned to stop worrying about making an impression and how to get on with directing actors' (Anonymous 1968). He also explored aesthetic approaches which predict those of his later television plays. Initially his stage work bore the influence of the Theatre of the Absurd, from the alienating use of masks painted on faces through to a more lasting concern with the use of space and minimalist set design. Clarke's continuous interrogation of staging both in the theatre and on television bears the influence of Bertolt Brecht, amongst whose pronouncements was the view that 'The theatre must acquire *qua* theatre the same fascinating reality as a sporting arena during a boxing match. The best thing is to show the machinery, the ropes and the flies' (Brecht 1978: 233). Clarke frequently did this, making his relationship with realism more complex than critics assumed.

One institutional factor in common with his television career was the need to direct whichever play he was assigned. Most of these plays operate outside what we may now identify as Clarke territory, though there are moments of recognition – for instance, *Neighbours* features a thorny problematising of liberal rhetoric with regards to race which will be explored more viscerally through Trevor in *Made in Britain* (Saunders 1968). Donald McWhinnie, who directed *No Quarter* on its professional debut five years after Clarke's staging, identified in Barry Bermange's writing a 'formal perfection' which worked as 'a counterpoint to the human, emotional factor'. But if this hints at Clarke's television career, so does McWhinnie's qualification that the director is restricted, unable to 'change a word or a sentence without doing damage' (Bermange 1969: 9). As on television, different forms provided opportunities to explore uncharacteristic techniques. In interview, the playwright Peter Whelan, who acted in *Krapp's Last Tape* and *Hecabe*, recalled Clarke's handling of the more epic *How I Assumed the Role of the Popular Dandy*, in which actors used 'the gantries, they were moving around above you, behind you, descending into the theatre to gnaw at a great banquet'.

Off-stage too there emerged a recognisable Alan Clarke. He had his first brush with controversy during a trip to perform *Neighbours* and *No Quarter* at Berlin's Akademie der Künste, during the West German drama festival Modernes Theatre auf Kleinen Bühnen. The interracial sexuality of *Neighbours* resulted in booing at the Berlin production, and trouble at the airport for black actor Wyllie Longmore (by contrast, the play was cheered in Paris). Meanwhile, as the aforementioned *Questopics* profile noted, 'Although disclaiming to be a theorist, he has some spikily unorthodox opinions'. Rather than being 'hampered by over-attention to realism', the theatre – in an interesting spin on Brecht's boxing analogy – should feature 'the spontaneity and uninhibited enthusiasm of a football game. As he puts it "Kick hell out of sacred cows".' Of these, the most sacred remained Shakespeare, as Clarke found with his controversially idiosyncratic production of *Macbeth*. This predicted two signatures of his later television work. *Thames Valley Times* described the play's 'violent changes between infernal noises and muted speech and utter darkness and brilliant light' (Anonymous 1966), thereby identifying one of these signatures, his willingness to shift perspective and objectivity by making the audience step back from the action. The production also demonstrated his concern with paring material down. In interview, Questors archivist Carla Field relayed the memories of some of those who experienced the process in an interview:

> He cut out a lot of the characters, and concentrated on the political bit of the story ... Alan had one audition, so they came to read for every single part, so there was a great crowd there, and as they came in, Alan said 'No, I won't be needing you, and I won't be needing you'. In fact, he had pared the play down so much that Peter Healy, who was reading for Macbeth, was a little bit worried that he was going to say that he didn't want any Macbeths either.

As Whelan recalled, some Questors were perturbed, as 'Shakespeare really was multifarious and all Alan was doing was a very spare, minimalistic version of it; but in terms of how it was done, it was tremendous – a bit like *Elephant*, endless repetitions down a kind of tunnel'. Clarke's visceral treatment included Macbeth vomiting after Duncan's murder. Before the production, expectations of its radicalism led Clarke to write a response for the *Questopics* newsletter (Clarke 1966):

> 'A new hard look' ... 'a contemporary re-appraisal' ... 'striking' ... 'original' ... 'imaginative'. All these punchy, rather high-sounding phrases and adjectives were to be found in the last issue of *Questopics* not, as we might be forgiven for assuming, in connection with a production we've already seen, but about one that's only just gone into rehearsal. It's not yet fully cast and already the notices seem to have been written; the actors don't even know their lines and already the audience has been told what to expect. So, if this production *isn't* striking, imaginative, contemporary and the rest of it somebody will be for it, and you can be sure that it won't be the *Questopics*' staff – it'll be the producer.
>
> For example, what would happen if, half-way through the rehearsal period, the producer decides that he's ruining a play, a great classic, by being 'striking', 'original' etc. and concludes that the style in which the play is usually interpreted and produced is the only way in which it can possibly be done? And it *has* happened! Should he hastily circulate all members of The Questors with the following black-bordered announcement:– 'We regret to announce that our forthcoming production will be

along the usual well-worn traditional lines and not imaginative, original, striking – as previously advertised. The producer deplores this change in the programme. Tickets bought on the strength of previous publicity cannot be exchanged but dissatisfied members will be allowed to picket this production. The picketing, incidentally, is to be organised not along the usual well-worn traditional lines but in an "original", "imaginative" and "striking" manner'.

Of course you can argue that I'm simply being facetious. Agreed – but my point is that these rather grand adjectives are meaningless to most producers. The audience may say that he seems to be approaching the play this way or that way; who cares? That's *their* problem – don't make it the producer's.

The truth is much more simple. The producer, if he is excited by the play he's doing, has an instinct, a profound involvement with play, and if it's realised in terms of performance, production and audience he's *ecstatic*; if not, he's *suicidal*. These two adjectives are the only ones that count – you know what you can do with all the others.

Slightly 'facetious', yes, but a lovely marking of territory. Clarke's investigation of theatrical form anticipated and arguably informed his later work. He directed vivid interpretations of the plays *The Love-Girl and the Innocent*, *Danton's Death* (1978) and *Baal* (1982), but the influence runs more deeply than that. Reviewing *Everybody Say Cheese* (1971), Donald Sartain (1971) noted from Clarke's handling of 'the techniques of classical comedy and music hall' that 'While most television directors continue to chase new concepts of "naturalism" in drama, Alan Clarke has introduced a vigorous theatricality into his work'. Sadly this is one of a number of Clarke's early plays no longer existing, rendering this glimpse into one strain of his career frustratingly unconfirmable. As we shall see, an element of 'theatricality' is ingrained in some of his compositional strategies, particularly in the 1970s. Overt theatricality resurfaces even in the kinetically cinematic *Road*, whilst *Billy the Kid and the Green Baize Vampire* features chorus scenes which resemble his staging of *Hecabe* (seen in photographs at Questors) and his studies of epic theatre at the Royal Shakespeare Company.

David Hare has argued that 'the thing that nobody who works in the British cinema likes to face, particularly people who hang around the British Film Institute, is that almost everything that's good in the British cinema has come out of the British theatre. And Alan, like other great British film directors, worked in the theatre first. And this meant that he understood actors' (*Own Man*). It is debatable whether Clarke's skill with actors was an inherently theatrical virtue, although George Costigan argued that Clarke's previous stage work showed in rehearsals 'because he knew how to build performances ... he knew how to talk to actors ... in a much deeper way than most film directors do' (*Director*). Mick Ford told Simon Rumley (1999: 80) that rehearsing the film version of *Scum* 'was very much like a theatre, we worked our way through the script, going through it in detail', and 'On set it was great because Alan Clarke had the cameraman, the crew he wanted and a rare thing among directors: he let everyone else get on with that and watched the acting'. Like Gary Oldman, Ray Winstone and many others, Tim Roth has praised Clarke's ability to nurture performances, recalling that 'Rehearsal was really meticulous ... you would get up and walk the scenes around ... perform over and over and over again', but within 'an atmosphere of humour and fun' in which 'you can get the work done much more efficiently' (*Tim Roth: Made in Britain*, 2002). Given the pejorative reading of 'theatricality' in film and television criticism, it is important to note that such verities are married with an increasingly distinctive cinematic vision. Rebuking Hare's polemic, Robert Chilcott (2001: 56) argued that, for many of the *Wednesday Play* generation, 'theatre was a way in', and that their 'chief visual and thematic inspirations' were 'the peak of auteur cinema – Italian neo-realism, Czech social comedies and the French New Wave'. Although I will return to these reference points, neither Hare's nor Chilcott's search for influence alters the fact that Clarke chose television rather than film or theatre, in spite of interest from the RSC and, later, Hollywood. A hugely popular figure on the floor at Rediffusion, he was turned down for their director's course by two selection boards until Stella Richman, the Head of Scripted Series, fought for him to be accepted, aware that 'there would have been a studio revolt if he hadn't' (Kelly 1998: 21). Following the late-night transmission on television in Berlin in early 1965 of his touring production of *Neighbours* and *No Quarter*, and an apprenticeship at Rediffusion directing Epilogues, Clarke's first full directorial credit came in May 1967.

To examine his style in the context of the practical limitations of production and institutional hierarchies which favoured writers, I will now discuss his collaborations at ITV with Alun Owen and Roy Minton, and an early collaboration at the BBC with Colin Welland.

Collaborations with Alun Owen, Roy Minton and Colin Welland

At ITV, between 1967 and 1969, Clarke directed fourteen single plays for the strands *Half Hour Story* (1967–68), *Company of Five* (1968) and *Saturday Night Theatre* (1969–71), and five episodes of the series *The Informer* (1966–67), *A Man of Our Times* (1968) and *The Gold Robbers*

(1969). It is more difficult here than in his later career to pin down Clarke's identity, as he is assigned material and is restricted by the nature of the productions, often conversation pieces on small sets. However, his work was so distinctive that ITV awarded him Director of the Year for 1967 (Anonymous 1968).

Given their similar backgrounds, and the role that Owen played in refining the scope of single drama with his scripts for *No Trams to Lime Street* (1959) and *Lena, O My Lena* (1960), it seems fitting that they became collaborators and friends. Owen's method was built on observation – he wrote *The Criminal* (1960) for Joseph Losey, who described him to Michel Ciment (1985: 184) as a 'self-made writer' who 'wrote with a tape-recorder'. In an interview with Sonia Copeland (1969) around the last of his six productions with Clarke, Owen described the collaborative process:

> once I know who's going to direct a play, somebody like Alan Clarke or Peter Hammond or the man I worked with for many years, Ted Kotcheff, then we sit down and tear the play to pieces – before the actors get anywhere near it. They've got to know what's going on in my mind ... Ted always used to say, and Alan says the same thing – that my plays are a bit ice-bergy. That it's not the top third, it's the two-thirds underneath ... The mid-twentieth century problem is the failure of people to communicate with each other.

This struggle for communication is a theme in Clarke's first transmitted play, *Shelter* (1967), which opened the first series of Rediffusion's *Half Hour Story*. A two-hander typifying much of Owen's short television work, *Shelter* features a 'Girl' (Wendy Craig) and a 'Man' (Colin Blakely) meeting in a park conservatory whilst seeking refuge from a thunderstorm. However, they are also sheltering in a figurative sense from respective emotional crises, and fleetingly connect through forced companionship and grudgingly earned revelation. She is quiet, he verbose, working through what N. Alice Frick (1967) called 'a play by play game of wits, of self-defensive feeling and attack, the battle of the sexes in fresh phrases'. These dialogue clashes reflect a linguistic conflict often noted within Owen himself, between a 'natural Welsh ... over-rich verbal fertility', and 'his Liverpool upbringing ... the language he heard on the streets' (Anonymous 1994).

Their meeting is complicated by emotional and social tensions, resulting in, according to Henry Raynor (1967a), 'a sensitive, terse, encounter of troubled people across class barriers'. As Blakely's character says, 'It came as a middling-sized shock to discover the paucity of the working man's basic word power. So I set about enlarging my own instanter.' This is contrasted with the emotional articulacy which the

Girl finds, as she reflects on her unhappiness with middle-class marriage. Superficial similarities with David Lean's *Brief Encounter* (1945) are reinforced by the man stereotyping her going to 'change your book at the Cash Chemist'. Drawn out of, or into, herself, she spars back. The developing relationship is captured through Clarke's fluid, fast cutting between big close-ups, a recurring feature of his early work. Then, when Craig's character finally breaks down, the intercutting stops, and she is given the space to express herself: 'the sameness starts and you lie to yourself ... And one day you run out into the Park and get caught in the rain and you run for shelter ... But there's no shelter, a man goes on and on at you and there's no shelter.' The man has learnt to listen as much as she's learnt to speak, but has the last word: 'We'll see what we can do when the rain stops.'

Although the play was denied a national profile by the vagaries of regional scheduling, it was the number one programme in the London area. It amply demonstrates the appeal of short drama, a form celebrated by Owen in an interview with Anthony Davis (1967). It is revealing to note the qualities which such an influential figure felt to be inherently televisual: 'The 30 minute play is to the short story what the longer play is to the novel. Television is not suited to the epic ... television is ideal for the small cast in a confined space, capturing a small moment in time.' It is a form with which he was associated, as Michael Billington (1968) noted: 'Alun Owen is an expert at the half-hour play. Knowing that too much incident can burst the form asunder, he usually concentrates on close examination of a single relationship; on top of this his dialogue almost invariably has a colloquial muscularity and exuberance.'

Owen's three subsequent *Half Hour Story* scripts for Clarke are also two-handers. *George's Room* (1967) also features a 'man' (John Neville) meeting a 'woman' (Geraldine Moffatt). She is a Northern widow looking to rent out a room; however, this is 'not merely a room', but has come to symbolise her inability to escape her dead husband's stranglehold and rebuild her self-esteem. George moved into the spare room having lost interest in sex, and she grew to fear this room during her Friday visits to collect the housekeeping money: 'I wasn't to knock, just wait until he called. Mind, I had to behave myself when I got in. None of my nonsense or I'd be sent packing until I came to my senses.' As in *Shelter*, a man tries to draw a woman into telling her story, but cannot simply summarise or rescue her self-image; the conversation is as much a play of identities, particularly the contested character of George. Although George didn't 'approve of femininity', the woman she had to be for him was no more a male construction of femininity than the newcomer's alternative: 'I like women. Whenever I see a pretty woman walking down the street I feel like giving her a 21-gun salute – I don't just accept them, I'm on their side, I'm delighted to be Adam's heir.' This invocation of Fall terminology problematises the sense that his move into the room, and his promise to let her 'fidget' in there to confront her fears, offer an escape.

George's Room stands out stylistically as it was the only *Half Hour Story* recorded in colour on 625-line videotape, a prestigious touch for a play which was ITV's entry for the Montreux television festival. However, in comparison with the inventive compositions of Clarke's other collaborations with Owen, this employs remarkably orthodox studio grammar, alternating mid- and close shots with the obligatory wide two-shot. Its deceptive simplicity prompted Henry Raynor (1967b) to suggest that this otherwise impressive production 'could easily pass as a radio play. It has almost no movement', with cameras left to just watch characters 'speaking or listening'. Clarke shared a humanistic concern with faces with others of his generation, most demonstrably Peter Watkins in *Culloden* (1964) and *The War Game* (1965), whilst Alan Plater argued that 'The thing that works best on television is a face talking – whether it's in a play or with newsreel cameras or anything – just a face talking, just a face looking. Eyes and a mouth' (Edmands and Hewitt 1968). However, these statements echo Troy Kennedy Martin's polemic on form, in which the close-up was described as a feature of television's evolution from a theatre of dialogue. Close-ups of 'faces talking and faces reacting' displayed 'a deep-rooted belief that the close-up of an actor's face somehow acts subjectively on the viewer' (1964: 24). The breakdown of *Shelter*'s heroine just before a commercial break brings to mind John McGrath's lecture in support of Kennedy Martin, claiming that for formal reasons 'the weeping close-up on television is rarely more than repelling' (McGrath 1977: 102). However, several directors have described the close-up as, in Jean Epstein's phrase, the 'soul of cinema' (Jacobs 2000: 122). Equally, across these pieces Clarke makes fresh use of the close-up, and demonstrates a keenness to harness his style to the expression of character. This striving for the means with which to synchronise character, equipment and viewer positioning (or, as he told *Questopics*, 'performance, production and audience') is a recurring feature in his work, long before its culmination with his discovery of Steadicam in the 1980s.

The next Owen–Clarke collaboration, *Stella* (1968), is a *tour-de-force* of imaginative camerawork in a one-set conversation piece, although such techniques were not always appreciated by reviewers. Michael Billington (1968) noted the economy and humour of Owen's writing, but his 'main reservation concerned Alan Clarke's direction which seemed rather mannered and self-advertising'. Whilst Billington found little aesthetic pleasure in 'endless shots up the boy friend's left nostril', Clarke's compositions within a tight set are frequently intriguing. The central relationship recalls the films of Michelangelo Antonioni; Richard Kelly's notes for a National Film Theatre screening evocatively described Geraldine Moffatt as Stella being 'lovingly framed by Clarke as though she were Monica Vitti' (Kelly 2002a). Another linguistic tussle is fought in *Stella*, over femininity, marriage and power. From an opening close-up of Stella contemplatively smoking, the play's early moments are wordless and languorous. At last, 'the man' (Ray Smith) abruptly enters, shot menacingly from an extreme low angle. We crab left to follow Stella into the bedroom. So far, we have heard only church bells. Finally, she speaks: 'Get out!' After a seven-day break from him, her boyfriend for the last two years, she tells him that 'our time is over … I've moved on'. During Clarke's intercutting, those stifling nasal close-ups enhance the play's exploration of human intimacy and its tensions, reinforcing his attempt to reclaim her: 'Look, Stella, you belong to me.' Later, from a similar angle he traps her against a wall, and proclaims that (like the camera) 'I attack you, I smother you'. Clarke uses two-shots to express distance, repeatedly foregrounding Stella screen left looking right, with the man in the background, centre of frame. Fittingly since we are disoriented by the fluctuation of power and accusation between them, our views of both are fragmented. In profile, she often appears as a disembodied leg subjected to our gaze as much as his, whilst our view of him shifts uncomfortably in regular changes in shot size, angle and framing.

At times Stella seems to be another frustrated housewife, dodging the restrictive marriages of *Shelter* or *George's Room*, declaring that 'you can get someone else to cook your chops'. Gender and power shift with language – it is Stella who says, 'If you could, you'd say you were having a baby and I'll have to marry you. Well, I'm not playing Sir Jasper to your orphan Annie.' Furthermore, 'You've been pretending to be a man for the last few years, and I suddenly realised – you aren't'. At the half-way point they go to bed, raising the possibility that we have witnessed a psychosexual game akin to Harold Pinter's *The Lover* (1963), but in fact this allows Owen to develop the association between sex and power. The second half begins with another evocative shot – Stella lies blankly on the bed, her face and body foregrounded, while in the background he looks smugly out of the window. Tolling bells add to the ambiguous mood, given their associations with both marriage and death. These recurring visual strategies emphasise the play's themes of distance and the construction of gender through images. Seven days apart prompt Stella to examine what binds people together, and the results are both witty and disturbing.

Clarke's style was particularly striking by the time of *Thief* (1968). On first seeing this play, Graham Benson noticed 'how different and original Alan was', and was 'surprised and excited by the technique ... It was filmic, it might have been imitated by others but it was Alan's style' (Kelly 1998: 24). This is hard to determine since the recording is now lost, but the camera script (Owen 1968) shows a continued use of low angles and conspicuous foregrounding, and supports its description by Henry Raynor (1968) as a 'powerful study of sexual attraction'. The play opens with 'A Man' (Alan Lake) attempting to attract 'A Girl' (Sian Phillips) by returning her cigarette case, which he had stolen at an earlier reception. During their conversation, theft is used metaphorically, to describe professionalism, sex – 'Some thieves reckon it's better than a woman' – and relationships, as 'Thieves don't like sharing, they want it all for themselves'.

There are thematic correlations between these four *Half Hour Story* plays which support a reading of meaning which prioritises the writer. There has been a progression in Owen's representation of the male–female relationship, with gender constructed along both psychological and social lines. The Fall is invoked in *Shelter* – contact is made in an Edenic setting, alongside a statue of manhood placed alongside the flawed reality, as 'They don't make us like that any more' – and *George's Room*, as 'Adam's heir' attempts to persuade 'woman' into a forbidden area. The social and economic limitations upon women also feature – in *George's Room*, a dominant patriarch can be escaped only through another male–female business transaction, the women of *Shelter* and *Stella* cannot escape the expected image of the wife, while even *Thief* could be read for a brutal subtext, as a relationship is contrasted with a potentially violating act of theft. From the natural daylight of *Shelter* to the late night of *Thief*, at root is the struggle for understanding, power or shared language between protagonists whose very names encourage a universal reading: man and woman. Though Owen is the dominant figure, the sheer scope of the ideas also qualifies his view that the television play is a 'small cast in a confined space, capturing a small moment in time', and its implied restrictions upon a director's style.

Such restrictions particularly apply to directors' work for drama series, which tend to require a fidelity to 'house style'. However, in his series work over 1967 and 1968, Clarke employs some of his distinctive motifs. For instance, Angela Moreton (1967), in her review of Clarke's episode of *The Informer*, noted the use of 'long searching close-ups'.

Equally, the acclaimed *A Man of Our Times* afforded scope for individual contributions; according to John L Phillips (1968), each episode could 'stand as a play in its own right'. James Towler (1970) eulogised that 'in retrospect it becomes abundantly clear what a landmark it was. As a study in present day human relationships it has never been equalled, let alone surpassed. Indeed such was the honesty of Julian Bond's story that, at times, it became so near to the bone as to make one feel distinctly uneasy'. He added that George Cole's performance 'will be remembered for as long as people talk about television'. The serial led Phillips to contrast serials favourably with single plays, arguing that their length provided an 'answer to the fact that television is an ephemeral medium', whilst their form made them 'perhaps the major contribution which television has made to the art of drama', through which 'the medium is now creating its own style'.

As at Questors, Clarke was in an arena in which he could develop. Welcoming the extension of *Half Hour Story* after its initial success, Stella Richman told *Television Today* that 'It has brought back to television writing a number of people who have become established and left the medium. Because the scripts have been good the series has also attracted high calibre actors and actresses. Further, we have been able to bring in a number of young directors to work with these very good casts' (Anonymous 1967). Of these, Clarke stood out, providing 'the most wonderful little two-handers – beautifully written, beautifully acted, but *masterly* direction' (Richman, *Own Man*). New writer Roy Minton was another to benefit, particularly from his pairing with Clarke. Although at this stage Clarke could not select material and collaborators, producers such as Richman and Irene Shubik at the BBC in effect made this authorial signature based on his perceived strengths. Arguing that producers must 'transpose the author's intention to the screen as faithfully as possible', Shubik (2000: 88) added that this involved finding 'the director whom he believes will be most closely in empathy with that particular writer or whose strengths ... will bring most to it'.

There was certainly empathy between Clarke and miner's son Minton, whose shared political and artistic sensibilities were drawn from similar experiences; as Clarke told Cas Cassidy (1979), 'Roy and I are working-class lads who were lucky enough to escape'. Discussing the themes of *Funny Farm* with Shiva Naipaul (1975), Clarke and Minton bounced off each other to form, as Naipaul observed, 'an articulate duet'. They met at Questors, but their first television collaboration was the now lost *Half Hour Story* play *The Gentleman Caller* (1967), the first of many Clarke portrayals of an authority figure – in this case a social security snooper – colliding with individuals. Over the next decade they worked together repeatedly, until disagreements over *Scum*. Minton's confrontational personality rubbed others up the wrong way – Shubik (2000: 92–5) recalled that *Sling Your Hook* (1969) was an unhappy collaboration. However, in the words of Graham Benson, 'Alan directed Roy Minton's work better than anybody else, and Roy wrote better when Alan Clarke was directing' (Kelly 1998: 48).

A fine early example of their collaboration can be found in *Goodnight Albert* (1968). The kind of 'small cast in a confined space' drama celebrated by Alun Owen, it focuses on the generational interplay between miner Albert (Victor Henry) and his Gran (Gwen Nelson). Sparkling with Minton's detailed and witty characterisation, the play was praised by Francis King (1968) as 'acted to perfection ... life-like, original and moving'. In a statement echoed by critics throughout Clarke's career, King added that this production made a welcome change from those 'in which working-class characters are treated either as comic cretins or ill-mannered and insensitive boors'. The play also anticipates later Clarke films such as *Rita, Sue and Bob Too* (1987) and *Road* by addressing changes in the role of masculinity in society, as Gran attempts to persuade Albert to move into a factory job. Albert plans an escape into the mythologised 1960s liberation, while the older generation details the realities of social mobility: 'I'm talking about government – your gaffers', Gran states.

Clarke again reinforces the impression of confined space through his highly characteristic use of big close-ups. But he also achieves this through other visual ideas, not least a nascent distanciation. In one cut from living room to kitchen, Clarke adds depth to the transition by repetition of framing. He places Gran in the bottom right of frame, and then cuts to the kitchen, in which a tap is framed in the same size and position as her. The cut between these shots leaves Gran in the viewer's perception, a claustrophobic companion following Albert into the next room. Clarke's use of angles lends unease as well as visual panache to a play whose 'kitchen sink' iconography may have led other directors to approach it in a more dour style. Clarke's bold foregrounding of objects such as the tap and a kettle coming to the boil resembles some of Joseph Losey's compositions, and its distanciating effects recall the strategies of Douglas Sirk. The familiar is thereby defamiliarised, from the very first shot, a disorienting close-up of a turning doorknob shot from an unusual angle. Equally, although there is a long conversation sequence employing big close-ups which implies a conventional approach, it is shot in a subtextually disturbing way. The two characters talk whilst lying in their own beds in separate rooms, but Clarke's use of positioning and the logic of alternating/reverse shots implies that they are in bed together, forming a subtle visual approximation of their claustrophobic relationship. 'There's only one bird for me, duck', Albert says, 'and that's you'.

Between the recording and transmission of Minton and Clarke's next television collaboration, *Stand by Your Screen* (1968), Clarke made his West End debut with Minton's *Funny Sunday*, featuring two of its cast, Gwen Watford and Patricia Lawrence. *Stand by Your Screen* was made for London Weekend Television because, after *Thief*, Clarke's previous ITV play (and the last regular *Half Hour Story*), LWT and Thames became the new franchise holders in the London region. One of six self-contained plays in the strand *Company of Five*, in which John Neville led a repertory company of actors (Alun Owen wrote Clarke's other contribution, *Gareth*), *Stand by Your Screen* is one of Minton's most wittily provocative scripts. Neville plays Christopher Gritter, who refuses to participate in the 'big, bad world', and lives behind screens in his parents' living room. He emerges to deposit a whoopee cushion, to jog to the door in crash helmet and goggles to destroy the newspaper, or to suggest a novel way for his mother's friend to celebrate getting her new television set: 'We'll make love on your new coat, our bodies suffused with telly tints as we gently rock to the lulling rhythms of the Epilogue.' She suggests that this 'spineless and sick in the head' individual 'should be locked up', but his parents have a different response – they refuse to even acknowledge his presence. The ensuing collisions are frequently hilarious, powered by an energetic performance from Neville, who brings out Christopher's mood swings from sombre reflection through verbal flights of fancy to nostril-flaringly camp provocation.

On one level, Christopher is a figure of revolt against suburban conformity. His father Norman (Cyril Luckham) delivers a bored monologue on the minutiae of his working day, and has a bathroom routine to which Christopher can set his clock. His parents have had a 'seeing is believing' faith in the media, and have been content to not think too much (when asked to consider the starving millions, Norman replies, 'Name two'). The internalisation of social pressures into the family unit is connected with the media through the central ambiguity raised in the title – the connection between the screens of the media and the 'screens' behind which Christopher hides. It is tempting to read Christopher as symbolising the single play itself. His attempts to bring the cultural revolution into the home from a screen in the corner of the room are ignored. His recurring question 'Is it time?' hints at direct action but is unanswered; he and Bess retire behind the screens for a bit of permissiveness; and his coded pronouncements (messages hidden in the settee) remain cryptic. It seems ironic, therefore, that one reviewer was stumped by the play's ambiguities, arguing that audiences might 'stick with obscurity ... to be enlightened in due course', but that obscurity should not 'develop into plain boredom' (Moreton 1968).

However, Minton's concern with communication is not obscure, but rooted in character. Christopher disturbs his mother Ada (Gwen Watford) by suggesting that she is lonely, prompting both parents to consider that their marriage has 'stagnated'. Although she believes that 'There's beauty in us' and that they need not 'die before we die', Norman is of the opinion that 'People like us don't talk, we just do, we carry on'. Given the impoverishment of discourse through the press, television and education, all of which reinforce the state's view that 'The world revolves around a pound note', all they can hold on to is, in Bess's words, 'a sort of communication words would destroy'. In this context, Christopher's flights of fancy are grounded in and by their social context, as he tests the limits of discourse, exploring the ways in which language now stultifies intimacy. Minton connects private and public spaces in Christopher's assertion to camera that 'If you're poor, you're mad; if you're rich, you're eccentric', and, with the purportedly liberating cultural revolution in full swing, prophetically observes: 'You can do anything, anything at all. If you can afford it. You'd better start saving'. He is last seen running on the spot, his movement as proscribed as Clarke's later protagonists, who are forced to go round in circles.

'Psychiatric therapy is fundamentally an agent for the state', Minton told Shiva Naipaul (1975) about *Funny Farm*, 'People are induced to accept rather than reject'. A similar point is made here, by Christopher's apparent acceptance of a traditional lifestyle, and by the play's connection of breakdown with institutionalisation, namely through his experiences of National Service. His reminiscences of very Clarkey off-duty exploits give way to disturbing memories of warfare – resembling, perhaps, Clarke's father's Second World War memories – and fascinatingly anticipate tropes in Clarke's later work. There are echoes of *Contact* in his description of waiting in the jungle for something to happen which remains unknowable to its protagonists: a fellow soldier's 'blood will spill on the soil of this alien land. And none of us knows why ... Fire we do. We were trained.' Like the military in those films, the Borstal trainees described by Archer in Minton's *Scum*, or children of the education system according to Trevor in *Made in Britain*, 'I am told not to think, but to do'. His mother and father have ignored much that he's said, but interject during this speech to directly address the audience with their own memories: 'Do you think he's alright?', 'He gets duty free cigarettes', 'He doesn't say much in his letters'. The shift in audience positioning caused by this intervention of direct address prefigures the moves between attachment with and detachment from protagonists in Clarke's 1980s work. This is particularly the case with *Elephant,* and much of Minton's dialogue here could be an epigram for that piece: 'Men are being killed ... by other men ... Down he goes, that unknown man ... Repetition breeds immunity, that's supposedly true. If so, I didn't get enough.'

To note such similarities is one thing, but to read Roy Minton's script in terms of its director's style two decades later is to risk imposing auteurist patterns. What of Clarke's handling of this script? Again, he is restricted by a single set, but provides images which are striking in themselves and which also reinforce theme. Sometimes Minton's swift call-and-response dialogue invites Clarke's hitherto trademark inter-cutting, but instead he holds on one character through several lines of dialogue, often from a surprising low angle from which the ceiling remains in shot. The play's opening caption is overlaid on a disorienting shot of a white surface which turns out to be close detail of the ceiling, followed by a sharp movement down to a face peering out between curtains – a monkey (Christopher in a mask) smoking a cigarette, the exotic made familiar by the screen in the corner of the room. This ever-present ceiling crucially delineates a claustrophobic space, which connects with Christopher's psychology and its relationship with family life and wider social factors. At one point he asks, 'Mummy, mummy, where is the womb? The security and comfort, the warmth, closeness, the inside better than the outside of the womb? Mother, why did you let me go? Why did you spew me out with that enormous shudder of pain and ecstasy into this temple of darkness?' The same could be asked of the army and other institutions which have left him adrift, unable to escape from the ultimate institution, the family. Spewed out from the 'womb' of the state, Christopher is as institutionalised as the patients who fear leaving a psychiatric hospital in *Funny Farm,* the trainees of *Scum,* the residents of an old people's home who return early from their honeymoon to that safe environment in *A Follower for Emily* (1974), and other figures in Clarke's work both with and without Minton.

Much of this work appeared at the BBC, which, as I will argue in Chapter 2, is where Clarke began to develop a truly individual voice. However, I am aware of the risk of evading the extent to which he was assigned work beyond his dominant thematic concerns; for instance, of his two *Wednesday Play* productions I discuss *Sovereign's Company* and not his less characteristic study in eccentricity *The Last Train Through Harecastle Tunnel* (1969). Therefore, I will reflect upon the 'studio system' of the single play which I described in my Introduction by discussing one of the less representative pieces with which Clarke developed his technique as a director on 16mm film: *The Hallelujah Handshake* (1970).

Following a superb year for Colin Welland, it is not surprising that reviewers privileged him as the author of *The Hallelujah Handshake*. This was one of four plays for which he won the Society of Film and Television Arts Award for best script, along with *Slattery's Mounted Feet*, *Say Goodnight to Your Grandma* and *Roll on Four O'Clock*. Although the play was largely well reviewed, it is worth focusing on a negative statement by John Lawrence (1970): 'Colin Welland has a strong sense of how people talk and behave, Alan Clarke an equally strong sense of how they move, but these two qualities remained separate.' Given the critical privileging of writers over directors, Lawrence's separation of their respective methods is interesting. Although the play features the embryonic use of Clarke's directorial signature of the camera following walking characters, his style is dedicated to 'serving' Welland's excellent script. Although Welland told Gordon Burn (1970) that this was his first play not to have 'come straight out of my own background and experience', he was still utilising the talent for observation which had prompted friends to say of *Bangelstein's Boys*: 'You didn't write that – you remembered it!' As he told Ian Greaves that a Methodist minister he knew in Barnes 'told me the story about this man who everybody tried to help but was totally without any responsibility ... you would find yourself let down by him and troubled by him and yet he had a charm and enthusiasm'. However, even in 'serving' Welland's script, there are again directorial touches from Clarke which both reflect and enhance its meanings.

The Hallelujah Handshake is the story of David Williams (Tony Calvin), although it is a mark of the play's structure that we do not discover his real identity until near the end. A small-time thief on a repetitive cycle of police warnings and short prison sentences, Williams is an inveterate liar who passes himself off as Henry Tobias Jones (a touring writer who once had a football trial), John Rhys Davies (BBC Welsh Orchestra) and others. We first glimpse Henry in a pub apparently with friends, but something seems wrong. Clarke neatly expresses Henry's alienation from the others through changes in positioning and framing: as he moves tighter on Henry's lost expression, the other characters become almost nebulous through their foregrounding in the frame, as shoulders that expel him from the group. This movingly effective device expresses two vital elements in the play: firstly, that the lonely Henry has tried to join a community but is estranged from it, and secondly that we too are estranged from him, watching from the outside with no access to his thoughts.

The scene in this pub is intercut with the community which he will go on to join, a Methodist congregation involved in the 'fellowship' of 'communal worship'. Their hymns are held over shots from the pub, as if enveloping Henry in that fellowship, offering the sanctuary of the hallelujah handshake – in his script, Welland (1970) describes the pub as 'a church substitute'. Unlike Henry's thoughts, those of the congregation are accessed, through brief interior monologues during the hymn: 'Please, God, a baby'; 'Christ! Why has your strident call to arms peppered your ranks with these post-menopausal monsters?'; 'Must remember to put the lamb in early'. The minister, Geoff, describes 'the gift of love' as 'the foundation of true happiness'. Arriving in search of this 'gift of love', Henry is welcomed into the group, but his keenness to please exposes his embroidered history. He volunteers a talk about his Bahamas visits, but it becomes clear he's never been, and conducts a choir with tremendous vigour but embarrassing inexpertise. He recruits children into Sunday school, and gives them a thunderous, disturbing lecture on sin, foaming at the mouth. This scene exemplifies Tony Calvin's superb performance, skillfully executing shifts in empathy. As the play's Assistant Floor Manager Graham Benson said, 'The whole difficulty of the piece was casting this lead role – a man slightly disturbed, and with a heightened imagination, capable of immense confidence and desperate shyness' (Kelly 1998: 36). However, speaking to Ian Greaves, although Welland thought Clarke was 'a terrific director', he reflected that the casting did not reflect the man on whom he was based: 'he was very very suave and totally presentable and without any obvious problems, whereas ... you would have had suspicions about ... the one that he cast in the play'.

Henry's loneliness seems so pervasive that it can no longer be cured by meeting people. He watches football with George's family, and seems to have found companionship, but – to quote the script – the 'normality of the family cuts his feet from under him'. The scene changes as he reaches out emotionally, heightened by Clarke's editing, an abrupt cut to find the family tense, exhausted and, according to the script, 'constipated by his flow of words' (Welland 1970). He tells them that 'nobody's ever listened – makes you think, you know, wonder if you've anything to say, you know, interesting, worthwhile ... Nobody tells you, you see, who you are ... But here today, you've all listened.' This brings to mind Ken Loach's *Kes* (1969), in which Welland played Mr Farthing, the only adult to listen to Billy Casper; however, although Farthing helped Billy briefly find his true voice, Henry's identity remains 'in limbo'. The end comes for Henry when worried parents demand his 'full case history'. The audience would like this too, having been told only what other characters think about him. Unable to give details because he lacks a sense of his own identity, it is only as Henry that he can sing, 'This is my story, this is my song'. He has also committed thefts, but the fact that these are not shown reinforces the sense that this is not why he 'conned' his way into the community; nor, perhaps, why they expel him. Trust works both ways – having reached out for love, he is told that 'we think you need treatment'. With his 'cry from the wilderness' unheard, he leaves; calling himself John, he joins an Anglo-Catholic congregation, gaining enough trust to give Communion. He is pursued by Geoff, who warns the Reverend Whitehead that 'he'll bring your church down', but Whitehead argues that 'it's because people have pasts that they come to us'. Ultimately, John betrays this trust by stealing and selling a raffle prize. Like Trevor in *Made in Britain*, his story is outranked by those of the police and magistrate, and his identity is finally removed through a spell in prison. Echoing the opening sequence, a shot of him washing in prison is overlaid with the sound-track of the Reverend Whitehead's congregation, a goodbye handshake as the community washes its hands of him.

If Henry/John/David's identity is 'in limbo', this limbo is the space between the stories he and other people tell to construct that identity. The crucial question asked by George's son – 'Why does Mister Jones tell lies?' – is beyond the adults because it is a call to understand rather than judge Henry, and also because it is a direct question which allows for none of the evasiveness of adult relationships. This is portrayed most disturbingly in a scene between Henry and Jim's wife, Brenda, both of whom have 'a hole in your life'. She is desperate for a baby, he for companionship; she seems to chat him up, he offers to provide her baby. Confusing with temporal ellipsis, Clarke cuts to shots with no narrative motivation – Henry at the children's playgroup, little girls on swings. And then, brutally, he cuts to the irretrievable breakdown of the argument, and Henry's outburst against her 'ogling me … undressing me. Why don't you leave me alone? Please leave me alone!' The scene raises questions about the story behind 'David', but they are not followed up, and the play refuses to judge or even articulate his thoughts. So why does Henry tell lies? The question directly follows his failed appeal to be embraced into the family, to 'sit in your branches', and as such implicates an increasingly alienating society. Looking back at Henry's speech to George's family, the repetition of 'you know' and 'you see' is striking because neither they nor the audience do. This impression is reinforced by Henry repeating his actions; though this plot repetition was bemoaned by critics as if unintended, it anticipates a key trope of Clarke's later work. The play ends with Henry striding off with his latest community, the Salvation Army. In spite of everything, if that way lies salvation, we hope he finds it.

Henry's fate confronts an individual identity with the judicial system, whose workings Clarke explores in greater depth in much of his subsequent work. The following section provides a case study of *To Encourage the Others*, to discuss the themes and visual approaches which mark it out as a landmark in Clarke's career, as well as the issues which it raises with regards to television direction.

To Encourage the Others (1972)

Nineteen-year-old Derek Bentley was the victim of one of the most horrific miscarriages of justice in British legal history. On the night of 2 November 1952, he and sixteen-year-old Christopher Craig attempted to break into a wholesaler's warehouse in Croydon. Disturbed by police, Craig drew a gun and a stand-off ensued, during which PC Sidney Miles was shot dead. When Craig was brought to trial at the Old Bailey, Bentley was in the dock with him. Although Bentley was unarmed and was under arrest at the time of the shooting, he was accused of inciting Craig, with the phrase – disputed, as we shall see – 'let him have it, Chris'. Both were found guilty of murder, but, because Craig was too young to hang, Bentley alone was sentenced to death. Despite widespread protests, the Home Secretary refused to intervene, and Bentley was hanged at Wandsworth Prison on 28 January 1953.

There began a long struggle to clear his name, crucial in which was David Yallop's book *To Encourage the Others*. Investigative journalist Yallop was another of Clarke's collaborators whose work explores similar areas. *Beyond Reasonable Doubt?* touches upon scapegoats and individual victims of injustice; *How They Stole the Game* studies FIFA President Dr João Havelenge, sharing with *The Firm* a concern with those feeding off football; while the semi-fictional *Unholy Alliance* – which Clarke and Yallop discussed filming – portrays a real-life global cartel dwarfing that portrayed by Clarke in *Beloved Enemy* (1981). Clarke and Yallop were of Craig's and Bentley's generation; Yallop witnessed the public response whilst growing up in their neighbourhood. Inspired by rigger John Silver, Yallop began research while still a floor manager, gaining the support of Bentley's family; Iris Bentley (1995: 12) felt that Yallop's work 'did the trick', as in 'twenty years since Derek had been hanged ... a whole generation had grown up not knowing anything about the Craig/Bentley case'. First published in 1971, Yallop's book remains a powerful documentation of a miscarriage of justice, from arrest and trial to appeal and executive non-intervention, as Yallop unpicks the contradictions, hypocrisies and downright fabrications which led to Bentley becoming 'the victim of judicial murder' (Yallop 1971: 14). Yallop developed a television play version, with Clarke involved from the beginning. They gained the support of script editor Margaret Hare (who as Margaret Matheson would later produce *Scum* and *Made in Britain*) and Mark Shivas, the play's producer and narrator, whose school had been barely a mile from the rooftop on which the shooting took place.

Yallop told *The Guardian*'s Michael Behr (1972) that 'It's because of Clarke's reputation as a director that I've got doors opened that I would never have got opened before'. And yet, the play's genesis was far from smooth. According to Yallop, Gerald Savory, BBC Head of Drama, 'said, "Where's the relevance for today in this play?" And Clarkey was enraged by that question. His response was, "They took the boy out and murdered him. There's the fucking relevance for today"' (Kelly 1998: 55). This 'crusading piece' achieved Shivas's stated aim to bring the 'injustice ... to the attention of parliament' (*Director*). Home Secretary Reginald Maudling responded that 'I have fully reviewed the facts of this case in the light of Mr. Yallop's book and television production ... I have found nothing to justify any action on my part ... Although there are some understandable discrepancies of detail in the account of witnesses of the confused events on the warehouse roof, the essential facts of the shooting are clear. There is no information before me to cause me to think that the verdict of the jury was wrong' (Hansard 1972). Part of Maudling's response was read out in a voice-over by Shivas which was added to the play's 1991 repeat. Though this repeat demonstrated the play's lasting impact, it seemed to no avail, as Shivas remarked: 'We had hoped for a posthumous pardon for Bentley, but it still to this day hasn't come' (*Director*). However, two years later, Bentley was granted a limited pardon, which accepted he should not have been hanged, but maintained his guilt. Finally, in the context of a new Criminal Cases Review Commission, Bentley was granted a full pardon on 30 July 1998.

The reading of personal style into this play demonstrates the limits of critical terminology. It was a real-life event which motivated its production, not an auteur's dominant themes. And yet, the presence of potential Clarke 'signatures' in the play provides a fascinating extra layer. Clarke directed Roy Minton's *Horace* for the same slot a week earlier, which also featured an innocent adult with a child's mental age, and a younger but more aware accomplice, ultimately swallowed up by institutions. As Shivas put it, Yallop's play 'appealed to Alan because

Alan's work was in particular always on the side of the underdog'
(*Director*). Clarke also uses Yallop's source material to explore discourses
on language and empowerment. Drawing its dramatic essence from the
book's investigative drive – uncovering the flaws and gaps in information presented to the jury – the play is located in a typical Clarke space,
addressing the difference between stories told by individuals and those
told about them. Chief among these is the phrase 'Let him have it',
which, as Yallop notes, has 'become a classic example' of the 'ambiguity
of our language' (Yallop 1971: 59). The phrase was challenged in court
in those terms – did Bentley mean 'let him have the gun, Chris' or
'shoot him, Chris'? As its title suggests, this is a major point in Peter
Medak's film treatment of the case, *Let Him Have It* (1991). The phrase
has appeared in countless articles and books, as well as songs, including
Elvis Costello's *Let Him Dangle* and Ralph McTell's *Bentley and Craig*.
However, none of these challenge the fact that, according to several
witnesses – among them one of the policemen never brought to court
(Trow 1990) – Bentley never actually said it. (Though Iris Bentley advised
the makers of *Let Him Have It*, she was critical of that title.) Also not
added to the available evidence was the fact that Bentley was unfit even
to stand trial because of his epilepsy and mental deficiency.

According to Steve Greenfield and Guy Osborn (1996: 1197), the
chief weakness of Medak's film was its 'failure to offer critical challenge
and to construct a "reality" while displacing or clouding the "authentic
reality"'. This is just one of the areas in which *To Encourage the Others*
surpasses *Let Him Have It* as an exploration of the case. As well as
recording the descriptions of 'Bentley', Clarke creates a space for the
real Bentley's story, or at least foregrounds its absence during the trial.
The play focuses for eighty minutes on events in the courtroom; by
contrast, these take up barely ten minutes of *Let Him Have It*. Yallop's
book and Medak's film both explore Bentley's childhood; the latter
opens with Derek's father rescuing him from beneath a bombed
building, establishing a contrast with his inability to rescue him from
the legal landslide which follows. The book details his medical history
and experiences of approved school. Both Medak and Yallop, therefore,
contrast the influence of Christopher Craig and his gang on Bentley –
and the Bentley family's attempts to keep them apart – with the
supposed 'influence' of Bentley on Craig on the night in question. By
contrast, *To Encourage the Others* opens with events on the roof, excising
Bentley's history until much later. Clarke lends extra weight to this
material through his two primary strategies – a drama-documentary
deployment of dramatisation with a scrupulous adherence to archive
material, and a highly expressive use of mise-en-scène.

John Caughie (1980) distinguished two forms of drama-documentary. Much of Clarke's work could be located within what Caughie called 'documentary drama', in which writers and directors create an essentially dramatic (albeit heavily researched) fiction, which they validate as a truth representation through the use of documentary visuals. However, *To Encourage the Others* resides in Caughie's other category, the 'dramatised documentary', in which research is conducted as rigorously as if for a documentary, often by journalists or current affairs departments, and is then dramatised, often around transcripted material. It is at heart a documentary – Clarke made the orthodox documentaries *Bukovsky* (1977), *Vodka Cola* (1980) on multinational corporations, and *The British Desk* (1984) on apartheid-era South Africa's intelligence operations in Britain. Reconstructing observed reality in a studio was a crucial element of early film documentary in Britain, even in the poetic *Night Mail* (1936), and similar technical constraints led the BBC to re-enact field research in such productions as *I Want to Be an Actor* (1946) and *Strike!* (1955). The format has its own space in the history of the radical single play, particularly those made by Granada which consciously pushed journalism on to the front pages, such as *Hillsborough* (1996) and *Who Bombed Birmingham?* (1990), an extension of *World in Action*. The courtroom scenes are all the more disturbing for having been taken from transcripts.

As with so many other drama-documentaries, the play had a problematic relationship with the reality it portrayed. Though impressed by the play, Graham Clarke (1972) argued that 'the full documentary force was lost to some extent when the author turned from hard fact to dramatisation', while John Bowen (1972) claimed that 'The formality of the dialogue taken from the court record fitted awkwardly with the stodginess of the invented or remembered scenes out of court'. The BBC were similarly wary of the presence of drama. Reacting to requests for a repeat, BBC2 Controller Robin Scott contacted the solicitor to check the Corporation's position following the then Home Secretary's decision to re-examine the case. Though keen on repeating this 'good production', Scott noted the possibility of refusing 'if I thought that its pleading was founded on spurious knowledge or trivial reasoning' (BBC WAC file T47/220/1). Meanwhile, the production team faced the ramifications of portraying real people, many of whom – the defence and prosecution counsels, Craig, Bentley's family – were still alive. Despite this, Shivas told Michael Behr that 'hardly any of the actors wished to meet them, or go back and look at them'. The exception, Yallop added in the same interview, was Charlie Bolton, who 'became emotionally involved with the family', and borrowed some of Derek's clothes to wear in the play. Such closeness between family and production team caused an unfamiliar problem for the play's designer, Daphne Shortman, when William Bentley contacted her to suggest the play should be shown on BBC1. Shortman noted in a memo, 'As I am one of his few points of contact, he thinks that I should be able to help him and it is difficult to explain that all I did was to design the play, however involved I privately became in his problems' (BBC WAC file T47/220/1). Meanwhile, the prospect of legal action led to the removal from all repeat transmissions of a section of voice-over regarding the pathologist Dr David Haler's statement on bullet calibration, although W. H. Allen had resisted a similar complaint against the original book (BBC WAC file T47/220/1).

The play's documentary material does not restrict its dramatic impact. It is a gripping and powerful courtroom drama, a form whose strengths and weaknesses were described by Steve Greenfield and Guy Osborn (1996: 1181):

> The process of 'the trial' has itself been seen as an arena with drama-turgical potential, and law, being predicated on a number of binary themes provides great scope for screenwriters and directors. Courtroom drama also allows actors to give full reign to their oratorical skills by giving the great plea in mitigation or through a withering cross-examination. Their portrayals are often romanticised, and the films tend to concentrate on specific areas that avoid the mundane and highlight the extraordinary.

Much of the play's 'dramatic' power is drawn from its 'documentary' use of transcripts. Take the summing-up by trial judge Lord Chief Justice Goddard (Roland Culver). With a theatrical flourish, he wields a knuckleduster at the jury to criticise Craig and Bentley, and also remarks, 'If I were to whip out a revolver and point it at you, it would be no answer for me to say "Oh, I didn't mean to kill him; I only meant to *wound* him"'. His mocking intonation reinforces the callous simplification of Craig's evidence, an act of malicious roleplay by the stereotypical eccentric judge. However, it is taken from the transcripts, even if Clarke and Yallop make it seem more abrupt by omitting a sentence in which Goddard introduced the statement as a legal hypothesis.

The play has moments of striking oratory and excellent performances, but avoids the 'extraordinary' moments which have led some directors to 'romanticise' the legal process. The play's chilling success lies in a striving for the opposite effect, as Clarke told Michael Behr: 'the main thing about the production was to keep it reasonably low-key. It's not by any means as theatrical and bizarre as the reality of it was. If you'd done it like that, people would have said, "No, you're laying it on too thickly".' It compares favourably with other miscarriage of justice films such as *In the Name of the Father* (1993), Jim Sheridan's film about the Guildford Four. Chief among Sheridan's dramatic devices was the stirring but invented High Court speech of a solicitor played by Emma Thompson. In such pieces rests the prosecution case against the fusion of dramatic and documentary forms. The idea that such personalising devices have to be used to gain an audience's empathy is a denial of the autonomous power of the facts, and of factual programming. The cornerstone of Sheridan's film is the relationship between father and son Guiseppe and Gerry Conlon, but many of the scenes between them are factually bogus because they never shared a cell. Phil Penfold (1994) argued that the film should not be condemned for such 'planned inaccuracies' when it remains a 'withering and aggressive attack on the lies, cover-ups and downright cruelty of the British establishment'. The use of true stories invites criticism over fictionalisation and dramatic compression, since real life has too many superfluous bit players and no convenient climaxes for commercial breaks. The problem lies not only in inevitable structural alterations but in Sheridan's manipulation of the date of Conlon's alibi. As Martin Bright (1994) stated, 'This is, after all, a film about a man who spent 14 years in prison because people made up stories about him'. *To Encourage the Others* is adamant that it will not 'make up stories' about its characters – this principle is ingrained in Clarke's style.

'Style' is a problematic term, with the play complicating discussion of authorship in two ways. Firstly, drama-documentary necessitates a fidelity to textual material, and a multi-layered process of 'adaptation' – from Yallop's book, his original interviews and court transcripts. This leaves the director a functional imperative, as Clarke told Michael Behr: 'The main thing was just to do it'. Citing this extra-textual social motivation – the single play's 'life-after-television ethic' – Andrew Clifford (1991) argued that in *To Encourage the Others* 'Clarke concentrated on the more material components of the drama: script, actors, plot'. Secondly, *To Encourage the Others* was shot not on film but on videotape in a television studio, employing a multi-camera set-up. These conditions of production suggest restrictions upon Clarke's technique. Apart from its filmed opening sequence and a flashback, over ninety minutes of videotaped material was shot over just three days. Given that all of Friday 11 February 1972 and most of the shooting days Saturday 12 and Sunday 13 were used for camera rehearsal, the total recording time was in fact just six hours (Yallop 1972, BBC WAC file R134/538/2).

It is much quicker to record a scene with several cameras simultaneously than it is to record a scene repeatedly from various angles with a single camera. However, the costs resulted in punishing schedules and hectic conditions, reducing the scope for individual expression. David Hare told Julian Petley (1985) that 'No director, no matter how good he is, can ignore the pressures of time and the technical process'. Not without reason were single play strands' rationed film slots so sought after. 'Advocates of working on film had a decisive argument when they spoke of "finesse",' wrote W. Stephen Gilbert (1995: 14), 'A cut created at leisure on the bench will always be sharper and more flattering than a switch between cameras directed at screech pitch in a sweltering studio gallery'. Furthermore, the studio is 'entrenched in the tradition of naturalism and all the political implications of how naturalism works as a broadcast code. For the studios are not manned by drama specialists ... The accumulated habits of creating a "look" in the studio are difficult to dislodge' (Gilbert 1980: 43). Stephen Frears remarked that Clarke's willingness to take on such productions may have made him seem a 'bread-and-butter director. He did tape as well as film, he did studio productions, which were somehow looked down upon in a rather silly, snobbish way' (Kelly 1998: 66). *To Encourage the Others* disproves the suggestion that multi-camera tape recording leads to anonymous direction. It contains many interesting visual ideas, which reflect the development of Clarke's individual style and reinforce the themes of the script.

He demonstrates a mastery of studio mise-en-scène. The play's first studio scene – following the opening filmed rooftop sequence – is directed with real economy. Clarke's use of fast pans, zooms and interrupted framing results in a disorienting portrayal of the Bentley family's induction into a Kafkaesque nightmare. Coming down the stairs to answer the door to the police, Iris Bentley is framed in a low-angle wide-shot. Rather than cutting to another camera, he pans left with her, and holds an over-the-shoulder shot as she opens the door. Although admittedly undeveloped, this demonstrates one of Clarke's visual tropes, the placing of the viewer on the side of a character by positioning us with them and, notably, against the state. Writing about Ken Loach's *The Big Flame* (1969), Raymond Williams (1977a: 70–1) remarked upon 'how regular and how naturalised the position of the camera *behind the police*' is in reports of social disturbance, to the extent that 'The police are seen *with* the camera' whilst the disturbance 'is the object'. From this, he observed that the conventions of actuality are 'inherently determined by viewpoint in the precise technical sense of the position of the camera'. The camera generally enters situations behind, or with, the police. Clarke's redirection of audience positioning is keenly felt given the preceding sequence – after all, the police are investigating the apparent murder of one of their own by an as-yet unsympathetic figure – and the context of the time. Such miscarriages of justice never filtered into the world of PC George Dixon, the archetypal English bobby of *The Blue Lamp* (1950) and *Dixon of Dock Green* (1955–74). *The Blue Lamp* was inspired by the murder of PC Nat Edgar by twenty-two-year-old army deserter Donald Thomas, and Yallop is among those who believe that the police's actions following Miles's death were motivated by anger at the refusal of the death penalty for Thomas. Unlike in *The Blue Lamp*, we see the consequences for the cop-killer after their capture. It is interesting, therefore, that Clarke's approach to this scene problematises the language of the cop show; as John Tulloch (1990: 64) argued, police series often excise two-thirds of the legal apparatus, including court and prison, creating the 'ideological effect of inscribing police *within* the genre as agents of an immediate and self-sufficient justice'. Clarke's work often examines this, opening with the after-effects of arrest in *A Life Is for Ever*, *Scum* and *Made in Britain*. Confusion reigns as the police burst into the Bentley home, and our sympathies are complicated by the hostility and suspicion of the family with whom we are initially positioned. A policeman emerges from upstairs with a knife, and is accused by Mrs Bentley of wanting to plant it on Derek. The accusation chimes with the shot structure; given the policeman's abrupt entry into and exit from the frame, the knife's convenient appearance does seem sinister.

In his treatment of the courtroom scenes, Clarke draws significant layers of meaning. With much of the play taking place on one set, the director's opportunities for visual innovation are limited, particularly within the givens of the courtroom framework. The interior setting is a given, as is the narrative drive (towards a verdict of guilty or not guilty). The adversarial symmetry of witnesses and legal figures on either side of the set is ideally suited to the oppositional placement of cameras in the conventional multi-camera set-up. Clarke employs these expertly, as in the evidence given by Craig's father. Defence questioning involves fifteen shots over three minutes, with Parris and Craig largely in mid-shot, with cuts to the conventional third camera position, a long-shot to establish space. There is also one shot from an angle which allows Parris and Christopher Craig to share the frame, with Parris made smaller by Craig's foregrounding, becoming almost an extension of him. Directly following this, the prosecution cross-examination is much more brutal, featuring fourteen shots in half the time. Mr Craig is isolated in mid-shots which exclude details of the court; as he wavers, these become medium close-ups, trapping him as the prosecution questions rain in. The shot of Craig looking on is echoed, recalling the previous sequence as its points are rebutted.

Multiple cameras allow for variety within the studio set-up. As in the courtroom scenes he shot later for *Horatio Bottomley* (1972), Clarke varies angles and employs cluttered framing, resulting in compositions which reinforce the play's wider implications. Craig and Bentley are often framed in the middle ground in shots which are mediated by the foregrounding of jurors, with society literally boxing them in. Our first view of Bentley in the dock is partially blocked by a nebulous fore-grounded juror – given the sentence which is to come, it is notable that we see him first as a disrupted body. As the accusation against them is read, a forced perspective shot obscures them with foregrounded law books and legal robes – Clarke cuts to this official view of them (from this angle, Goddard's view) directly on the words 'together murdered a policeman'. Similar shot strategies recur with an even greater sense of fatalism in the Convention scenes in *Danton's Death*, as armed guards frame the authority figures who look on at Danton's impassioned but doomed defence. Another crucial part of *To Encourage the Others* is elegantly summed up in one cut: as the jury are counselled that Craig and Bentley should be tried 'on the evidence alone', Clarke cuts to the Bentley family waiting outside. They have Derek's coat, which could provide evidence that Derek wasn't dragged along the roof by Sergeant Fairfax as the police claim, but which will not be produced in court. The cumulative effect is to draw attention to the essential limits of the discourse: the things that the jury do not see. Unlike the jury, we have been made aware that Derek has recently been assaulted, that the prosecution were present at a meeting during which the defence explained their entire argument, and that Bentley's own defence counsel stated that 'I think both the little bastards ought to swing'.

The cramped mise-en-scène, with compositions cluttered by on-lookers, reinforces the vicarious act of looking on, an idea pursued as relentlessly here as in David Lean's treatment of courtroom scenes in *Madeleine* (1950). Vicarious activity is a major theme, capturing the tensions surrounding emerging youth culture in the 1950s – Clarke, sharing Yallop's belief that this was 'a rationed generation', wanted to shoot in black and white (*Director*). The trial revolved around inter-twined notions of vicarious responsibility: the inactive politicians and appeal judges who allowed Bentley to hang, the protesting crowds, and the nature of both the crime (Bentley was only ever looking-on) and its punishment. As John Parris, Craig's defence counsel, told Yallop (1971: 13), 'Bentley was a vicarious sacrifice, the innocent scapegoat released into the desert to die and thus bear away into oblivion the guilt of a whole people'. It was, therefore, 'in the public interest that somebody, anybody, should die because a police officer had been killed'. Like the gangsters of contemporaneous British social problem films, Bentley and Craig became 'folk devils', to employ Stanley Cohen's term for those people inscribed with the 'set of images of who constitutes the typical deviant' (Cohen 1980: 16). In *Stand by Your Screen*, Christopher describes himself as 'one of them what people don't like but find necessary to convince themselves of their own sanity'. Clarke repeatedly gives a voice to these figures, who have been exiled from societies whose worst features they embody.

It is over an hour into the play that documentary voice-over intervenes to present a direct rebuttal of the prosecution case, outlining the key facts of which the jury were unaware. Some might see this as a collapsing of the dramatic form. However, in such productions it is necessary to reclaim drama-documentary from debates over colliding epistemologies to argue for its formal specificity; *To Encourage the Others* offers, in Derek Paget's wider description of the genre, something 'that no other form can achieve, uniting within one text television's historic popular mission to inform and to entertain' (Paget 1998a: 3). Much of the play's power comes from the jarring moments in which the unfolding drama is interrupted by documentary voice-over. As a device this replicates the sheer power of Yallop's original journalism, and reflects the horror of the case without a fictionalised on-screen representative spelling it out. Of course, part of the Bentley tragedy is that – unlike Goddard, who made some 250 interruptions to proceedings, many reinforcing the prosecution case – there was no 'character' in the 'drama' who spoke out in such a way. Furthermore, this shift to documentary address is evidence of a more complex discursive relationship at work. Clarke had already made conventional attempts to reflect both the inner and externally imposed stories of individuals, for instance in the intercutting and voice-overs of *The Hallelujah Handshake*, or, in *I Can't See My Little Willie* (1970), the way in which Arthur's inner life is reflected in the use of Donald McGill seaside postcards. *To Encourage the Others* represents the starting point for Clarke's analysis of form in the telling of stories about individuals, a motif which reaches its peak in the late 1980s. Christmas Humphries makes this reply to Derek Bentley's inarticulate denials: 'So, all these officers who've given evidence about what you said are not speaking the truth. Is that your story?' From the composition in which Craig and Bentley are obscured by law books, it is clear that only one story applies during the studio sequences: the official state story. Their statements are ignored, mocked or even invented. 'Let him have it, Chris' is just one of the 'verbals' attributed to Bentley or Craig by the police and reinforced by the legal and media apparatus. The consistency with which aggressive shot sequences mirror prosecution questions implicates the studio sequences themselves; Bentley's and Craig's stories are told only when the dramatic form gives way to documentary voice-over and, intriguingly, in the play's only filmed sequences. The two are interlinked when the voice-over introduces a flashback to a scene which was not reported in the trial, in which Bentley helped the police by trying to talk Craig into giving up.

'Piebald' filming – the mixture of videotaped interiors and filmed exteriors – has since become deeply unfashionable, but Clarke makes this necessity of production a strength. The play opens with the events on the rooftop, shot on the actual Croydon warehouse on which the real events took place (see Gillman 1972). This is their story, shot in the language of the comics and gangster movies so enjoyed by Craig and Bentley. Clarke's rapid intercutting generates suspense; sweat-drained close-ups add to the thriller style; Craig and Bentley wear the kind of suits seen in gangster movies. When Fairfax's description of the scene is given, it is contradicted in the same language, through photographs replicating not only documentary reportage but also frames of film. During the trial, the viewer is frustrated by the disparity between our memory of the opening scene (in which nobody says 'let him have it') and the way it is described. The shooting itself is also much less straightforward than its reporting in the studio. Whereas *Let Him Have It* films the gunshot from behind Craig's arm, leaving the audience in little doubt of his guilt, Yallop was convinced by various anomalies – not least the inaccuracy of Craig's weapon, exacerbated by the smaller-calibre bullets he used in it – that 'whoever did kill PC Miles, it was certainly not Christopher Craig' (Yallop 1971: 168). Although the aforementioned cuts to the script removed this statement, this scene heavily implies that he was accidentally shot by a police marksman. As Miles moves up the staircase, Clarke cuts quickly between Craig and various policemen taking aim, and employs parallel zooms to roughly match their framing, implicitly connecting them. With the protagonists framed in mid- and close-shots which exclude the weapons, the gunshot is not directly attributed.

After Shivas's voice-over deconstructs the trial, the final half-hour is a heart-rending portrayal of the Bentley family's frustrated campaign for a reprieve, and Bentley's final days in his death cell. Clarke's customary attention to detail led the nation's hangman, Albert Pierrepoint, to supervise the hanging scene. As Mark Shivas told Richard

Kelly, such things are 'more horrifying in reality, and the sheer banality of how this was done was particularly nasty'. It seems fitting that the director of *Christine* (1987) and *Elephant* should be exposed to horrifying banality. Unimpressed by an actor's attempts to secure the rope, Pierrepoint himself 'fixed it on Charlie Bolton's neck, just a bit too tight. And Charlie let out a scream because he was so psyched up.' After the shot was completed, nobody helped him remove the items, or talked to him, as 'the reality of it had just hit them very hard, and Albert was someone they wanted to be rid of as fast as possible' (Kelly 1998: 56–8).

Bentley's hanging is a stunningly realised piece of studio direction, a near-silent seventeen-shot sequence of brutal efficiency. Clarke cuts from the newspaper headline 'Bentley must hang' to Bentley hunched over a table with his warders. He is in profile, his warders sitting screen left, one with his back to us obscuring the other. Trapped in the frame by faceless figures of authority, Bentley swallows as if already grasping for breath. He is encouraged to stand as the anonymous agents of capital punishment move through the door behind him. A close shot captures Bentley's warder tying his hands behind his back; in wide shot a wardrobe is moved, uncovering the door to the next room. From another angle, the other warder's back obscures Bentley, who slowly turns to his left, at which point Clarke cuts to a shot from over his shoulder – between him and the warder, just as Bentley had been between the two warders, is the noose in the other room. Briefly returning to a full-shot of Bentley facing his fate, Clarke then brutally articulates that fate, cutting to a shot in which the noose replaces him in the centre of the frame. He zooms out as everyone enters the room, some faces disconcertingly seen through the noose, behind which Bentley eventually takes his place.

Again, Clarke moves from wide shot – obscured by the foregrounded hangman, onlookers settle into position – to close detail as Bentley's feet are ushered into their place between two planks. Clarke cuts to mid-shot with arms placing a white hood over Bentley's head, then returns to the previous shot to observe his legs being strapped up. Finally, in mid-shot, the hangman places the noose over Bentley's head and secures it. He removes his hand, and another mid-shot shows Bentley with the hood over his head and noose curled around him, a guard at his side clutching a securing rope. His fate sealed, Bentley speaks: 'I didn't tell him. I never told him to shoot that policeman.' And then, in a distressingly rapid piece of editing, he is killed. A figure disembodied in the frame presses down on the lever. In fact, his left hand appears to press down on the arm holding the lever, a gesture which reinforces the anonymity of the act, as the second hand creates the impression of him subconsciously wanting to restrain himself. Bentley's head appears very briefly in a medium close-up, in which onlookers are framed behind each shoulder, then falls out of the frame. Clarke cuts to the most graphic image, a low-angle shot with Bentley falling through the trap door and the rope tightening. He is surrounded, by the hangman on the lever, the warder holding the rope, and the rest – warders, priest, officials – disembodied or obscured, their identities irrelevant. The sequence has shown the enactment of legal *process* beyond the autonomy of its exponents, a process whose relentlessness is exacerbated by the mode of production. The machine which moved into gear with the opening of the first door has been captured in almost live action as part of another process. Far from suffering for not being a cinematic assemblage of individual shots, this sequence epitomises the way in which drama-documentary makers introduced, according to John Caughie (2000a: 122), 'a new form to twentieth-century art', building upon 'the specificities of the televisual' and its 'unique capabilities for the representation of the social real'. Our awkward positioning as spectators in this scene is derived precisely from the way the multi-camera set-up 'makes it difficult to cut into the middle' of a scene and 'identify the look of the spectator with the look of the character' as in narrative cinema, whilst at the same time demonstrating television's specific recourse to 'the *possibility* of the immediate'. This summary simplifies Caughie's position – the formal complexities of this '*aesthetics of immediacy*' will re-emerge later – but demonstrates the need for further critical exploration of a visual language too often ignored as an institutional compromise.

The sense of this sequence being unstoppable is reinforced by Clarke's framing of hands and feet, which excludes the rest of their owners' bodies. The effect is strangely unsettling, and can be compared with Charles Barr's analysis of Robert Bresson's framing of a hand in *Au hasard, Balthazar*: 'we are shown the *act* in isolation', a hand's 'isolation in the frame indicating its independence of ... conscious will' (1969: 108). Whereas such strategies represented in André Bazin's terms (1969) the phenomenology of grace, a deference to the spiritual, the automation of Bentley's jailers represents an emptying deference to the processes of law. Clarke returns to the frame from which Bentley dropped, with the rope moving where he had been standing. He holds a shot of two onlookers shifting uneasily, overlaying captions which quote the complacent belief of the Home Secretary, shortly before the Bentley incident, that an MP was 'moving in a realm of fantasy' if he thought every stage of the judicial system could go fundamentally wrong. Over a shot of the tightened rope slowly swaying comes the final observation:

'This has been the true story of how one teenager moved into that realm of fantasy.' This was a movement which Clarke himself would make in the borderline fantasy *Penda's Fen*. The next section provides a case study of this play, which shows Clarke's 16mm film technique and issues of authorship in a very different light.

Penda's Fen (1974)

An overtly traditional view of England is established in the opening sequence of *Penda's Fen*, only to be instantly problematised. What filmic language could be more familiar than a long shot of an English landscape scored by classical music? Particularly when it is the music of Sir Edward Elgar; the distinctively English heritage with which he is associated implies a cultural layering, akin to the Arcadian topography established by Chaucerian quotation in the evocative opening of Michael Powell and Emeric Pressburger's *A Canterbury Tale* (1944). This site is particularly rich: pastoral Worcestershire, with the purple line of the Malvern Hills in the distance. In this part of the country the mythic continuity of Englishness is seeped in the soil, from Shropshire – Housman's half-imaginary 'land of lost content' – to these Malvern Hills, traversed and celebrated by Elgar. His visionary oratorio conceived in that landscape, *The Dream of Gerontius*, underscores the voice of Stephen Franklin (Spencer Banks) as he addresses it, a voice described in the playscript (Rudkin 1975) as 'Adolescent, dark smouldering Midlands quality, overlaid with schooling'. 'Oh my country,' he begins, 'I say over and over: I *am* one of your sons, it is true; I am, I *am*. Yet how shall I show my love?'

But there is something unsettling in the troubled insistence of his assertion, and in this particular piece of Elgar's, distinctly darker than the imperial marches which led to his appropriation as a troubadour of jingoistic nationalism. Instead we hear *Oh Happy Suffering Soul*, and upon its 'fearful dissonance' lines of barbed wire are superimposed over that landscape. Imposed, a layer upon a layer. They frame the hills as a composition, an image of Englishness, and perversely resemble the lines for musical notation as if also framing the composition of the score. The serrated edge running along that landscape imprisons the image, but also resists something lurking within. A scarred arm reaches from the bottom of the screen; its hand grasps the barbed wire only to slip away. In this movement lies the core of the next ninety minutes: Stephen's attempt to grasp certainties and thereby escape them, and to question who 'I *am*', in the context of national identity. These counties trace their roots back before any other part of England, before Anglo-Saxon, Christian or Roman invasion. Its author explained in an introduction to a 1990 repeat that the 'English' name of the Malvern Hills actually 'has been pure Welsh, or British, for a good two thousand years'. In this landscape lies 'Layer upon layer upon layer of inheritance. What's in a name? The devil of a lot. Or, in the light of this film, the demon of a lot.' Another layer, credits, superimposed. This is Penda's fen. It is also *Penda's Fen*, by David Rudkin.

The disturbance of Stephen's sense of belonging enriches the play's evocation of adolescence. The pastor's son, nearing the end of his schooldays and the start of adulthood, has, to quote Rudkin (2003), 'his idealistic value-system and the precious tokens of his self-image all broken away – his parentage, his nationality, his sexuality, his conventional patriotism and faith'. The play quickly establishes these certainties. 'Overlaid with schooling', he has on his bookshelves Aeschylus and Euripides, historical sources with mythic resonance. He welcomes an injunction granted against *Who Was Jesus?*, by a woman not dissimilar to the 'clean-up TV' campaigner Mary Whitehouse, eulogising her and her husband for exercising 'eternal vigilance' to 'uphold our erring national family on its Christian path'. Like Trevor in *Made in Britain*, Stephen's national pride is built on a dangerously Aryan exclusion of external influence. As Robin Carmody (2001) noted, when *Penda's Fen* was transmitted, something else lurked within this part of England: the National Front had won a record by-election share at West Bromwich in 1971, and Enoch Powell, whose constituency was Wolverhampton, gave his Rivers of Blood speech in Smethwick. Defending English freedoms against Left-wing conspiracy theories, Stephen admires the purity of Elgar – purity of religious spirit and nationality as well as of composition. *The Dream of Gerontius* 'poses the most important question: what is to happen to my soul?' This question generates a profound dissonance to match that which occurs in the music, a dissonance focused on a central motif of a questioning of origins.

His 'conventional patriotism' has been institutionally reinforced. Stephen is 'learning to defend my country', alongside other 'sons of England' in a militaristic cadet force within his grammar school. In one beautifully mounted sequence, Stephen investigates motifs in the school's architecture. Comforted by his sense of his 'own participation in the English myth of historical harmony and social continuity' (Rabey 1997: 63), Stephen reads mottoes which despite their libertarian ethos are literally set in stone. Though Honeybone facetiously translates 'fiat lux' as 'the car and soap flakes', Stephen corrects him: 'let there be light'. The emblem 'discover thyself' becomes in Honeybone's terms 'uncover thy arse, more like'. In his own way Honeybone is prepared to interact with these signs whilst Stephen is not. Signs from the past retain a capacity for renewal; in extreme close-up we see on the printed score of *The Dream of Gerontius*, 'Copyright renewed, 1928'. But their interpretation is rendered invisible, their voices appearing only in voice-over imposed on the images. *Jerusalem*, which is sung by the boys, becomes an equally fixed sign; it is described blandly as 'every English-man's alternative national hymn', which, given the revolutionary connotations of Blake's words, parallels this song with *Land of Hope and Glory*, that reconfiguration of Elgar's *Pomp and Circumstance* of whose words the composer himself partly disapproved. *Jerusalem*'s split personality often inspires radical texts to employ its language – many of its lines have become titles of plays and films – and to invoke its spirit. 'England's green and pleasant land' is subversively intercut with a Borstal beating in *The Loneliness of the Long Distance Runner* (1962) and public-school brutality in Lindsay Anderson's *If* (1968) and Dennis Potter's *Traitor* (1970). Showing the influence of Anderson, *Penda's Fen* conflates religious, educational and military figures, culminating in the moment in which a mother finds three such authority figures, unexplained, around her burnt son's hospital bed.

Reinforcing this is the sexuality which forms a crucial area of Stephen's self-discovery. At the start, he condemns as 'unearthly' the angel who meets Gerontius's soul, because although it is male, it sings in a woman's voice. His subconscious reveals his homosexuality to him, employing the language of a 'Manichean dream' which he had earlier described, in which a demon appeared on his father's church tower, only for Stephen to turn it into an angel. His father, the Reverend Franklin (John Atkinson), explained that to the Manicheans, 'Light was a vulnerable spark to man under constant attack from forces of darkness', and that they hoped for 'some great son of light himself to come' (their heresy being that Jesus was 'one of many'). This imagery informs one of Clarke/Rudkin's most beautifully realised sequences. In a brief montage, we are moved into the rectory at night, but establishing shots give way to a pan from an open window to Stephen asleep, a shift in language suggesting that something has gained access. In his dream, an angel rises over the Malvern Hills, made indistinct by a play of light. Dream logic takes him to a Lindsay-Anderson-style depiction of the heaving limbs of a rugby scrum in the school gym. Wearing a white shirt, Stephen stands against a white background, connoting an almost unnatural purity which is then soiled as he is pelted with mud. More explicit imagery follows: naked, Joel the local milk-boy looms over the low-angled camera. Stephen's hand reaches up to him, slowly caresses his chest, and moves downwards. But this way lies flame, and the movement of Stephen's hand produces a spark. An angel rises over the church roof – where now the demon?

After the soundtrack's flourish comes silence. Stephen wakes, noticing the open window. Something is sitting on his bed. Momentarily it has Joel's face, but then is revealed in a big close-up, a gargoyle, an incubus. Initially static, Stephen gradually moves to turn on a light – but it is still there, very much real. Only when he reaches out to touch it does it disappear, just as Joel had. The only word Stephen speaks is 'Unnatural'. Dennis Potter (1974) felt it was 'a mistake to give literal solidity' to this 'all-too-visible demon', which though 'terrifyingly real when trapped behind the eyelids' becomes on screen 'little more than a comically inflated carnival novelty'. However, the incubus/succubus succeeds on a symbolic level as an expression of sexuality, an impurity from within made corporeal. Paul Oppenheimer (1996: 140) argued that films such as Robert Altman's *Images* (1972) 'take it as a premise that the demonic dominates all types of love, that demon-lovers invade and wrestle through the bodies of all men and women, not simply those committed to evil or disdainful of humanity'. The angel re-appears in daylight, prompting a discussion between writer and director, as Rudkin recalled:

> Alan said, 'This angel, have you written it in the right order ... he sits in front of the stream, we look across the stream and there's an angel behind him. And then we see Stephen's point of view of the reflection of the angel in the stream. Shouldn't he see the angel before we do?' I said, 'No, totally different meaning. To present it the other way round is to explain the angel and imply that it's Stephen's hallucination. But the angel is really in the field.' Alan said, 'OK.' It's a beautiful moment, it has a sort of Buñuel-like quality of the apocalyptic, but in the landscape. It's treated like any old thing in creation that happens to pass by. (Kelly 1998: 72)

The incubus sequence was not dissipated by a stock dramatic realisation that it was 'just a dream'. As Stephen's father told him, dreams do not *come* true, 'they *are* true – a dream tells you a truth about yourself, a truth you hide from yourself for your well-being'.

Stephen's dream state of terror exists also in the waking world as realisation of his sexuality sets in; a waking paralysis stops him warning Joel about a bird resting beneath a wheel of his milk float, and it is killed. The conflation of Joel and demon reoccurs, when the incubus's face zooms towards him while he's riding his bike, and he crashes. Coming round from unconsciousness, he realises that this was actually Joel on his float. Joel helps him up, but is troubled by Stephen clinging to him for a moment too long, and, with a girl waiting for him, says firmly 'that's *all*'. In the handling of such small moments of yearning lies Clarke's most sympathetic portrayal of homosexuality. His previous attempts drew mixed reactions. In *Under the Age* (1972), Paul Angelis played 'Susie', a jealous and manipulative barman in make-up. Although Angelis's performance is sensitive, the play's motivations were questioned by a member of the Gay Liberation Front on *Late Night Line-Up*. Ted Whitehead defended his play against accusations that, like so much other media coverage, it had represented the 'freak end' of homosexual characters (see Anonymous 1972). This had arguably been the case with the comic stereotyping of Peter Terson's *The Last Train Through Harecastle Tunnel*. Irene Shubik (2000: 85) felt that Johnson's rejection of a fellow prisoner's advances in *A Life Is For Ever* constituted 'the first convincing homosexual scene I had seen on television'. Stephen's sexual awakening is also a key part of his alienation. In the gym, the setting of his earlier dream, he is caught in a different scrum, as mocking lads put pink ribbons in his hair. Stephen stares them down – Clarke holds on one youth slowly losing his smile as he identifies Stephen's defiance – and emerges triumphant. As Stephen's certainties in other areas erode, he addresses Mrs Arne with the direct question, 'Can a homosexual have children?' In his discussion of gay, bisexual and transgender images in broadcasting, Steven Capsuto (2003) praised *Penda's Fen* as 'a notable point of contrast for the tame dramas that were appearing at the time in other countries', either of the 'teen' or 'issue of the week' variety. In particular, there is no equivocation: Stephen is gay, and the play 'acknowledges homosexuality as something erotic, not just conceptual or theoretical'.

The exploration of Stephen's political value-system provides another broad section. Troubled by the radical playwright Arne (Ian Hogg), Stephen responds that 'you can tell he's not a nice man from his television plays ... There's always somebody in them unnatural.' Arne confronts the manipulation of language, noting that pensioners die of 'cold' during strikes and 'hypothermia' when the cause is state greed, while the 'psychopaths' with real power behind democratically elected 'figureheads' calculate the numbers of 'strategically expendable' in a nuclear war. The ancient fen, with its apparent fixity and permanence of meaning, becomes a battleground of signifiers. Of this landscape 'hymned' by poets and 'enshrined' by 'our greatest composer', there is according to Arne something 'hollow beneath your feet'. Echoing the empirical hollowness underpinning Stephen's experiences, Arne is concerned with modernity masked by the invocation of culture, and abetted by a public content with received wisdom. 'What is it hidden beneath this shell of lovely earth? Some hideous angel of technocratic death? An alternative city for government from beneath? Oh, you say, it must be something to protect us ...' This speech is illustrated with imagery which subverts the seemingly pastoral use of landscape with which the play opened. Those images are mirrored in shots of a radio telescope and of trees, which under prolonged gaze resemble mushroom clouds. As with atom bomb tests on venerated Native American ground, the apparent desire to 'bottle the primal genie of the earth' conflates scientific rationalism and pagan mysticism. This is also explored in horror film language: a car blaring out loud music arrives near Pinvin, and one of the teenage passengers gets out to urinate, walking out of shot. Clarke holds still on a very long shot of the car while we wait, with only sounds from the car breaking up its hypnotic effect, until the youth eventually returns. As a girl screams we cut to the car, seeing that he is badly burnt; he says only 'The man ... in the fire'.

The play's narrative and thematic strands coalesce around the story's location. The misspelling of Pinvin as Pinfin becomes a focus for the erosion of Stephen's notions of purity and inheritance, and for the play's historical layering. Pinfin is a corruption of a corruption of its pre-Christian name, a semiotic slippage which could just be, as Rudkin (1974) put it, 'the old, primeval "demon" of the place opening half an eye'. As in the play's opening sequence, the sense of a settled landscape is disrupted by the lingering grasp of its ancient inhabitants, particularly England's last pagan king, Penda. Later, Michael Williams's gorgeous magic-hour photography frames father and son in darkening landscape as they discuss Penda's 'fall', an apocalyptic mirroring of the departing 'son of light' with the setting sun. At first, Stephen attempted to close this 'eye', correcting a sign-writer. However, when his accident renders him unconscious, this becomes a catalyst for a disturbing vision. In this vision, Stephen is struck by the fact that the Pinvin sign's 'v' has been peeled away, a point whose metaphorical importance is emphasised by Clarke's staggered zoom. In a shift to hand-held camera, we follow Stephen's dream-walk across a field. Moving into the garden of a country house towards a thudding sound, he finds a scene of outward normality rendered disturbing by the sleepy dream logic of its compositions. Couples and children sit happily. A jovial older man encourages a child and her mother to a block. Contentedly she holds out her hands, and he chops them off. Smiling broadly, she dances around the garden. Into this dream of emasculation, in the language of masturbation anxiety and castration, enter the couple admired by Stephen for gaining the injunction on *Who Was Jesus?*, their arms triumphantly aloft in the pose of their press photograph. They beckon towards

Stephen to join them, at which point he wakes. In this landscape, so reminiscent of William Blake, David Ian Rabey (1997: 64) observed that 'self-styled moral guardians preside over rites of sacrifice and complicity in mutilation'. Mere plot synopsis cannot describe the mood of this disorienting sequence, to which Clarke brings a crucial stillness; David Rose observed that 'even when it came to the supernatural, he treated it for real' (*Director*). Such scenes gain force from the way in which Stephen, according to Dennis Potter (1974), was 'struggling in a real place, a patch of landscape and so of mindscape'. Anticipating his own *Blue Remembered Hills* (1979), Potter added that the place where we grow up 'is always beyond the reach of the cartographer and forever charged with the intensity of those first perceptions which turn words or songs heard in the head into particular configurations of local topography'. According to Rabey (1994: 826), Rudkin often constructed 'moral landscapes that uniquely externalise inner traumas'. The discovery that Pinvin/Pinfin was Pendefen/Penda's fen unites questions of origins, inheritance and permanence, underscoring a process by which Stephen's own sense of roots – nationality and family – crumbles.

In another vision, he meets the ghost of Elgar. *Penda's Fen* is often a fabulously evocative postscript to Ken Russell's *Monitor* profile of the composer in 1962, particularly in sequences of Stephen cycling around the countryside to the *Introduction and Allegro for Strings*. Rudkin (1974) explained that 'it's more than Elgar's music that haunts *Penda's Fen*; there's something of his spirit, too'. Stephen initially shared the view of Elgar as 'the archetypal country gentleman whose music enshrines the noblest sentiments of patriotism and faith', but Rudkin noted that Elgar was 'a tradesman's son who married above himself and was socially oversensitive all his life'. Largely self-taught, Elgar invites Stephen to respond more creatively than his regimented education has allowed. 'Gerontius's transcendental death-bed cry', he tells Stephen, was actually 'music from the whine of a dog for his bone'. Nobody will crack the secrets of his *Enigma Variations* whilst 'they have no demon for counterpoint'. Elgar undermines Stephen's simplistic use of him as a signifier of nationhood and 'purity' (he had Welsh blood in him, and lamented the appropriation of *Land and Hope and Glory* to attack his beloved Germany), and the boy's awareness of his own impurities is echoed gruesomely in Elgar's description of watching his own cancer being cut out. Howard Schuman (1998: 19) identified this as a key scene, in which Stephen 'is made to understand that even the most lofty music of England is connected to nature, bodily functions and popular art – a crucial way-station to embracing both mystical paganism and a radical view of Jesus'.

Stephen's sense of self is rooted in problematically intertwined concerns with parentage and origins. Looking for a place-name book to explore Pinvin, he finds *The Buried Jesus*, his father's manuscript arguing that Jesus has been misappropriated, 'dangled like a halo above a sick culture centred on authority and death'. Earlier, when Stephen described the vigilant watchdogs as 'a mother and father above all parents', Clarke cut devastatingly to his parents' discussion on whether to break a secret to him, as agreed, on his eighteenth birthday. Now we discover that secret: he is adopted. This loss of parentage echoes his ebbing sense of nationhood, as the clergyman counsels: 'You are like the English language ... You have foreign parents too'. Stephen's conception of origins and nationality have in fact broadened, as his resistance to external influence has diminished. He has been arguing with the past, which Marina Warner (1994: 94) described as 'a vital part of being a member of society'. The realisation that 'No home is an island, no homegrown culture can thrive' is a central part of self-definition; ultimately 'We earn home, like everything else'. Having earlier played *Jerusalem* for the school, Stephen sits at the church organ to play the Angel's triumph from *Gerontius*. In an ambitious matte shot, the ground cracks. Penda speaks, in language similar to that of the clergyman's manuscript: 'Stephen Franklin, unbury me.' On a hilltop, the 'mother and father of England' covet Stephen as 'our child of light'. But, at the end of his journey of discovery, Stephen rejects their rhetoric, grasping that nationality is mutable: 'I am nothing pure ... my race is mixed, my sex is mixed, I am woman with man, light with darkness ... I am mud and flame.' Like Raymond Williams's (1971: 28) description of D. H. Lawrence's belief in 'England my England', identifying *his* England is 'an assertion, a declaration of independence, a challenge'. The mother replies: 'If we cannot have him, darkness must not.' They burn his photograph, upon which – fittingly, given Stephen's troubled inter-mingling of image and reality – he catches fire. As in *Gerontius*, there is a 'brief fearful dissonance' in the apocalyptic soundtrack, until Stephen's invocations to Penda bring 'the moment of the glance of God'. Penda destroys those 'true dark enemies of England, sick father and mother who would have us children forever'. He asks Stephen, 'our sacred demon of ungovernableness', to 'cherish the flame til we can safely wake again'. The visions cease. Stephen walks back down the hill.

Clarke's contribution is impressive, but Rudkin is undeniably the play's dominant author. As a 'son of light' using fire from the gods, Stephen exemplifies Rudkin's Promethean protagonists, 'determined to break interpretative restrictions and so radically transform the designated norm', accepting the dangers of 'isolation, excommunication, scorn, and destruction' (Rabey 1994: 827). As well as the playwright Arne, searchers for Rudkin self-portraits may seize on his bisexuality, and the fact that he is a clergyman's son, to read Rudkin into the similarly named Stephen Franklin. For four decades, Rudkin has carved a unique path through such landscapes of myth, memory and identity. Musically trained and a classical scholar, he is as much a poet as a playwright, a composer of language, his subject matter ranging from Euripides to Mahler to Hitchcock, each resonating equally to that sensitive ear. Alongside his operatic, theatrical and radio work, by *Penda's Fen* he had been writing hugely original television plays for a decade. His first, *The Stone Dance* (1963), introduced themes and imagery to which Rudkin returns in *Penda's Fen*, including a pastor's son sensing 'fire' within himself, difference portrayed in demonic terms and surroundings with pagan resonances.

As rural as much of Clarke's work is urban, as lyrical as he is often elliptical, the play operates in areas of imagery removed from the socially concerned realism with which he is associated. Producer David Rose's choice of Clarke to direct a production since described by James Saynor (1992: 30) as a 'fantasia' and 'a bizarre BBC art movie' was as surprising as it was inspired. Howard Schuman (1998: 19) noted that the director 'rides the intellectual and emotional whirlwind of *Penda's Fen* – with its ton and a half of symbolic, poetic, theological and political freight – with a firm sense of rhythm, clean uncluttered framing and elegant camera movement'. Schuman's language implies a hierarchy, and Clarke does serve the script superbly, but it also constitutes a refinement of his personal style. 'Alan had tremendous nerve, and he showed it time and time again in *Penda's Fen*', Rose recalled, 'within drama that was bustling and hustling and trying to compete with the American pace, suddenly you rested' (*Director*). The stillness of Clarke's technique generated multiple effects; in the beautiful montage of establishing shots which introduces Stephen, or a scene of harmony at the bedside of the late Mr Kings, Clarke would, in the words of Peter Whelan, 'put the camera on it and just leave it ... you just looked at the same thing to the point at which it really sank in on you in a most extraordinary sort of way'. Furthermore, according to David Hare (1990), Clarke possessed 'a strange mix of romance and realism', and *Penda's Fen* showed a side to him 'streaked with a romantic intensity which was almost mystical'.

Although not in Clarke's usual register, it is in his frame of reference. It shares with *Sovereign's Company* and *Scum* a concern with the institutionalisation of youth, alienation and the initiations of adolescence; thematically it is *To Encourage the Others* taken into 'a realm of fantasy'.

It shares the complexities of *Made in Britain* and *The Firm*, with its protagonist's contradictory motivations, competing identities and inner demons. Like Blake, this piece combines spiritual and religious visions with an underlying socio-political drive. Protagonists such as Stephen allow Rudkin to address 'the fiction of being English, conventionally predicated on the twinned illusions of the continuity of social form and of the objectivity of law' (Rabey 1997: 63), and 'refuse incorporation into any social fiction that does not acknowledge their self-invented uniqueness' (Rabey 1994: 826). Clarke too goes on to explore the interlinked social, political and cultural underpinning of Britishness – the external and internal workings of repression, Blake's 'mind-forg'd manacles' – and his protagonists' rejection of imposed narratives, reinforced in complex ways by Clarke's aesthetic strategies. At one point Stephen's mother drives him up the motorway into the city, providing a shocking interruption of modernity. 'The belt moves on, regardless of the needs of man', she tells him, 'The whole rhythm of his life is chained to the machine'. Hope lies in anarchism, a 'Second Coming' in his father's terms, brought about by man 'through some last disobedience and new resurrection'. It is Stephen's inheritance to lead this 'revolt from the monolith' back to 'the village'. Man's only hope, according to Arne, is that, when 'the great concrete megacity chokes the globe from pole to pole', it contains the 'sacred seed' of its own collapse. Many of Clarke's protagonists – like, reputedly, Clarke himself – share this anarchistic tenet, exponents of 'disobedience' and 'chaos', pounding at concrete, exhausting the megacity. Although Clarke was 'wary of the story's frames of scholarly reference' (Rudkin 2003), he triumphed with the play's core: a representation of individualism and institutions, revolt and the urge to obey, and of the conflation of individual and British identities.

A third voice must be added to those of Rudkin and Clarke. *Penda's Fen* exemplifies the contribution made to *Play for Today* and other single play strands such as *Thirty Minute Theatre* (1965–73) and its regional offshoot *Second City Firsts* (1973–78) by BBC English Regions (Drama) Television, based at BBC Birmingham under David Rose. If the single play represented a studio system, BBC Birmingham – with Rose exercising his relative autonomy from London and his brief to provide an outlet for regional voices – became its independent studio. David Hare recalled that he and Clarke were on the same corridor as Frears, Leigh, Alan Bleasdale and others, benefiting from the 'BBC Birmingham culture', with Rose 'letting people do what they wanted ... "The earth splits open? Oh yeah?" There's just no way a London producer and script editor would have been having that' (Kelly 1998: 69). Describing his work for the BBC and later Film on Four, James Saynor (1992: 30) argued that 'Rose's cinema represented an intense amalgam of realism and fantasy', responding to 'the "need" of a concrete locale combined with the writerly "leaping" of a talented dramatist'. *Penda's Fen* and Bleasdale's *Boys from the Blackstuff* (1982), Saynor added, were 'probably the twin peaks of this Rosean tradition on television'. Indeed, Rose himself has described *Penda's Fen* as 'a milestone, if not the milestone, of my career' (*Director*).

Like so much of BBC Birmingham's richly varied output, including *Boys from the Blackstuff*, Philip Martin's *Gangsters* (1975–78) and Alan Plater's *Trinity Tales* (1975), *Penda's Fen* is rooted in its landscape in a more complex way than a tokenistic attempt to set a play in the provinces; rather than telling Rudkin to 'let me have something about Warwickshire', the point was to get writers to 'mirror some aspect of a community' (Campbell 1972). This affected the form, as Rose told Bob Millington and Robin Nelson (1986: 25–6): 'to reflect regional life, the landscape and the community, we tried to make as many ... *Play for Todays* on film as possible, to somehow get a feeling of the outlook of the regions ... Space is created!' Rudkin (1974) confirmed that the piece was 'conceived as a film and written visually'. Furthermore, he dismissed the prevailing hierarchy within which 'visual questions are none of the writer's business', and writers must 'leave it to the director to picture it all out'. This statement was a clear demarcation of Clarke's role as a metteur-en-scène, although it is worth noting that Rose believed in 'the director being in on the play at the earliest possible moment' (Campbell 1972). Rudkin's statement, however, failed to impress some critics. Nancy Banks-Smith (1974) protested that the way Rudkin 'pictures it out himself' shows 'little faith in our imagination'. Similarly, though otherwise impressed, James Murray (1974) found the play 'awash with self-indulgent symbolism'. In the discussion programme *Real Time* broadcast on BBC2 the same night, Rudkin explained that many of its ideas were initially intended to be separate works, but came together to form the play's 'diversity'; seizing on this, Peter Lawson (1974) complained that the play was 'about too much', full of 'unrelated material, which never fused into a coherent whole'.

Clearly those critics had trouble with the play's ambitious scope – Banks-Smith added that 'it was not a TV play' – but others appreciated it as something special. Dennis Potter (1974) memorably wrote that '*Penda's Fen* demonstrated that the *Play for Today* slot has become ... the major area left on TV still capable of transmitting the nourishing zest of an individual imagination which necessarily cares not a controller's fart for ratings'. Taking Rudkin's point that 'TV trash is sapping our brains',

Mary Malone (1974) believed that with such plays 'the magic box earns its keep'. In 1990, Channel Four repeated *Penda's Fen* just two days before Clarke's death. W. Stephen Gilbert (1990) summed up the press reaction: 'Its special effects may have revealed its age but so did its seriousness and its power: contemporary television simply doesn't explore ideas as dangerous as these.' *Penda's Fen* provides a reminder that public service broadcasting included in its scope a broad plurality of views in fiction, and also that critics' understanding of single drama's aesthetic 'radicalism' has become narrowed. Rudkin's *House of Character* (1968) and *Blodwen, Home from Rachel's Marriage* (1969), according to their producer Irene Shubik (2000: 77), broadened the viewing experiences and expectations of millions and moved beyond 'the normal composition of audience for this sort of work' in avant-garde cinema. *Penda's Fen* retained its potency for other practitioners. Stephen Poliakoff cited this 'extremely imaginative and quite demanding' but also 'very popular' play to demonstrate that 'It's not true that the television audience just wants easy to understand plays' (Anonymous 1982a), while Peter Ansorge (2003) singled it out as 'one work that illustrates what viewers have lost through the dismantlement of the single play on television'. The next chapter covers a period during which the space in which such plays could be made came under threat, and in which Clarke began to assert his individual identity.

Realism and censorship in the 1970s

In the previous chapter I sought elements of personal style exercised by a director working within collaborative institutional processes, reading his signatures within pieces whose writers had a predominant authorial investment or whose conditions of production restricted the critical construction of the director as unifying figure. To continue Clarke's analogy between single drama and classic Hollywood, this put me in a similar position to early auteur critics as they compared directors working within the studio system, seeking evidence of individuality whilst accepting that, as Andrew Sarris (1968: 36) put it, 'All directors, and not just in Hollywood, are imprisoned by the conditions of their craft and their culture'. In this chapter I trace the development of his dominant themes and aesthetic approaches as he negotiates this kind of 'imprisonment', the restrictions which I articulated in Chapter 1, to assert his individual voice as a director.

In the opening section, I trace the development of this voice in several of his productions from the 1970s, placing their concern with realism and narrative in the context of the approaches of other practitioners of his generation and some of his cinematic influences. The restrictions on his voice are demonstrated by the banning of *Scum* and the shelving of both *Bukovsky* and two episodes of *Love for Lydia* (1976, eventual series 1977). Much of the chapter is devoted to *Scum*; in two sections, I discuss the issues raised by its banning, including the changing status of radical single drama, administrative intervention and censorship and the concern of both practitioners and theorists with realism and 'progressive' form. Arguably catalysed by the banning of *Scum*, Clarke had emerged by the start of the 1980s as one of Britain's most distinctive directors. Far from being trapped, Clarke was 'lucky', according to David Thomson (2002), 'to be a director in a writers' medium. Every film school in the world would benefit from seeing how a directorial personality can be sharpened and matured by keeping company with adventurous producers and good writing.' Clarke learnt 'to acquire versatility with the camera and sure speed with the actors', and when his 'own style and preoccupations' emerged, 'they were all the stronger in their solid grounding'.

'Imprisoned' – themes and approaches in the 1970s

Following on from the previous chapter, I will now explore more of Clarke's 1970s productions, this time focusing on the development of his 'own style and preoccupations'. I maintain my interest in the contexts in which he worked, but my emphasis has changed: as well as providing an administrative space, the 'studio system' of the single play connoted themes and approaches within which Clarke's own voice thrived. Despite restrictions of technology, contested authorship and executive intervention, his plays feature repetitions of style and theme which demonstrate his growing authorial centrality. I agree with Simon Hattenstone's argument (1998) that 'Although Clarke hardly ever wrote his own films, he was an auteur. He cajoled and teased every nuance out of the scripts, and the finished work always seemed to belong more to him than the writer.' Clarke's 1970s style has qualities of sparseness and stillness which have drawn comparison with that fellow director of ascetic subtlety, Robert Bresson, featuring performances of searing honesty undisturbed by stylistic flourishes or narrative embellishment. His de-emphasising of narrative causality is deeply felt in this period, although his interrogation of narrative structure is manifested in a more complex way in his 1980s work. Among his thematic concerns are individuality, authority and institutionalisation, and an interest in incarceration in both literal and figurative terms. Speaking to Benedict Nightingale in 1981, Clarke identified in his own work an interest in 'boxes – people being somewhere they don't want to be, or wanting to be somewhere they can't get into'.

The tone of his major work clearly emerges in *Sovereign's Company*, his second *Wednesday Play*. A powerful exploration of masculine psychology, violence and Britishness, Don Shaw's play is based around the training of officers at the Royal Military Academy, Sandhurst. The play opens with the arrival of new cadets at Blenheim Company, among them Alan Dawkins (James Hazeldine). Embarrassed by his proud parents in this upper-class atmosphere, Dawkins makes painful attempts to bond with others through reminiscences of scaling a fence, which seems appropriate as he has a social barrier to climb. In contrast with the easy communality of 'gentlemen' cadets, he is sneered at by Dexter

(Clive Francis). The class dynamic of Sandhurst was a topical area; it was among the aspects explored a year earlier by Trevor Philpott in his BBC documentary series *The Philpott File*. In a preview, Philpott (1969) noted that, for much of its hundred-year existence, 'only those with the right education and background stood any chance of entering the Academy gates. Cadets came from selected public schools, many of them from traditionally "army" families.'

From a particularly traditional 'army' family comes Andrew Cantfield (Gareth Forwood), who arrives in a chauffeur-driven car with his grandfather, Major General Cantfield (Roland Culver). Unlike Dawkins, Andrew settles easily among his own kind, but once training is under way his unsuitability becomes apparent on a level beyond social mores, with his withdrawn and sullen body language and a telltale involuntary trembling of his leg during drill. What this signifies becomes clear during a staged inter-company fight, a pivotal sequence which is handled superbly by Clarke. Before the battle, he generates suspense by cutting between close-ups of members of Blenheim Company waiting in their corridor and the invading company's legs pounding down flights of stairs. The subsequent battle in a corridor is chilling more for the claustrophobia of its realisation than for any graphic shots of violence. Clarke places a hand-held camera in the middle of the tightly packed corridor, the static mass of bodies contrasting with movement provided by the jarring of the camera caught up in the mêlée. Cantfield runs away, locking himself in the toilet. The difference between his behaviour and that expected from him is emphasised through a beautifully executed mid-action cut between medium close-ups of Cantfield in the toilet and Dexter, placed identically in the frame, fighting the enemy. Blenheim Company are triumphant, but Cantfield cowers in bed, trembling in shock. He arranges to see the Commandant, apparently to leave, but has a change of heart when the only witness to his cowardice is coincidentally kicked out. Cantfield is offered an acceptable way out – his stipulated regiment, that of his grandfather, seems set to be disbanded, leaving him free to activate an escape clause – but he refuses it.

Cantfield strives for an image of masculinity. As the Company celebrate one of their own winning the Sword of Honour, Clarke holds on a two-shot of Cantfield and Dexter singing 'For he's a jolly good fellow'. Dexter again seems to be Cantfield's mirror, and his lusty bellowing of the words, and occasional validating looks to Cantfield, encourage the latter not only to match Dexter's enthusiasm but also to ape his body language. The calling of 'hooray!' is held over a cut to Cantfield later practising a salute in front of the mirror, in effect saluting the image he seeks for himself. This image is frequently associated with his grandfather. At a family reception, the General seethes during a discussion of former cadets now fighting against each other for India and Pakistan, proof of their status as 'trained professionals' shifting loyalties in the modern world. Dawkins's father puts it more bluntly – 'Not necessarily tied to any country' – prompting Cantfield to speak the General's unspoken thoughts: 'Rubbish!' Humiliated, Cantfield stands at a drinks table with his back to the room, on the verge of tears, and tells Dawkins to go away. 'Where to?', Dawkins replies, 'A convenient lavatory?' The image slips away – failing to replicate the behaviour at drill, he is charged with being inattentive on parade. But he gets an unexpected opportunity to prove himself when 'yobbos' break in to the old swimming pool. Dawkins and Cantfield capture one of them. Whereas Dexter resolved his antagonism with Sender through a fight, Cantfield displaces his, taking the initiative from Dawkins and trying to impress the others by assaulting the youth, dangerously losing control. Dismissal follows.

Although the General tells him that 'I didn't push you into it', Cantfield has been motivated by a need to fit the group ethic and the ideals of masculinity and Britishness represented by the regiment of his grandfather, who told him that 'You're going to an idea'. The play opens and closes with *Marching with the Coldstream Guards* played over portraits of military figures. These images, of the kind to which the cadets must aspire, are static and historical, reinforcing the apparent inflexibility of these ideals. The virtues of the Academy are extolled in the Indian Museum amidst the paraphernalia of empire and anachronistic swords and pig-sticking trophies. Such relics 'remind us of our great spirit of the past', as British leaders need to 'know what and why you're leading'. Then there is the title itself. Blenheim Company holds for this term the banner Sovereign's Company, first presented by King George in 1914, an honour the cadets must battle to retain. These ideals exist for king and country, a phrase I use deliberately to invoke Joseph Losey's 1964 film. *King and Country* opens with a similarly evocative use of heroic iconography which has become stultified, the Hyde Park monument to the dead of the First World War. Losey's film is powered by class tensions and mutual sacrifice between an officer and the deserting working-class soldier he is called upon to punish, and *Sovereign's Company* updates and explores this dynamic with comparable sophistication. Both productions seek aesthetic strategies with which to historicise the values portrayed, with Losey using 'a kind of sepia tint all the way through to recall old photographs from the period' (Ciment 1985: 248). On *Sovereign's Company*, film cameraman Peter Hall uses sunlight and organic colours to imbue scenes with a golden light, a nostalgic haze with an arguably subversive effect, making the contemporary appear dated. Clarke reinforces this sense of tradition with the occasional self-announcing switch to orthodox film grammar, for instance in a lengthy tracking shot along the Company standing to toast the Queen (replicated in the boys' rendition of *Jerusalem* in *Penda's Fen*).

Simon Hattenstone (1998) observed 'many hints of his future work' in *Sovereign's Company*, particularly its non-judgemental invitation to 'observe the class system, the macho hierarchies and tyranny of rules', and a similiarity to Robert Bresson's work in 'the stillness of the camera and the stillness of the boy's eyes'. Clarke returned to this similarity between educational and military institutions in the later *Penda's Fen*, in which Stephen was taught 'to defend my country' in the cadets, and the inter-company rivalry of *Scum*. This is also an early Clarke study of repetition, with training called (by Sanders on boot polishing) 'a cycle you pedal every night til you're exhausted'. Clarke captures the uniformity and confinement of movement through compositional strategies and the occasional temporal ellipsis, not least one elegant cut from the calling of Cantfield's name in roll call to his reaction later during drill. A similar contrast between repetition and movement occurs in the later *Fast Hands* (1976), in equally drill-like montages of boxer Jimmy's training. Sender's opinion on drill is that 'because we give orders, to kill, or to save lives ... they have to take away our individual reactions, make it uniform'. There is even a glimpse of the structural circularity which marks Clarke's later work, as the play ends as it had begun in the Cantfield car, with the same shot structure and the General's interpretation of tradition serving to deny the progression of the narrative, as he claims that 'even if the regiment were to go, they can't take away its past. They can't touch us. And that's what matters, isn't it?'

I will return to Clarke's recurring motif of movement and the ways in which it is restricted, but it is worth noting his comments during a chance meeting with director Paul Greengrass. One morning in 1981, Greengrass attended a court-martial for a nineteen-year-old soldier whose career was effectively ended because of his sexuality. There he found Clarke, who was considering dramatising the trial:

> There were a lot of parallels with *Sovereign's Company* in Colchester barracks that day, we agreed – mostly in the way the army was terrorising a vulnerable young boy to prove its manhood ... I asked him what he took from the day. 'Bastards, weren't they? ... Look at the way they move, and the way he looks. Poor kid's shitting himself ... he showed me unwittingly all the essential tools of my trade ... it's all in the looks and the movement. (Greengrass 2002)

Like many of Clarke's plays, *Sovereign's Company* proved to be contro-versial. One reason for this was its representation of Sandhurst. On an edition of *Late Night Line-Up* broadcast on the same night, Shaw was interviewed alongside a representative of Sandhurst, although 'a member of wartime intelligence' later told him that this 'nice chap' was 'a deliberate plant to give the lie to my gallery of villains' (Shaw 1970). Complaints reached Parliament, although tellingly these were related to the perceived documentary elements of Clarke's style. Following a discussion on encouraging more young people into the Services, Conservative MP Cransley Onslow expressed his concern with the BBC's 'anxiety to present as authentic what was in fact a fictional and deplorable travesty of conditions at R.M.A. Sandhurst'. Ian Gilmour, Under Secretary of State for Defence, maintained that 'the Department refused to co-operate in the making of the film because it realised from the script that it would produce a thoroughly distorted picture of cadet life at Sandhurst' (Hansard 1970). As a result, as producer Irene Shubik (2000: 143–4) recalled, designer Colin Pigott had to build 'his own Sandhurst, down to the Indian Museum' at a deserted school near Windsor; unsurprisingly this play 'turned out to be enormously expen-sive'. The body of Onslow's complaint was related to fictional form, as Shaw (1970) identified: 'The fact that drama is fictional does not mean any loss of reality nor that it is inferior to the documentary method when dealing with actuality. In fact it is often a better medium in which to demonstrate truth, admittedly a truth which is personal to the writer'. Form was 'the crux of the problem', with his 'integrity' in doubt because this fictional play was reductively 'challenged as a documentary'. Responding to the idea that, as one headline put it, 'Sandhurst was never like this', Shaw maintained that 'it was exactly like this'. Shaw was a former Sandhurst cadet who had left without graduating; he could also quote a former staff officer and lecturer at Sandhurst who thought he had 'dealt with a difficult set of circumstances with a remarkable lack of bias'.

Another area of controversy, which would become a recurring problem for Clarke, was the depiction of violence. In the BBC audience research department report *Violence on Television*, some viewers objected to 'the violent streak running through the whole play', feeling 'horrified' or 'frustrated' by 'the violent and bullying attitude of the cadets to one another'; another put it more simply: 'the fighting made me feel sick'; 51 per cent described the play as 'very' or 'quite' violent, although, unlike other programmes analysed, it features only two scenes of violence (BBC 1972: 144). The difference between this and other 'committed' pieces in the study lay in Clarke's handling, as the 'realism of fictional

violence' stemmed from the '*vividness* of the picture of the consequences', from the sense of '*distance*', and from the viewer's '*ability to
identify* with the characters involved' (167, emphases in original). Such
debates over the fusion of drama and documentary, violence and
realism would become more ideologically charged over Clarke's
contributions to *Play for Today* (as *The Wednesday Play* was renamed
following a change in the night of transmission).

Another milestone in Clarke's career is *A Life Is For Ever* (1972) by
Tony Parker, a respected oral historian who crafted dramas around
meticulous observation and research. His factual work often recorded
the experiences of prison inmates. His first book *The Courage of His
Convictions* was co-credited to its subject Robert Allerton, *A Man Inside*
was a compendium of prisoners' writing, conversation and art, and the
Omnibus programme *Art in Prison*, according to Allerton, gave 'more of
the feel of what being in prison is like' than most things he'd seen
(Parker 1973: 7). The inspiration for *A Life Is For Ever* came from
Parker's 1970 book *The Frying-Pan*, for which he lived in the progressive
psychiatric prison HMP Grendon Underwood, recording interviews
with inmates and staff. Chapter 12, 'A Life Is For Ever', focused on life
imprisonment through the case of 'Derek'. Following *To Encourage the
Others*, Clarke's portrayal of another 'Derek' also punished for a
policeman's murder, *A Life Is For Ever* shows a year in the life sentence
of Johnson, and constitutes Clarke's first fully worked-through study of
incarceration. It was a fruitful collaboration; producer Irene Shubik
(2000: 85) recalled introducing writer and director at the first draft stage
'so that Alan had the chance to gain all the knowledge of prison he could
from Parker'. Parker detailed his research in an introduction to his
original script. This set out elements of style which became central to
Clarke's work in this period. Parker's suggestions included generating
an 'undramatic' atmosphere, representing 'self-destroying monotony',
and producing a detailed 'sound-score' because 'the incessant noise of
prison life is important as, and certainly more immediately striking
than, the undercurrent of the general atmosphere' (Parker 1972). So
realistic were these aspects that, as Shubik (2000: 85) recalled, 'the
Home Office phoned up a day after transmission to find out how we had
managed to get into a prison to film without their permission. Later they
asked to borrow the film as training material for the prison service.'
This is particularly impressive given that Clarke was denied permission
to shoot inside a real prison. The verisimilitude of the studio recon-
struction was aided by shooting location material on video, avoiding a
'phoney' contrast with filmed exteriors.

But the play's fidelity to prison experience is ingrained in the production more deeply than in its design. 'To an outsider', wrote Sean Day-Lewis (1972), 'the claustrophobia, repetitiveness, tensions and cross-currents of prison life appeared to be brilliantly recreated under Alan Clarke's direction'. A judge's voice-over statement, that 'For you there is absolutely nothing to be said', becomes the play's defining principle. Parker saw his role as interviewer 'to be quietly attentive, to record without comment or judgement' (Anonymous 1996), and the play's monotonous and repetitious depiction of prison life is predicated upon an avoidance of commenting upon or judging Johnson. This helps the play capture the depersonalisation described by one of Parker's interviewees: 'Everything's taken from you and put away in store until the time for your release ... including your personality ... which isn't handed back again because it doesn't exist anymore' (Parker 1973: 28). Instead of being rehabilitated, prisoners whittle away time on trivial tasks, losing identity and autonomy to the extent that many are unable to conceive a life without prison. Parker observed of the lifer 'Derek' that 'outside that context nothing had meaning any more', leaving 'only this bleak emptiness to cling to'. As a result of this he 'knew no words to say that spoke as clear or loud as all his considered silences' (Parker 1970: 240), which became a feature of the play, as Nancy Banks-Smith (1972) made clear: 'I don't remember another play ... in which the lead says so little ... Certainly nothing in his own defence.'

In his script note (1972), Parker wrote that in prison 'Nothing other than the passing of time happens', or 'if it does, it doesn't happen for long and before long has become forgotten because it was irrelevant ... last week was the same as this week, and next week will be the same as this'. Bronco McLoughlin recalled Clarke saying he wanted to show 'Working the machine shop, stitching the mailbags. No drama, every day boring. I wanna bore the fuckin' audience' (Kelly 1998: 61). As a result, the play avoids imposing the narrative clichés of the prison genre: Johnson half-heartedly considers breaking out but betrays the others, and later attempts suicide but fails. Faced with this 'remnant of a man', according to Stewart Lowe (1972), we wonder what 'society achieved by this kind of punishment – apart from revenge'. If this sounds alienating, it is worth noting Irene Shubik's observation that 'Like all Parker's plays it had a large audience viewing figure and generally appreciative reviews'. Importantly, she added that 'rather than being blatantly propagandist, it showed all sides of the story and left the audience to think and draw their own conclusions' (Shubik 2000: 85–6). Parker and Clarke refuse to impose dramatic neatness or a unifying overview, leaving the rough edges intact to replicate witnessed experience and to respect their own distance from the protagonists' experience – as lifer 'Roy S.' told Parker (1973: 17), 'Reading all the books there've ever been about prisons won't bring you anywhere near it'. The play seems a formative moment in Clarke's style. According to Colin Ward (1996), Parker's work opposed the fact that 'Most of us are not neutral observers and arrange the evidence to support a point of view'; Clarke's work similarly opposes this position.

A sensitive study of repetition, *A Life Is For Ever* operates in the same areas as Robert Bresson's prison masterpiece, *Un condamné à mort s'est échappé* (*A Man Escaped*, 1956). Peter Black's review (1972) indicated a Bressonian approach to acting: 'Alan Clarke's direction scrupulously dramatised Parker's carefully flat avoidance of obvious dramatics ... Maurice O'Connell played Johnson by emptying his face of emotion and leaving the audience's imagination to fill in the blanks.' This 'emptying' quality recalls Bresson's methodology with actors, or, as he tellingly defined them, *modèles*. In his *Notes sur le cinématographe* (1997: 32), Bresson described seeking automatic behaviour from his *modèles* through repetition, upon which 'their relationships with the objects and persons around them will be *right* because they will not be *thought*'. Susan Hayward (1993: 181) saw Bresson's essence within 'this unadorned style', in which his 'protagonist remains as impassive as the camera', and, by intoning rather than performing his role, 'interprets nothing'. One of the techniques which Bresson used to avoid '*thought*' perform-ances, also employed by the likes of Humphrey Jennings, Jean Renoir and the Italian neo-realists, was his use of non-professional actors. The casting of O'Connell, a saxophonist new to acting, demonstrates that Clarke, like Ken Loach and others of his generation, shared the belief of André Bazin (1967: 23–4) that the absence of professional actors, and particularly 'the rejection of the star concept' with its baggage of audience identification, produced an 'extraordinary feeling of truth'. As John Caughie argued, one of the ways in which acting could be prevented from being one of the 'corrosions of the real' outlined by Bazin was through the use of 'actors who could pretend not to be actors, who could sound unrehearsed, and who brought no history of pretending with them'. In drama documentary, 'classical acting skills seem to be reserved for officialdom or authority in a neat reversal where the traditional skills of impersonation came to mean insincerity, and not quite knowing your lines meant you were speaking the truth'. There-fore, performers play a role in film-makers' negotiation of the space between 'representation as construction of meaning and representation as reflection', although, as Caughie noted, there has been an 'absence of theoretically informed critical writing about acting' for television (Caughie 2000b: 162, 164–6).

Diane (1975) is similarly Bressonian in its 'unadorned style'. Initially a two-part play called *All the Saints*, it was edited down to ninety minutes, more the result of transmission details changing because of a strike than Clarke paring down, although the changes led Jonathan Hales to remove his writing credit (Kelly 1998: 76–7). The title change reflects its greater emphasis on Diane, with whom Clarke finds his first Bressonian heroine. In the first half, set against bleak yet sunlit surroundings, she is a prickly schoolgirl experiencing the problems of growing up. In one well-observed scene she takes the lead when her would-be boyfriend Jim nervously prevaricates in kissing her, while in others she experiences the arbitrary callousness and crudity of male youths. Her character, particularly after she leaves school and is fired from various jobs for insolence, and those elements of religious imagery which remain from the original, make this a fascinating companion piece to Bresson's *Mouchette* (1967), thoroughly integrated into 1970s Britain. We are denied access to her motivations, heightening the shock when she is incarcerated for disposing of a baby which she had conceived to her father. The scene in which Diane explains this represents, as Richard Kelly put it, 'an uncommonly overt and entirely Bressonian piece of direction' (1998: xxiii). Janine Duvitski recalled planning to play the scene with a lot of emotion, but Clarke asked her for technical reasons to 'just keep your face completely still and just say it'. She was upset to find that he intended to use that version. 'He said "trust me, that'll be fine", and of course it was so much better than me just moving my face all over the place' (*Director*). Duvitski was unfairly self-deprecating, but her inexperience at that stage reinforces the impression of the director seizing control in the cutting room, employing – as Bresson told Jean-Luc Godard – 'the clumsiest young girl, the one who is least an actress' in order to 'extract from her everything she does not suspect me of extracting from her' (Reader 2000: 90).

The second half of the play takes up Diane's story after her release three years later, as she adjusts to adult life. Her maturity and confidence, as she finds a job, home and new boyfriend and recovers enough emotionally to look after her housemate's baby, prompted Charles Barron (1975) to read the play as almost 'a commercial for the penal system; being institutionalised made a woman of Diane'. But scars of her abuse remain as she resists physical and emotional connection. The play explores the nature of dependency as her father tracks her down after his release from prison, in search of reconciliation. Under Clarke's direction this potentially depressing 'issue' drama is a beautiful work of emotional sensitivity and visual depth, although his use of wipes is perhaps a 'cinematic' touch too many. Viewers responded; head of plays Christopher Morahan was 'very excited when we got a very large audience for *Diane*', particularly 'considering it was summer and BBC2'. After all, the BBC 'want to produce plays that are seen. We're not in a minority business' (Anonymous 1975). Though audience research found that some viewers objected to 'the dreariness of its theme, the excessive use of bad language and the fact that it was disjointed and difficult to follow', others were 'completely absorbed by it', finding it 'Unusual, interesting and moving' (Anonymous 1977a).

My use of cinematic references is not intended as a checklist of Clarke's influences; according to David Rudkin, 'Alan would have said "Bollocks" to a comparison with Bresson' (Kelly 1998: 74). However, it is useful to contextualise Clarke's style within the approaches of other practitioners of his generation. His filmed plays share Ken Loach's approach to photography: namely, as Loach told Graham Fuller, an attempt to match the 'immense respect for people' demonstrated by Czech and Italian neo-realist cinema. Loach sought 'a more reflective, observed, sympathetically lit style of photography', lighting the space rather than privileging a lead actor, with the camera observing with 'the placidity of a fixed lens', a 'slightly narrow ... but not telephoto lens'. Clarke shares Loach's tenet that 'If you give people space, it gives them a dignity' (Fuller 1998: 38–41). The rhetoric of observation and objectivity also rejects the ways in which conventional cinema takes its structure and elements of its meaning, according to Bazin (1971a: 65), from the lead protagonist: 'The structures of the mise-en-scène flow from it: décor, lighting, the angle and framing of the shots, will be more or less expressionistic in their relation to the behaviour of the actor.' Conversely, in neo-realist films such as Roberto Rossellini's *Paisà* (1946), the camera 'makes no pretence at being psychologically subjective' and, 'as if making an impartial report, confines itself to following' its characters. The style of Clarke, Loach and others shares these elements of impartiality, observation and reporting, often with the use of long unbroken takes, which Bazin praised in conjunction with the deep focus techniques of directors such as Orson Welles and William Wyler. However, as Jamie Sexton observed, it is important to note the 'relationship between aesthetic innovation and technological change'. The use of 16mm film and lightweight cameras affected the development of the form employed by many practitioners, with its 'more journalistic than aesthetic' connotations (Sexton 2003: 429, 431).

Mark Shivas observed that Clarke's 1970s work often employed a 'rather tranquil camera' which 'allowed you to watch within the frame' (*Director*). In *Diane*, one scene features the camera holding on the table at which her father sits, while she is seen through a window in another room in the background; another shows a youth mending his bicycle, waiting in the foreground as Diane slowly walks to join him from the distant background. Of Clarke's 'emblematic' style, Christopher Morahan argued that for a decade 'his camera placement was open to parody'. He 'would hold a frame for a very long time because the life was in the frame, an Ozu kind of style' displaying 'rigidity' and 'classicism' (Kelly 1998: 80). Taken together, these techniques represented for Bazin a way of preserving the integrity of the filmic space. Constructions within the frame maintained spacial and perceptual reality, allowing viewers to gaze within that frame and make their own reading, rather than be enslaved to readings encoded by the juxtaposition of images through montage. The rhetoric of objectivity therefore offered an alternative to the psychological subjectivity upon which classical or 'seamless' realism depends: a position from which the spectator is stitched into the film's diegetic world by its structures of narration, taking a position like that encouraged by the third-person narrator in the novel. It is unsurprising that this generation of programme makers maintained a belief in the radicalism of these techniques. As Robert P. Kolker (1998: 17) summarised, citing Godard, Truffaut, Antonioni and Terence Davies as examples, 'any filmmaker who sets out to make a film that is counter to the structure of the dominant Hollywood cinema turns not to Eisenstein, but to the cinema that Bazin applauded and championed, the cinema of the long take, of coherent mise-en-scène'. However, the phenomenological or even empirical connotations of Bazin's conception of realism have drawn critical dissent; as we shall see, in the shifting ideological terrain of film criticism, Clarke, Loach and others were to face considerable opposition to their techniques later in the decade.

Another factor connecting this generation to the neo-realists was their approach to narrative. In plays such as *Horace* and *Diane*, Clarke began to address the role of narrative in terms similar to those proposed by Bazin and by the crucial neo-realist thinker Cesare Zavattini, screenwriter of Vittorio De Sica's *Ladri di biciclette* (*Bicycle Thieves*, 1948). Chief among these are an inversion of the classical use of characters as functionaries of plot, and an attempt to capture without embellishment the 'dailiness' of everyday life. Since 'our first, and most superficial, reaction to daily existence is boredom', Zavattini claimed, it was 'not surprising that the cinema has always felt the "natural" and practically inevitable necessity of inserting a story into reality in order to make it thrilling and spectacular'. Rejecting this became the 'essential innovation' of neo-realism. Denying accusations that 'everyday occurrences are not interesting' and 'do not constitute a dramatic spectacle', Zavattini (1978:

67, 74) argued that 'When a director evades the analysis of "every day occurrences" he obeys the more or less expressed desires of the capitalistic system of cinema production ... The putting together of one situation after another in a narrative line is not so very difficult. The analysis of a situation or an action in depth is extremely difficult.' Each event would be allowed to retain its own integrity rather than being subordinated to the cause-and-effect logic of classical narrative cinema, because 'a stone is a stone, not a stepping stone to something else', or, in the phrase of Kristin Thompson and David Bordwell (1994: 419), 'Scene B is apt to follow Scene A because B happened later, not because scene A made it happen'. Therefore, when Bazin (1971b: 58) argued that 'the very principle of *Ladri di Biciclette* is the disappearance of a story', he meant less the absence of a story than the loosening of causal connection. In these terms, Bazin's prediction that Italian neo-realism would leave 'No more drama' is echoed by Clarke's attempts to produce 'No drama' in *A Life Is For Ever*.

Clarke's work during this period features episodic and elliptical narrative structure. The randomness of experience is often emphasised by ellipses, employed shockingly in *Diane*, which does not show the discovery of the dead baby, Diane's confessions or her and her father's arrests. Instead, Diane is suddenly in a room with the vicar, and only gradually during their conversation do we realise what has happened. The narrative episodically follows Diane's experiences, a structure similar to that of *Horace* (1972). This portrait of two children – one an adult with a child's mental age – is a delightful example of Roy Minton's rich combination of harshness and dark humour. Both characters are in search of fantasy and protection, with Horace obsessed with toy jokes and Gordon refusing to be deprived of his 'magic cape'. Their adventures result in two of Minton's most unsettling images: the diabetic Horace fading into illness wearing his joke face mask – a juxtaposition which recalls Clarke's Absurdist use of masks in the theatre – and the sad spasm of a joke spider on a table in front of Horace as he is left in an institution. The play's episodic portrayal of the experiences of an adult and child wandering the streets make this a distant, Northern, cousin of *Bicycle Thieves*, which in terms of narrative 'unfolds on the level of pure accident', and treats each event according to its 'phenomenological integrity' (Bazin 1971b: 59, 52). With their stories structured in this way, the characters Horace and Diane become the organisers of narrative time and the defining principle of their titular plays.

However, to focus on Clarke's filmed plays with reference to art cinema risks misrepresenting his experiences as a director. *The Love-Girl and the Innocent* (1973) was shot on location on videotape, and was not written for television but adapted from Alexander Solzhenitsyn's stage play. Like *Danton's Death*, *The Love-Girl and the Innocent* was made for BBC1's *Play of the Month* (1965–83), the type of prestigious strand in which classics were brought to mainstream audiences, encoding television drama's cultural seriousness. Set in a labour camp in 1945, the play features an archetypal Solzhenitsyn scenario: the daily moral choices of protagonists in a harsh environment. The 'innocent' of the title is Nemov (David Leland), who refuses to take advantage of his position as production chief to commit the expected abuses of power; his insistence that 'I'm not going to be turned into a bastard like other people in the camps' anticipates Archer's assertion in *Scum* that 'They're not getting me, the bastards'. Undermined by ruthless Khomich (Richard Durden) and corrupt doctor Mereshchun (John Quarmby), he ends up working in the foundry. Now powerless, he falls in love with Lyuba (Gabrielle Lloyd), whose own tactic for avoiding the regime's worst excesses has been to become a 'love-girl'. Mirroring the banners specified in the play text, Stalin's mantra that 'people are the most valuable capital' (Solzhenitsyn 1969), this relationship helps them reclaim their brutalised humanity. Nemov feels 'as if you've released me' and, although their relationship is doomed, refuses Lyuba's pragmatic offer to share her with Mereshchun. After an accident befalls Nemov, she takes the doctor's offer. It is not difficult to read Clarke's authority into this adaptation, the survival of individuality and beauty within an oppressive institution. Clarke's Orwellian concern with 'a boot stamping on a human face' (Orwell 1949) is always most concerned with the human face: see the alternative transcript reading near the end of *To Encourage the Others*, Derek Bentley's death-cell dictation of his last letter, or Archer in *Scum* reading a letter for a fellow Borstal trainee, an oasis of tenderness in a dehumanising regime built on denying such narratives.

Like much of Clarke's work, *The Love-Girl and the Innocent* explores a landscape of private histories silenced by public narratives. Himself exiled to a labour camp between 1945 and 1953, Solzhenitsyn reported on Stalinist excesses with the encouragement of Khrushchev, until history again changed sides. Though the West awarded him the Nobel Prize for Literature in 1970, at home he was expelled from the Writers' Union and excluded from the *Literaturnaya Entsiklopediya*. Solzhenitsyn's only stage play, *The Love-Girl and the Innocent* was banned, and just before the BBC version's transmission he warned that 'If I am declared killed or suddenly mysteriously dead, you can infallibly conclude that I have been killed with the approval of the KGB or by it' (Miller 1973). The play could be taken as a topical piece metaphorically reflecting

Solzhenitsyn's plight as much as it is a representation of Solzhenitsyn's gulag past; Leland, later the writer of three of Clarke's incendiary studies of 1980s Britain, argued that 'No matter the period, everything that Alan did related to the present' (*Director*).

The play's events are caught up in competing discourses which complicate its status as historical representation. The narratives with which the Soviet Union appropriated and then denounced Solzhenitsyn's work, like Clarke's sympathetic dissemination of his work within a prestigious theatre strand and the ideologically loaded expectations of the subjects fit for costume drama, demonstrate Keith Tribe's assertion that the 'lessons of history' become less the empirical observation of the past than 'the product of a construction of a history which can be deployed in contemporary arguments' (Tribe 1977/8). This location, which Khomich observes 'isn't in the geography books or the philosophy books or the history books', constitutes – as Solzhenitsyn described imprisonment elsewhere (1974: 24) – an 'almost invisible, almost imperceptible country' populated by 'a silent people, without a literary voice'. Khomich's assertion articulates the way in which history becomes, in Tribe's phrase, a collision of 'a non-discursive past and a discursive present'. In this, the play resembles Ken Loach's more comprehensively worked-through alternative historical serial *Days of Hope* (1975), which according to Loach examined 'Who creates history and who it belongs to' (Fuller 1998: 50). The play's representation of history is complicated by its visual rhetoric, as the immediacy of video lends an intrusion of modernity which risks reducing representation to a 'recognition effect', generated not by 'the historicity of the plot' but by 'the manipulation of the image' (Tribe 1977/8). Therefore, part of the *Radio Times* preview discussed the play's meticulous recreation of reality. Although celebrating Clarke's talent, this served also to detail the orthodox signifiers of costume drama – design, sets, costumes and expense. A Siberian labour camp was recreated at a disused RAF camp at Cromer on the Norfolk coast. David Leland told Russell Miller that the cast 'almost began to believe that it was happening to us. The location and the costumes were so convincing that at times one doubted that the cameras were real'. Polish actor Jan Conrad, himself one of Stalin's victims, vouched for the building site and foundry sets: 'It was incredible. I looked around me and I thought: yes ... This is how it was. It was like going back in time 30 years' (Miller 1973).

Though a triumph of design, the play's success lies in its hugely evocative atmosphere, which, as Patrick Campbell (1973) argued, was 'admirably created and sustained by Alan Clarke in a meticulous and disciplined piece of direction'. Learning from Tony Parker, his approach is understated and sparse, according to Campbell 'sparing us the expected incidental and title music and reminding us what an impact silence can make'. This distinctive production is testament to Clarke's expertise in location video recording, the technology for which was still relatively crude. Not until *The Actual Woman*, made by BBC Birmingham a year later, was the potential of Outside Broadcast for drama widely accepted, with the innovative use of the LMCR (Lightweight Manual Control Room) as a studio gallery. Given modern television drama's anally clenched desire to look like film, for instance treating video images with the FRV (Field Removed Video) process, the phase of OB drama recording in the 1970s and 1980s seems bold. Its merits were partly aesthetic, providing a matching grain for studio interiors rather than the 'piebald' system which had awkwardly evolved. However, its obvious benefit was that, as Bob Millington (1984: 6) noted, 'BBC production schedules are based on a film unit achieving between 3 and 4 minutes of Drama programme-time a day, whereas an OB unit, rigged normally, records between 9 and 20 minutes of material in the same time'. Video allowed a quicker turnover than film even on single-camera productions, but the multi-camera set-up, allied with the director's ability to consult monitors, reduced the need for extra coverage (although video duping of film feeds was also becoming widespread). However, if the benefits of multi-camera were brought on to location, so were the restrictions, with aesthetic consequences for directors. Stephen Poliakoff spoke for many in seeing OB as 'a real danger to drama', a 'poor relation to film' resulting in a loss of 'atmosphere and depth' (Anonymous 1982a).

Clarke, however, moulded his signatures to location video. Recurring framing strategies, sparse mise-en-scène and repetition feature in the successive studies of institutionalisation *A Follower for Emily* (1974) and *Funny Farm* (1975). In the latter, Clarke develops his emergent motif of following walking characters, accompanying a demotivated male nurse around a psychiatric hospital. But Clarke's experiences with location video recording were mixed, as is demonstrated by a comparison of *The Love-Girl and the Innocent* and *Love for Lydia*. The former draws much of its power from Clarke's technique. Preparing to walk to the doctor's hut, Lyuba turns to answer a question about Nemov's health. There is something unsettling beneath the apparently conventional medium close-up – the background is fuzzy, nebulous, reinforcing her mental abstraction. It is a device which Clarke returns to, demonstrating a preoccupation with lenses. Designer Stuart Walker explained its idiosyncratic use on *Danton's Death*: 'he was the first television director who'd raised the topic with me. It's common enough in film, but in television you've got zoom lenses and it's all close-ups, mid-shots, one-shots ... we ended up with the cameras right on the perimeter of the studio, shooting close-ups of actors right at the other end' (Kelly 1998: 100). The effect in both plays is to create 'a very different feel than moving in tight and doing the same close-up on a wider lens'. Lyuba then sets off, captured – in direct contrast with the kinetic attachment of Steadicam to later walking protagonists – in a static long shot. Her protracted walk along a light-lined street towards the camera recalls the ending of *The Third Man* (1949), a similarly troubling coda to a tale of shifting loyalties against a morally barren landscape. The length that the shot is held emphasises a paradox in the composition – despite her freedom to walk, and the space around her in the frame, she is constrained by that frame, and can leave it only by arriving at her terrible destination. The shot therefore reinforces her predicament within that landscape. Another videotaped play, *Fast Hands*, has similar sequences near its ending, as boxer Jimmy, brain-damaged after being over-matched in a fight by his manager, walks painfully slowly out of shot. The change in body language is reinforced by the static long-shot, which contrasts with the rapid cutting and changes in angles during earlier montages of Jimmy's training.

However, Clarke's fascination with the long-shot was less welcomed on *Love for Lydia*, a major ITV adaptation which reunited him with producer Richard Bates and writer Julian Bond after *A Man of Our Times* and *Horatio Bottomley*. The producer maintained that the serial would be 'very, very faithful to the mood and intention' of his father H. E. Bates's book (Anonymous 1976a). It would be video-recorded on location, a technique which he had been lobbying other producers to use for a decade – importantly for Clarke, Bates added that 'any director who works with me has no alternative'. Clarke's experience on *Love for Lydia* in effect demonstrated that aesthetic experimentation, whilst encouraged in single drama, was frowned upon in popular series. David Yallop recalled Clarke's plan to 'begin the first episode on wide shots, hold those right the way through. And as the story progressed, week by week, he'd tighten the shot – so you'd end up with the last episode all in close-up' (Kelly 1998: 88). This fascinating manifestation of Clarke's concern with composition faced considerable hostility. Bates left the programme after three episodes were completed (two by Clarke, one by John Glenister), although Bond's scripts for the thirteen-part serial and the casting which Bates had approved remained unchanged (Anonymous 1976b). The Association of Directors and Producers protested against his 'dismissal', accusing ITV of actions more befitting 1930s Hollywood. On 14 May 1976, Bates and Clarke were 'summoned to meet

Cyril Bennett, programme controller for London Weekend and congratulated on the style and the casting' of episode one. However, 'after a rough cut of episode two had been seen, Bates was removed from the project and instructions given for both episodes to be reshot', because Bennett 'could not see the actors' faces'. *Television Today* expressed surprise that 'Alan Clarke, who might have been expected to be held responsible for the style of the direction, was not dismissed' (Anonymous 1976c), but he too soon left. Cyril Bennett (1976) denied congratulating Bates, stressed his consultations with LWT's Chairman and Managing Director, and quoted ADP President Piers Haggard's agreement that 'despite the outstanding sense of atmosphere and period, and the stunning quality of the visuals, the lack of close shots does seem perverse and could alienate an audience'. When the remade series aired, Stewart Knowles (1977) argued that Bennett had been 'vindicated' by this 'series that refused to die'. Others were less kind; Clarke's approach was partly vindicated by the opinion of Patrick Campbell (1977) that viewers should have been spared its unadventurous style, 'interminable close-ups on the same four faces registering the same single reaction'.

Popular drama had, therefore, proved a contentious area for Clarke, but so far the single play had been an ideal forum for dissent and experimentation. *Scum* exemplifies this, as Clarke told Cas Cassidy (1979): 'There is a tradition in *Play for Today* that it unearths a lot more shit than normal ... we lifted up a respectable rock of the establishment and we found what was underneath was corrupt and rotten, so we reported it'. However, in testing the limits of that space, Clarke found that the rules were changing.

'No barbed wire': *Scum* (1977, 1979)

Scum has been dogged by controversy since the banning of Clarke's original television play in 1977, heightened by the reactions to his 1979 cinema remake and its television transmission in 1983. The fact that its star Ray Winstone recently fronted advertisements describing one lager as 'the daddy', trading on his character's iconography, demonstrates that this notoriety has made it Clarke's best-known production. However, it has also given this skilful piece of film-making an unfairly reductive reputation, overshadowing it to the extent that the cover of Roy Minton's novelisation featured the word 'BANNED' more prominently than the title. Though Clarke told David Hare that he did not want it to become 'the defining event of his life', the banning of *Scum* was a pivotal moment in his career. It engendered in him, according to Hare, 'a sense of hopelessness about anything in Britain ever really changing' (*Own Man*). In this and the subsequent section, I place *Scum* in the context of concurrent debates among practitioners and critics – on the future of single drama, censorship and realism – to trace the manifestation of these concerns in his work. This transitional text marks a crucial step towards Clarke's discovery of his own distinctive voice.

Closer to a James Cagney prison movie than the propagandist pseudo-documentary described by critics, *Scum* is, as W. Stephen Gilbert (1978) argued, 'a rattling good tale in the staunch tradition of Hollywood liberalism – the hero, a clear victim of injustice, overcomes the system, holds to his integrity, vanquishes the villains and establishes a new and, it's implied, more principled order'. The setting is a Borstal which, although designed to rehabilitate young offenders, encourages criminality, violence and racism. *Scum* derived its claim to the real as a 'documentary drama' from the scope of the research which it dramatised. Minton interviewed 'between 80 and 100 people', including 'inmates, staff, ex-matrons, psychiatrists, teachers, probation officers, police, parents and a Borstal governor' (Murray 1978). Though the BBC's Managing Director Alasdair Milne questioned its veracity, commenting on *Tonight* that Minton and Clarke 'went into a Borstal – for a day anyway', Clarke told *The South Bank Show* that 'each person and each incident' was taken from those interviews (for details see Kelly 1998 and *Scum* DVD). They 'got the boys back' when they thought 'maybe that sounds a little exaggerated' and 'double-checked their story, because it's very important that what goes on there is ... based on total truth'.

Both versions open with the arrival of Carlin, Davis and Angel, who are immediately verbally and physically bullied. The television version opens with Davis being recaptured after fleeing an open Borstal. He runs across open fields but is imprisoned by Clarke's framing of him through the windscreen of the pursuing warders' car, a shot in which the warders are also confined. The cinema version opens by focusing instead on Carlin, who is first seen as an anonymous pair of cuffed hands, recalling the opening shots of Bresson's *A Man Escaped*. Transferred from another Borstal after retaliating against a warder, Carlin is violently warned off similar behaviour here by officers and by Banks, the 'daddy' of his wing. After continual provocation, Carlin attacks Banks's stooge Richards with billiard balls in a sock, and then beats Banks, telling him 'I'm the daddy now'. He strengthens his control by beating Baldy, the black daddy of another wing. Our identification with Carlin at these points is heightened by Clarke's attachment of the viewer to him through the positioning of his hand-held camera. Although employed in previous productions, this stylistic strategy is here consummated as a Clarke signature, connecting the viewer with the character's physicality. Initially, Carlin's 'very presence is a challenge to the screw' because he has '*his own* knowledge and authority intact' (Minton 1979: 14, my emphasis). Through the distorting lens of hindsight, Clarke's work seems to build to this study of incarceration and institutional violence, combining in Carlin's swaggering Borstal walks the attempts of his previous protagonists to assert their individual identities.

Archer (David Threlfall in the original, Mick Ford in the remake) embodies a different form of rebellion, digging beneath the system's rhetoric of rehabilitation, with 'a constant and cynical erosion of the system's oppressive certitudes' (Walker 1985: 156). Among his tricks to inconvenience the system, he claims his entitlement as an aetheist (despite previously proclaiming himself Christ) to be supervised alone rather than going to chapel, prompting a crucial scene with warder Duke. Asserting that 'more criminal acts are imposed on prisoners than by prisoners on society', Archer asks, 'How can anyone build character in a regime based on deprivation?' Connecting warders and trainees, he notes that Duke has served a 'hefty sentence' working in institutions, and, in one of the play's phallic symbols, argues that the length of his key chain demonstrates his failure to gain promotion, a 'daily humiliation' for which he makes the cons pay. Duke charges Archer with insolence, and responds in the traditional depersonalising language of the prison film, ordering him to stand and give his number. The conversation is mirrored in Clarke's shot structure. The scene opens in long-shot, but as they talk Clarke cuts between mid-shots in a conventional shot/reverse-shot structure, a reversibility which heightens their interaction. But as the officer snaps, both revert to their place in the system, reflected in the circularity of the scene's return to long-shot. This scene demonstrates, according to Minton's novelisation (1979: 101), that Archer 'has finally captured Duke'.

Drawing from the familial discourses of Borstals, Minton focuses on the battle to become the 'daddy' to explore masculinity through the central theme of the family. Borstal 'trainees' are inculcated through the authority's use of each 'daddy' to supervise them in the domestic space. The Gritters in *Stand by Your Screen* had demonstrated the internalisation of the dominant ideology into the family unit, in line with Antonio Gramsci's reading of consensus in his prison notebooks as 'the "spontaneous" consent given by the great masses of the population to the general direction imposed on social life by the dominant fundamental group' (Gramsci 1971: 12). Warders privilege Carlin in return for using his influence 'to keep things down'. The conflation of public and domestic authority figures is symbolised in the image of the daddy which the boys either obey or seek to attain. The nearest to an affectionate mothering figure is the unsuitable Miss Biggs, whose class-bound matriarchy leads her to respond with the views of 'Her Majesty and her representatives' (like, perhaps, Auntie Beeb). She is 'establishment, a front, a token', who 'cannot – or will not – relate to their actual experience' (Minton 1979: 30). She mistakes Toyne's grief over the death of his wife for that of a pet, after which he commits suicide, though this was cut from the television version. When a trainee gets married on day release, he is welcomed back with a mock ceremony involving a trainee dressed as his wife. The family subtexts are partly lost in the film, largely owing to the simple fact that the actors are older. The original is more effective at demonstrating that vulnerable young people are being driven to such acts because of its fresh-faced cast – for instance, John Blundell's voice creaks during one of Banks's threats. The film becomes a conventional brutal prison confrontation between fully formed and therefore apparently more independent adults.

The final member of the family appears only in the television version. 'Daddy' Carlin asks pretty boy Rhodes to be his 'missus', in a scene which immediately follows his victory over Baldy. This juxtaposition of brutality and nervous emotion powerfully demonstrates Carlin's vulnerability, and its removal from the cinema version undermines the complexity of his character. His ultimatum to Rhodes, to choose between having a hard time or easy time, is disturbingly similar to that offered by Mereshchun to Lyuba in *The Love-Girl and the Innocent*. When Davis, traumatised after being raped, visits Carlin for help, the latter refuses to make his 'missus' leave to allow a private conversation. This makes Carlin less sympathetic as his 'missus' legitimises the link between prison sexuality and power about which Davis is so distraught. This scene starts with a familiar Clarke shot, the camera outside the room looking in at action framed in the doorway. This connects Carlin with the two other scenes in the television version which use this shot, both featuring brutality against the trainees who entered Borstal with him – Davis being tricked by Eckersley and punished by Sands, and Angel being attacked – making him seem no better the officer who fatally ignores Davis's final cry for help. He becomes a tool of the authorities like the weapon he brandishes at Baldy in *Scum*'s most iconic exchange of dialogue: 'Where's your tool?'; 'What fucking tool?'; '*This* fucking tool' (Black and Decker have missed a trick in not arranging their own advertising campaign ...). There is a different type of doorway framing used at the end of this scene in the cinema version, with the composition of Carlin's swagger away from Baldy recalling a motif of John Ford's in *The Searchers* (1956). As well as recalling that film's use of landscape as conditioning factor in notions of civilisation and the complex morality of violence, this shot affirms that Carlin has become every inch the Western hero (in contrast with Archer, who, after being refused Dostoevsky's *Crime and Punishment*, bemoans the undemanding adventure books on offer: 'I don't know whether to be Roy Rogers or Nanook of the North').

Clarke's compositions reinforce this impression that, like Johnson in *A Life Is For Ever*, Carlin has become institutionalised. When facing the Governor, Carlin is in close-up, enclosed in the frame by two warders. Clarke then cuts to wide-shots, characteristically standing back from identification to take a detached view of trainees to match that taken by the system. These wide-shots are filmed with an almost fish-eye lens which heightens the claustrophobia of Clarke's highly formal compositions, based around a paralleling of straight lines and repetition of groups of three. Carlin is flanked by two warders facing three officials sitting at a desk, and is then connected with these officials as Clarke cuts to a reverse-shot positioned similarly from behind the Governor. A similar shot appears at a crucial point in *The Love-Girl and the Innocent*, to reinforce Nemov's proscribed options within the labour camp power structure. Throughout *Scum* social structures are mirrored in the geometry of framing. Some of these relate to the play's class subtexts, the way 'the system ... divides and rules the working class' (Gilbert 1978), which Clarke articulated to Cas Cassidy (1979): 'It is not without significance that the boys in Borstal are working class, all of them, and the warders are largely uneducated also ... the alsatians of the working class are looking after the rats of the working class'. In several layered compositions, he frames Borstal trainees in the bottom third of the frame, just as they are locked firmly into the bottom third of society. The Victorian location occupies the higher two-thirds, which, bearing in mind the frequently Dickensian imagery on display, notably in the cinema version's sequence of youths shovelling coal in the snow, emphasises the system's recourse to Victorian values: the workhouse, the undeserving poor and the Gradgrind approach to education (the latter resonating particularly alongside Prime Minister James Callaghan's 'Great Debate' on education). These long shots from side-on, resembling tableaux, are a recurring motif of Clarke's in this period, as beautifully handled as similar strategies being explored contemporaneously by Stanley Kubrick, particularly in *Barry Lyndon* (1975). Like the 'eighteenth-century paintings and engravings of French society' which designer

Stuart Walker recalls Clarke consulting for *Danton's Death* (Kelly 1998: 110), in *Scum, Baal, Psy-Warriors* and other plays Clarke stresses the position of individuals within society, or their alienation from it, by framing 'tiny figures in big rooms and surroundings'.

As we have seen, much of Clarke's work in this period depicts institutionalisation, and allies technique to the depiction of individuals whose movement is restricted and made uniform. *Scum* epitomises these approaches, contrasting the individuality of Carlin and Archer with the physical uniformity encouraged by the institution as a preparation for useful labour, expressed in collective walks and machine-like tasks. Like many other prison films, *Scum* operates in similar areas to those articulated by the theorist and penal historian Michel Foucault. Foucault's *Discipline and Punish: The Birth of the Prison* charted punishment's shift from the public destruction of human bodies to the disciplining of bodies in prisons. Therefore, as Danaher, Schirato and Webb (2000: 52) summarised, prisoners would be 'coerced, monitored, trained', '"drilled" in labour gangs' and 'made to perform routine tasks in a repetitive manner'. By 'regulating the space of prisoners', such 'machinery was created to work through the prisoners' bodies'. With the regulatory disciplines of bio-power inscribing power relations upon the body, the resulting docile bodies became, in effect, self-regulating.

Archer's comparison of these institutional practices with the world beyond the Borstal walls reflects what Foucault described as a 'carceral continuum', the spread of penal procedures and coercive forces throughout society. The journey taken by Carlin reflects that taken into other institutions throughout Clarke's work: the army in *Sovereign's Company*, prison in *A Life Is For Ever*, a mental hospital in *Funny Farm*, a school with militaristic overtones in *Penda's Fen*, even the detention centre resembling an 'English public school' (Leland 1986: 46) to which Trevor was sent in the deleted ending of *Made in Britain*. Their connectedness is heightened by Clarke's application of recurring motifs, and was almost made more explicitly, as *Scum* was devised as part of an unrealised trilogy of plays about the institutionalisation of young men into the police, the army and Borstal (Kelly 1998: 92). This correlation recalls Foucault's question: 'Is it surprising that prisons resemble factories, barracks, hospitals, which all resemble prisons?' (Foucalt 1991: 228). *Scum*, therefore, is not simply an effective prison film, but the thematic core of Clarke's work. Archer, successor to Chris Gritter in *Stand by Your Screen*, argues that, whilst in Borstal 'you act, you're punished, you're free', whereas in the outside world 'you act, you're punished by your own guilt complexes, and are never free'. Just as Foucault saw prison as both a micro-society and a model for society, the

Borstal in *Scum* became, according to David Thomson (1993: 80), 'a universal metaphor, a place for the invisible members of society, and a mercy for those who preferred not to look'.

Ultimately Davis commits suicide, and after Carlin refuses to quell ensuing tensions a riot breaks out. The play ends with a shot which echoes the opening shot of Davis through a windscreen: the trainees in the yard are framed by a doorway, and yet are in the open in comparison with the officers cramped in the dark door frame. Comparing *Scum* with Losey's *The Criminal*, Thomson observed that officers and inmates share 'a dreadful pact' and 'interdependent servitude'. Both films are 'lucid about this social dynamics', revealing 'a curious liberty for the prisoners and a fearful mental shackling on the part of the warders' (1993: 80). Minton developed these ideas in his novelisation: trainees see inside the religious Governor's puritanically sparse cell-like room, and Miss Biggs gets locked in E Wing, screaming the closing words 'GET ME OUT OF HERE' (Minton 1979: 128).

It is tempting to read the backlash against the riot as a prediction of the play's own banning, as three protagonists – for whom we could substitute Clarke, Minton and Matheson – are dragged through the corridors of an institution. This reading is inspired by Dennis Potter's mischievous paralleling of institutions in his review of *Funny Farm*, which he felt successfully captured 'the pace and moods of any institution for the unwell, such as a crowded ward ... or the Television Centre ... The patients didn't seem to watch much television, another disturbing similarity to the inmates whose doors open onto a long corridor that goes round the Television Centre and never quite makes it out into the real world' (Potter 1975). W. Stephen Gilbert (1978) also noted similarities between the BBC's actions and Duke putting Archer 'on report for insolence'. Minton's novelisation addressed the play's relationship with authority discourses. Lucas's diary is criticised by the Governor because, though 'extraordinarily well-written', it 'does not paint a very flattering picture of our life here', whilst, in an opening pastiche of Aldous Huxley's *Brave New World* (1932), Home Office figures are given an airbrushed tour around an open Borstal, in which there is none of the rumoured 'brutality', as the visitors can 'see for themselves' (Minton 1979: 106, 5). *Scum* is dedicated to breaking through rhetoric to allow the viewers to see for themselves.

This is not to deny that it heavily loads its case. On *The South Bank Show*, former Borstal deputy governor Mike Whitlam spoke for many in calling it a 'very biased' film, but importantly he added that this bias represented 'the boys' perception of a Borstal' and accepted that he might be biased 'from the staff point of view'. Whitlam argued that

Scum neglected to mention that 'quite a large number of them actually do come out with skills and training', and that 'the vast number of prison officers are caring people'. Clarke's reply articulates a recurring theme in his work: 'okay, "the vast number ... some violence does go on, some suicides do go on, some rapes do go on, but they don't go on with everybody", *statistically* it's alright'. His response is reminiscent of Charles Dickens's response to the 'refined and delicate' critics of his exposure of conditions in *Oliver Twist*: 'I am glad to have had it doubted, for in that circumstance I find a sufficient assurance that it needed to be told' (Dickens 1874: vii, x). *Scum* was intended, Clarke told *The South Bank Show*, to make 'the case for' the 'underdog' in Borstal, and to deliver its 'main thesis' that 'Borstal doesn't work'. Indeed, the National Association for the Care and Rehabilitation of Offenders had recently released a damning report on Borstals, and the institutions were phased out in 1983. But the BBC suppressed the play – with major consequences for Clarke's career and the future of British television drama.

   The television version was filmed between 7 March and 5 April 1977 in a former old people's home in Redhill. Producer Margaret Matheson highlighted it in her plans for the 1977–78 run of *Play for Today* as 'an original piece of dramatic writing ... wholly truthful, very harrowing and a brilliant piece of film-making' (Anonymous 1977b). Approved by the BBC at every stage from its Early Warning Synopsis onwards, details of the completed *Scum* were passed to the *Radio Times* for the issue dated 5 November 1977. However, in October rumours circulated that the play would not be shown; Clarke told *The South Bank Show* that 'we actually weren't notified ... we found out in the corridor'. Taking over as Controller of BBC1 from Bryan Cowgill, Bill Cotton postponed the play, requesting cuts to the swearing, rape and billiard ball attack and the removal of the first suicide (Kelly 1998: 103). Clarke observed that the television version became a 'negotiated one with the BBC before their nerve finally went, having gone through this awful democratic phoney process of "yes, take a little bit out there, take a bit out there, we'll think about it" ... and even then they wouldn't accept that' (*South Bank*). Clarke told the BBC that such cuts were self-defeating: 'if we take any more out ... the kids will think it's bloody Butlins in there; they'll be arriving in bloody coaches for holiday weekends at Borstals!' (Cassidy 1979). Clarke, Matheson and Minton went public. *The Guardian*'s Peter Fiddick (1977, 1978) was smuggled into Television Centre to view the play soon after his similar experience with Dennis Potter's *Brimstone and Treacle* (1976, banned until 1987), and at a controversial screening on Wardour Street on 20 January 1978 Minton gave out his polemical press release on this 'Billy Cotton Banned Show'.

Several reasons were suggested for the ban. The most frequently repeated accusation was that it was too violent. Head of Drama Shaun Sutton told Richard Last (1978) that he 'would like to see *Scum* get a transmission' but 'in its present form I don't think this is possible. The violence is too dense.' Milne improbably claimed on *Arena* in 1978 that *Scum* was 'probably the most violent thing we've ever made' but added, for reasons which will become clear, that 'we could have handled that'. Some critics supported Milne – Richard Afton (1978) praised him for having 'the courage to forbid this ... reprehensible ... play being shown in any form' – but Shaun Usher (1978) responded that it contained 'less bad language than many recent documentaries, and no more violence than the occasional thriller'. The same could not be said of the cinema remake, which Howard Schuman (1998: 20) justifiably argued was 'one of the few times Clarke allowed already hot material to overheat'. Filmed between 10 January and 17 February 1979 with a budget of £250,000 (Walker 1985: 155), the remake is much more explicit in its depiction of violence, swearing and also the rape of Davis, resulting in a film which is cult viewing for 'lad' magazines and football hooligans, one of whom described it as a film 'to get you in the mood' (Tordoff 2002: 243). Clarke rejected claims he had spiced up the remake, stating that he had 'done the original' by restoring material cut by the BBC 'with all the language that a place like that would actually have' and which was 'violent because the original script was more violent' (*South Bank*). However, Jan Dawson (1979) argued that Carlin's characterisation undermined the film's case: 'Exonerated in advance by the unfairness of the system within which he tries to protect himself, he can later perform no act too atrocious for the camera to justify.' The film's 'own directorial and dramatic strategies are about as democratic as the rape it so pruriently observes'. Gordon Gow (1979) agreed that it 'states its case so vigorously that it can hardly help looking like sensationalism'. Describing the original as 'one of the most brutal and sickening pieces of work I have ever had to sit through', Margaret Forwood (1983) wrote a scaremongering preview of the cinema version's television transmission. Following this late-night censored broadcast on Channel Four on 10 June 1983, Mary Whitehouse took legal action against the IBA for allowing its transmission. The Divisional Court agreed that the IBA had made 'a grave error of judgement', but, when the Court of Appeal over-turned this verdict, Geoffrey Robertson QC (1985) dismissed accusa-tions that *Scum* was 'an exploitation film with stereotype characters'. The IBA Director General's informed opinion as founder of a prisoners' trust was that *Scum* was a 'serious dramatic work based on tensions and violence that are a feature of a closed prison society'. (For transcripts of the case and its crucial wider implications for the IBA and media censorship see Anonymous 1984 and 1985, Hewson 1984, Robertson 1985.)

Mike Whitlam suggested that Clarke had 'missed the point of the violence', making a film 'which shows the violence in order to sell it'. Clarke's reply – 'No, no no no' – demonstrates his weary familiarity with such misreadings. In this case, they were exacerbated by tales of Clarke achieving realistic scenes by stirring up violence between the cast and kids from Leytonstone youth club (see Kelly 1998). Visiting filming of the cinema version, Alan Road (1979) noted that Clarke was 'worried that things could get out of hand' with the climactic riot scene. That day, 'a wardrobe mistress discovered a length of lead piping in the sleeve of one lad's jacket. A spot check revealed a number of hidden chair legs and wire coat-hangers crudely adapted into offensive weapons. There have been rumours of racial tensions and settling old scores. Clarke explains that grievous bodily harm is not in the script and would, indeed, ruin the ending of his film.' His search for realistic violence had already exceeded expected limits in the boxing drama *Fast Hands*. Bill Buffery, an undergraduate in his first acting job, fought eight rounds with professional welterweight boxer Paul Davis at a public hall. The result was a brutal eight-minute sequence intended, as producer Barry Hanson told Dermod Hill (1976), to show 'exactly what the experience of a fight, of being hurt, is', because 'it is something that has never successfully been faked'. The fight ended earlier than planned, with Buffery able only to repeat: 'I'm dead. I can't move.' Clarke offered a realistic rather than an exploitative portrayal of violence and in *Scum*, as in later films such as *Elephant* and *The Firm*, provided 'a serious view of violence and the way it breeds on violence' which exposed the way most programmes use 'easy brutality to provide amusement and entertainment' (Anonymous 1978a). The repetition of such scenes comments on the power structure, as violence performed on the trainees renders rehabilitation impossible. Filmed by *The South Bank Show*, Clarke explained to the cast of the 'murderball' sequence that the trainees put in some 'fist' to release their frustration. This culminates in the riot in which those vilified as 'scum' live up to their training, led by Carlin, who constantly asserted his desire to serve his time peacefully.

Therefore, *Scum* got into trouble precisely because the violence *did* have a serious point. Talk show host Michael Parkinson (1978) attacked this 'horrendously disturbing play with a theme of unrelenting degradation', arguing that if it was 'true', then 'the Prime Minister should consider immediately closing all Borstals and arresting large members of staff on criminal charges'. However, if it was 'dramatic exaggeration, then *Scum* is a very dangerous play, indeed, which gives a documentary impression of life in Borstal as one of unredeemed horror'. Parkinson added that if the writer was 'so passionately committed to exposing Borstal conditions', he should campaign 'to correct abuses as vigorously as he has bewailed the fate of his play', which seems unfair given that Minton had been prevented from doing so through his drama. Clarke summarised the BBC's response: '"the violence between the boys we can take, the language and the coarseness and the fact that it doesn't look like a play, it looks like it's real" and all that rubbish, "we can take all that" ... the main point of the film is its criticism of the way that the prison officers behave towards the boys ... and it's on that basis that the BBC banned it' (*South Bank*). Recalling that Cotton told him that 'he didn't want it on his channel', Clarke suggested that Cotton may have been motivated by vested interests: 'three or four times during the conversation he said that the fact he was a magistrate had nothing to do with it' (Road 1979). In his autobiography, the 'unrepentant' Cotton rejected such speculation: 'studying defendants in the dock, I used to wonder what had possessed them to behave so appallingly, and I had an uneasy niggle at the back of my mind that the television industry to which I had given my life might in some ways be implicated'. Referring to the 'sickening violence' of the billiard ball attack, he said that 'I felt this scene was not just brutal, but that it would brutalise those who watched it' (Cotton 2000: 175).

Responding to complaints that 'the Borstal service would have no comparably effective way of setting the record straight' (Anonymous 1978b), Patricia Williams (1978) argued that it was 'up to the Home Office to refute the allegations in the play rather than the BBC', and cogently asked why it should be 'singled out for protection as opposed to other government departments which are frequently the subject of plays'. According to W. Stephen Gilbert (1978), the Home Office, which was responsible for both the penal system and television, 'would not be glad of such a film', and in the uncertainty surrounding the Annan report on broadcasting, 'The BBC, cap in hand for a long-term licence, cannot afford to excite the Home Secretary's wrath'. For the same reasons, David Leland introduced the play's 1991 transmission with the opinion that this represented 'political censorship'. Milne stressed that he had not had contact with the Home Office, and that the decision had nothing to do with the licence fee – Minton had mischeviously called for an official investigation into the waste of £120,609 'at a time when the BBC is demanding further licence increases' (Last 1978).

There followed a period of retrenchment at the BBC. In February 1978, the general advisory council 'commended' Milne in their quarterly

meeting (Anonymous 1978c), and Milne addressed the drama department, although Shaun Sutton rejected press reports of an emergency
summoning to insist this was 'normal practice' (Anonymous 1978d).
Director General Ian Trethowan told a Writers' Club lunch that he
preferred to waste money on *Scum* 'to ensure that programmes like
Scum were produced'. He argued that 'people would feel that they had
to be careful earlier' if a play 'had to be shown' once it was 'on the studio
floor', and therefore *Scum* 'is part of the price to be paid for quality'
(Anonymous 1978e). Elaborating on the labelling by John Caughie
(1980) of television's separate 'official' and 'creative' discourses, John
Cook (1998: 96–7) wrote that broadcasting institutions, 'always trying
to curb and restrain', are faced with practitioners aiming 'to challenge
conventional television thinking' and extend 'the boundaries of what
was permissible on screen'. Trethowan's statement illustrates Cook's
point that the institution 'tacitly *invited* and supported' such practitioners because it was 'in the best interests of its own health and long-
term survival to do so'. Similarly, Peter Fiddick (1991) observed that
Margaret Matheson's reputation as 'a producer of challenging drama'
and defender of her writers made her both a 'periodic thorn in the side
of the BBC hierarchy' *and* 'someone in whom they took some pride'.
Drawing attention to the 650 plays he had not banned, Milne
reaffirmed his support for political plays such as *Destiny* (1978) and *The
Spongers* (1979), which proved it was 'sometimes useful' to 'shock
audiences into awareness' (Williams 1978). Derek Paget (1998b: 110)
remarked upon this 'institutional trait' while placing Clarke's *Road* in
the context of the Royal Court Theatre, noting that 'The turbulence
attendant upon controversy can be read as a cultural index both of the
importance of the subject under discussion, and of the virility of the
institution originating it'.

But the willingness of broadcasters to maintain this support
appeared to be weakening. An economically driven move towards series
and serials exacerbated a cultural shift away from single drama which
for some practitioners signalled a decline in the core beliefs of broadcasting's golden age. When Clarke and Minton's *Fast Hands* aired as
part of *Plays for Britain* (1976), ITV sought to redress the negative
signals sent out by their cancellation of *Armchair Theatre* with advertisements which proclaimed this strand its 'successor' (Anonymous 1976d),
while producer Barry Hanson reaffirmed its typically contemporary
issue-led remit: 'People are obsessed with Britain at the moment, re-
examining the myths by which we used to live' (Anonymous 1976e).
Former *Wednesday Play* script editor David Benedictus (1975) reiterated
that plays exist 'to ask questions', and that the best practitioners have

'broken the rules'. *Scum* epitomised such drama, but came to symbolise its decline; Dennis Potter's defence of the play reads like a eulogy: 'You are forced to react, to think, to argue, to attack or defend, and if drama is never allowed to do that, what on earth can we expect from the rest of television?' (Cassidy 1979). Assessing the BBC's handling of banned plays including *Scum*, Melvyn Bragg and Tony Cash (1979) worried about Milne's 'refusal to be open to debate, to questioning and to any democratic discussion either inside or outside the BBC', and its consequences for this 'true national theatre'. At Clarke's memorial service in 1990, David Hare argued that the BBC's willingness to censor itself in line with government had serious repercussions for its independence: 'Along the fault line created by the banning of *Scum* flowed all the lousy decisions and abject behaviour which left the BBC ten years later having to fight to justify its very existence to government' (Kelly 1998: 105).

Dramas had been 'banned' in previous periods. In the 1960s, alongside the notorious banning of Peter Watkins's *The War Game*, David Osborne's *Three on a Gas Ring* (1960) was withdrawn, whilst the BBC picked up John Osborne's *A Subject for Scandal and Concern* (1960) and Clive Exton's *The Big Eat* (1962) after ITV backed out. However, censorship clearly increased in the 1970s. Political bias, violence, language and sexual content were among the reasons given for a variety of delays and cuts. Victims included several Ken Loach plays, Barrie Keefe's *Gotcha* (1977) and *Champions* (1978), even the *Doctor Who* serial *The Deadly Assassin* (1976), which prompted an apology to the previously marginalised Mary Whitehouse and the removal of a scene from its master tape. This is without touching upon dramas in effect 'banned' by not being made, of which Ian McEwan's *Solid Geometry* in 1979 and Ian Curteis's *The Falklands Play* in 1986 achieved the highest profile. Several productions were shelved like *Scum* including Potter's *Brimstone and Treacle* and, ironically, an episode of *Doomwatch* attacking censorship, *Sex and Violence* (1972). *Article Five*, Brian Phelan's play on British human rights abuses, was pulled in 1975, and attacked as 'a bad play' by Shaun Sutton despite John Bowen's opinion on behalf of the Writers' Guild that this 'serious play on an important subject' was 'at least as well acted and directed as the majority of the BBC's drama output' (see Munro 1979). Others included Howard Barker's *Prowling Offensive*, Howard Schuman's *Censored Scenes from King Kong* (rescheduled for three years after 1974 until Schuman withdrew it to assist his stage version), Richard Eyre's *Pillion* for *Play for Today* (1979) and the *Horizon* drama-documentary *The Black Pool* (1980) written by Alan Plater, withdrawn by Milne when others had passed it. *Scum* was relegated to the BBC's vaults, though it served as a demo tape to aid the negotiation of a deal for the cinema version (one consequence of which was the abandonment of a stage production by the Royal Shakespeare Company). Following the unbannings of *The War Game* and *Brimstone and Treacle* in the 1980s, in 1991 the original *Scum* was given a posthumous screening (albeit with some cuts) just before midnight on BBC2 on a Saturday night in summer. While welcoming the broadcast, Peter Fiddick (1991) observed that 'there is limited credit in screening, 13 years on', the one banned play 'that most aimed to confront an audience with a problem of its day'. Equally, this screening itself suffered further brief cuts, as Matheson pointed out in her commentary on the play's 2004 DVD release, its 'first intact' availability (see Lucas 2004).

Clarke told Cas Cassidy in 1979 that *Scum* might have gone out unchallenged just four years earlier: 'The climate then was tangibly, well, less Right-wing than it is at present. It's hard to pin down precisely what's going on politically at present when you're right in the middle of it: but there's this creeping Right-wing atmosphere affecting most things. God knows how serious it will become.' *Scum* emerged during a period of establishment retrenchment in Britain in response to political unrest. It was not only Harold Wilson's Labour government which suffered 'dirty tricks'. MI5, according to Mike Hollingsworth and Richard Norton-Taylor (1988), had been politically vetting BBC employees since 1937, and were now briefed to uncover 'subversives'. Given the Left-wing politics of some plays, Drama was an obvious place to start. With reference to *Brimstone and Treacle* and the perceived politics of producer Kenith Trodd, Milne told John Cook (1998: 99) that 'the climate in '76 was difficult', and that it 'might have coloured my judgement'. Like the Borstal officers who bloodied the noses of ringleaders, the BBC's actions against Potter and Clarke served to encourage the others by striking at two practitioners who were hugely respected within the industry for their devotion to television. At the height of the controversy, W. Stephen Gilbert (1978) argued that *Scum* was 'one of the finest pieces of work ever made by BBC Drama Group. Like most good art, it works on more than one level ... director Alan Clarke's style is realistic, the familiar telenaturalism look.' However, this 'look' was to be seized on by critics to ignite simmering tensions over techniques which fused drama and documentary.

Scum, documentary drama and progressive form

In this section, I will unpick *Scum*'s status as a documentary drama and discuss the formal debates which sprang from it, to assess how these crucial issues reflected upon Clarke's technique as a director. This involves placing its dramatic features – the 'excess' of narrative and performance, and authorial subjectivity or 'bias' – alongside (but not *against*) the claim to objectivity of documentary language. Drama-documentaries are often attacked for propagandistic intermingling of fact and fiction. One critic suggested that *Scum*'s subject matter should not be tackled within 'the bastard art form of documentary fiction', within which the writer sought 'the freedom of creative drama and the licence this gives him' but also 'the credibility which his claim to background research gives him', as if 'asking to have his cake and eat it' (Anonymous 1978b). The BBC argued in a crucial statement that 'Every incident in *Scum* may be accurately documented, but packing them into one 90 minute play is a distortion of conditions at a Borstal' (Murray 1978). On *Tonight*, Milne reiterated that his advisers were 'sure ... that incidents of that kind must and do occur', but only 'over a long period of time', and so this 'compendium' would 'distort' the facts 'under the guise of a dramatic truth'. Minton understandably replied that 'one of the most elementary skills of the dramatist is his ability to condense his material into a period of actual time that will retain his audience's interest while not abusing its credulity' (Hunt 1981: 30). However, the problem goes beyond inevitable dramatic compression, extending to a distrust of the imposition of a dramatic narrative. In contrast with the avoidance of narrative embellishment in *A Life Is For Ever*, *Scum* focuses a melodramatic narrative around an anti-hero protagonist. As such it resembles the American docudrama which emerged from similar social problem roots, as opposed to the documentary lineage from which the British model developed (see Chapter 1), and which featured according to Todd Gitlin 'melodramas whose stereotypes ... disclose the point of view of historical victims' (Gitlin 1994: 62). Though British academics were able to explore a more radical form within culturally privileged radical single drama (see Paget 1998a) than the exploitative 'Disease-of-the-Week weepies' (Kelly 1998: xvi) associated with the American model, both share core issues such as the use of narrative which led Bill Nichols to define docudramas as an inherently fictional form existing outside the 'discourse of sobriety' (1991: 60). And yet, the relationship between narrative and representation is more complex than an imposition of drama onto fact. The 'narrative turn' through which social reality is emplotted is as much a feature of documentary as it is of drama, and after *Scum* Clarke builds on his characteristic paring-down to investigate the ideological workings of narrative.

The notion of 'duping' persisted, despite its dependence upon a dismissive view of audiences passively receiving media which was out of touch with concurrent audience research methods stressing the 'uses and gratifications' approach 'to see audiences as active participants in the creation of meaning' (Casey *et al.* 2002: 19). Interviewed on *Arena*, critic Joseph Hone argued that programme makers were trying to 'seduce' viewers into thinking they were watching reality, whilst documentary maker Denis Mitchell voiced a concern that if viewers joined *Scum* late, this 'large naïve – from a film point of view – mass of people' might wonder if it was real. Alasdair Milne argued on *Tonight* that viewers 'should not be given, in the guise of a play, what was essentially a documentary – a polemic' (see Kenneth Robinson 1978). In this debate, according to Michael Church (1978), 'everyone is on thin ice. The BBC because "distort" is a pretty odd word to apply to a play. (Did Genet "distort"?) The author, because with his emphasis on research he does make implicit documentary claims. The director, because *Scum* somehow feels like a drama-documentary.'

The BBC's position had not substantially changed since a mysterious editorial appeared in the *Radio Times* in January 1969. An unattributed author argued that the viewer had 'learned to distinguish between those programmes which he knows to be fact and those he knows to be fiction by means of a series of conventions which he has come to respect', maintaining the dichotomy between documentary as a 'photographic record of real events' and drama as 'art presented as art'. This 'simple situation has been complicated' by plays such as *Cathy Come Home* and Tony Parker's *Mrs Lawrence Will Look After It* (1969), 'well-acted dramas' making 'a deliberate comment' on social problems through use of 'real-life material'. Reassuring readers against the danger that 'these new programme techniques' might be 'taken too far', the BBC sought 'to keep faith with the viewers', who 'have a right to know what they are looking at' (Anonymous 1969). In response, referring to Parker and Roy Battersby's 'banned' *Five Women* (subsequently trimmed so much it was renamed *Some Women*), eight practitioners including Garnett, Trodd and Loach interpreted this as a warning: 'if you refuse to take our gentlemanly hints, we shall censor or ban any of your programmes which deal in social and political attitudes not acceptable to us'. Occasionally a rebel may be allowed 'an isolated event', as this 'helps to preserve our liberal and independent image', but not a 'movement'. Because nobody was said to have been 'duped' by Alf Garnett's appearance in a real football crowd, 'this is an argument about content, not about form' (Garnett *et al.* 1969). To a certain extent with *Scum*, as John Corner (1996: 39) observed with regard to *The War Game*, 'objections which were primarily about the substantive content and viewpoint expressed were strategically displaced into becoming objections about the unacceptability of the form itself'. Asking whether Milne would argue that *Gangsters* or *Porridge* (1973–77) were more 'true' than *Scum*, Peter Buckman (1978) argued that it was 'indefensible' to 'elevate the debate to the plane of philosophical abstractions', since television had always 'formed for us its own version of reality'. Similarly, Jeremy Isaacs, whose Channel Four screened the remake, argued that 'This insistence on the Aristotelian unities did not seem appropriate ... for the film medium, in which time and place can be altered at will by a single cut. To insist in fiction on journalistic literalism seemed harsh on the makers of a tough but particularly well-made, and even moral, movie' (Isaacs 1989: 117).

Milne qualified such concerns, arguing on *Arena* that 'It's only worrying if the labelling goes wrong'. Confusingly given his decision over *Scum*, he added that even if a *Play for Today* 'looks like a documentary', 'people ought to know by now that it's a *Play for Today* and purports, therefore, to be a dramatised version of some truth'. Rather than the play's violence, he was concerned that he 'didn't believe that the ambience that they were dramatising was in any way real, thus I asked the question, of what truth is this the dramatic expression?' Tony Garnett responded by stressing that film-makers 'go with prejudices, but we go to dig at reality' and to 'make *our* sense of it'. This notion of a subjective truth illustrates one of the precepts of radical drama – as Albert Hunt summarised, Minton's comment that 'nobody "likes" *Scum*' (including Minton himself) implied that 'the play contains some "truth" that we ought to be told about, whether we "like" it or not' (Hunt 1981: 30). Similarly, Clarke told Jennifer Selway (1979) that 'I'm carrying the message into the open. That's my responsibility. Don't shoot the messenger!' However, that was precisely what did happen, as this belief came into collision with the conviction among executives in the objective truth of factual broadcasting, particularly in 'documentary's cultural status as a kind of faith' (Paget 1998a: 1). It seems unlikely that, as James Murray (1979) argued, the film 'might have been better if Minton and Clarke had attempted a factual Rampton-type documentary and let their real witnesses talk for themselves'. Given the way interviewees used false names and insisted on avoiding other former trainees, they may not have spoken on camera; equally, there would have been access problems given the lack of Home Office approval. But the feeling remained, particularly among BBC journalists, that 'some controversial plays are not completely thought-out and lack balance' (Anonymous 1978f).

Like other practitioners, Clarke belittled the naivety of this concept of 'balance', describing it in dismissively formulaic terms as being '50% critical and 50% uncritical' (Selway 1979). In Marxist media writing, 'balance' and 'objectivity' are themselves ideologically loaded terms, presupposing a fidelity to 'the ideas of the economically dominant class' which through power over the media and cultural institutions come to predominate as the 'dominant ideology' (for a recent definition tailored to television, see Casey *et al.* 2002: 24). Raymond Williams (1976: 145) defined hegemony as representing not simply direct political control but 'a more general predominance which includes, as one of its key features, a particular way of seeing the world', dependent 'not only on its expression of the interests of a ruling class but also on its acceptance as "normal reality" or "commonsense" by those in practice subordinated to it'. Jack Gold told *Arena* that there is 'no such thing as an objective documentary. Merely by choosing the subject or choosing where the camera's going or choosing which particular incident you're going to film, you immediately interfere with objectivity'. On the same programme, Tony Garnett argued that factual programmes 'contain, personally and uniquely, an imaginative response' bringing to 'that narration of fact' the 'filter' of 'their own authorial preconceptions'.

Loach, like Clarke, was not trying to 'dupe' viewers into accepting that dramatic events were real. Generating immediacy is a dramatic device, based around, as Loach told John Hill, relatively conventional film-making techniques: 'I shoot a scene from two or three angles so that you can cut it together. I repeat the action for each set-up.' He 'couldn't make these films in a documentary way' as he would have to 'go in with a wide-ish angle and stand in the doorway'. His films were 'set up like a piece of fiction', although he crucially noted the use of 'little tricks of the trade to try and make it look as though it is happening for the first time' (Hill 1997a: 169). The use of documentary language is part of his personal style, just as W. Stephen Gilbert described 'Alan Clarke's style' above, and not an absence of style as this criticism would imply. Clarke told *Arena* in similar terms that *Scum* 'is a play, it's not a documentary, there's been such a lot of I think rubbish talked about what's a drama, what's a drama documentary ... a documentary is one in which people portray themselves, and a drama is one in which actors are paid to portray other people. *Scum* is the latter.' Acting represents another crucial tension between drama and documentary; Derek Paget (1998a: 126) observed that 'rehearsed and performed drama', when compared with 'real-world drama', is always 'excessive' in that 'the pro-filmic is different in both degree and kind', and so regardless of the primacy of factual material 'the performed drama will always be an "excess"', which some critics construct as 'a gap in credibility'. This 'excess' extends to its style, including expressive long shots and conventional reverse shots which require a scene to be filmed over and over again, which undermine claims that *Scum* is stylistically a pseudo-documentary. That it could be condemned as such calls into question the expertise of executives in the grammar of drama, as W. Stephen Gilbert (1978) pointed out: 'No one from Drama has ever risen as high as BBC Channel Controller. Milne is from Current Affairs, Cotton from Light Entertainment.' Consequently, according to Kenith Trodd, controllers struggled to deal with drama, 'especially if it spilled over into current affairs or moral issues that forced it out of the television viewers' page and on to the front pages' (Cook 1998: 96).

Clarke does use 'tricks of the trade' to generate spontaneity. He uses mid-shots which react to characters' movement, occasionally stands 'in the doorway' with a 'wide-ish angle', and jerkily observes Winstone in the bath in the television version, with Winstone almost acknowledging the presence of the camera. Margaret Matheson admired 'The performances that Alan got from actors – and the way that he got the camera into the action, where he chose to put his camera, how he chose to move his camera' which created an 'exciting' feeling 'that it's very immediate, that it's real' (*Director*). But these practitioners would share the view of André Bazin that 'realism in art can only be achieved in one way – through artifice' (Bazin 1967: 23). Indeed, documentary language acknowledges this artifice, unlike the dominant cinematic form – 'classic realism' – which employs techniques of editing, close-ups, reaction shots and other devices to render the camera an impossibly invisible presence and to stitch the spectator into the action through empathy with character in terms of narrative and positioning. Clarke and Loach were among the leading exponents of a camera style which often seems to react to events in a technique described by John Caughie (1980: 28) as the 'rhetoric of the "unplanned" or "unpremeditated" shot: the camera surprised by the action'. This documentary language involves 'systems of mediation (hand-held camera, loss of focus, awkward framing) so visible as to become immediate, apparently unrehearsed, and therefore authentic', in contrast to the 'classic paradox' of the 'dramatic look' of conventional screen grammar, which 'creates its "reality effect" by a process of mediation so conventionalized as to become invisible'.

The 'telenaturalism' style of these practitioners has been placed in the tradition of literary naturalism developed by writers such as Emile

Zola. Using Zola to describe Loach's methodology, Deborah Knight observed that 'Like the experimental scientist, the naturalist does not set out merely to record or to document some aspect of the observed world; instead, in an attempt to explain what she has observed, the naturalist records in controlled conditions – in the novelist's case, in the novel itself – something she has previously observed in an actual environment' (Knight 1997: 61). As we have seen, various practitioners, including Clarke in plays such as *A Life Is For Ever*, predicated their technique upon generating such responses and positioning themselves as observers. As in *Scum* it is the setting, and the ways in which the narrative is focused around its debilitating nature, which creates the 'naturalistic perspective' and 'asks us to recognize that, given the social and cultural contexts in which these characters act, things could scarcely have been otherwise' (Knight 1977: 76–7). Despite continued controversy over the form, many practitioners favoured it over more expressionistic modes to confront large audiences, following in visual terms George Orwell's maxim that 'Good prose is like a window pane' (1968: 30). According to Trevor Griffiths, given that 'the popular imagination ... has been shaped by naturalism', the 'demystifying, undistorted, more accurate, counter descriptions of political processes and social reality' of such modes offered a potential 'struggle for the popular imagination', rather than 'talking to 38 university graduates in a cellar in Soho' (Cooke 2003: 98). This sense of engagement is distinct from the critical construction of single drama as arthouse television, a ghetto lost in the postmodern 'flow' of broadcasting. Realist texts actively generated extra meanings from their place in the schedules, as Ken Loach noted: 'we were following the news so we tried to work in the style of *World in Action* and other current affairs programmes so that people didn't think "we have had the facts and now we will have the fiction" but rather "we've had the facts – now here's some more facts with a different point of view"' (Hill 1997a: 160). This engagement carried menace, according to Colin McArthur (1981: 294): 'Inherent in the characteristic bourgeois separation between art and social life is the view that so long as the media-worker is clearly seen to be producing fiction, then what he/she does is of little political consequence. The moment, however, that the forms he/she uses cease to be unambiguously "fictional" and begin to look like the "factual" production of the media, then he/she is seen to pose a political threat.'

The academic Left, however, questioned the extent to which naturalistic modes constituted a worked-through 'political threat' in a series of debates which took place around Loach's *The Big Flame* (1969) and *Days of Hope* in the film journal *Screen* (see MacCabe 1974 and 1976,

McArthur 1975/6, Williams 1977a, Caughie 1980 and 2000a). The work of Clarke, like that of Loach, clearly demonstrated a progressive incorporation of new content, akin to 'the revolutionary force of Tolstoy's texts which ushered the Russian peasant onto the stage of history' (MacCabe 1974: 16), and texts such as *Days of Hope* addressed wide audiences through the accessibility of naturalistic form (McArthur 1975/6). In response to Georg Lukács's discussion of the terrain between naturalism and realism, Bertolt Brecht argued that this making visible was not sufficient; naturalism and conventional dramatic identification served to naturalise existing political systems: 'The dramatic spectator says: Yes, I have felt like that too – Just like me – It's only natural – It'll never change – The sufferings of this man appal me, because they are inescapable – That's great art' (Bloch *et al.* 1977: 71). As a result, as Raymond Williams (1977b: 5) summarised, 'Naturalism as a doctrine of character formed by environment could emerge ... as a passive form: people were stuck where they were'. Loach's style was therefore 'not political in the right sort of way' (Knight 1997: 70) because, according to Colin MacCabe, it lacked the self-consciousness or self-reflexivity of a Brechtian conception of cinema. Realism as a political form should, according to Brecht, be based upon 'discovering the causal complexes of society' and 'unmasking the prevailing view of things as the view of those who are in power' (Bloch *et al.* 1977: 82). Challenging the dominant ideology through cinematic language involved creating the space for wider change, reflecting a Marxist 'counter sense of realism' which 'insisted on the dynamic quality of all "environments", and on the possibility of intervention to change them' (Williams 1977b: 5).

Penny Boumelha (1987: 19) noted that debates on 'classic realism' in literature had exposed the 'bourgeois and humanistic epistemological bases of the "great tradition"', showing 'the political content built into ... narrative tactics'. The classic realist text employed 'a form of closure – not simply formal, but ideological – by which the reader is continually produced and addressed as a unified individual human subject through such means as the convergence at a single and uniform ideological position of a set of hierarchised discourses of which one is always a controlling "truth-voice"'. Examining such hierarchised discourses in the cinema, John Caughie distinguished between 'the fascination with which the documentary camera appropriates its object and renders it passive and the active look which is exchanged between agents of the drama'. The 'dramatic look' places the spectator in 'quite literal identification' with 'the hero', both 'empathising' and seeing 'the fictional world and the action through his point of view'. The 'documentary gaze' is not 'cut into the narrative space' in this way, but stands outside, 'exploiting the "objectivity" of the camera to constitute its object as "document"', and denying the sense of 'reversibility' given to characters who 'look and are looked at', 'both in the play and in play'. The problem with this 'hierarchy' is that the documentary and dramatic discourses 'are integrated to produce a self-confirming discourse of truth' (Caughie 2000a: 111–12). In Marxist terms, contrary to the 'position of superior knowledge' taken by spectators of the realist text, whose visual narration presupposes a 'secure equilibrium' based upon the 'restoration of order', the revolutionary subject 'must experience itself as being in contradiction', that 'motor which drives history' (Caughie 2000a: 105). According to Colin MacCabe (1976: 100), the classic realist text may 'state a contradiction which it has already resolved' rather than 'produce a contradiction which remains unresolved and is thus left for the reader to resolve and act out'. Critics were left to decode a 'contradiction in the text' rather than exploring 'how contradiction is produced in the audience' (MacCabe 1976: 100), and the working class became 'the object of a gaze' in texts such as *Days of Hope* instead of being 'the subject of history' (Caughie 2000a: 112).

In such summaries lies the danger of essentialism; descriptive naturalism possesses its own ideological dynamism. Observing that the 'classic realist text' was used 'as the straw man against which both Modernist innovation and critical realism in a Brechtian mode were measured', Bignell, Lacey and Macmurraugh-Kavanagh (2000: 88) noted that 1960s drama-documentaries could be seen as 'modernist rather than realist, with their concern to explore issues of form and their sense of engagement with the contemporary'. This was Dennis Potter's view in the 1970s; even whilst arguing for non-naturalistic practices as the most valuable methodology with which to 'disorientate the viewer', Potter observed that 'the best naturalist or realist drama, of the Garnett-Loach-Allen school for instance', resists offering viewers a cosy 'means of orientating themselves towards the generally received notions of "reality" ...by the vigour, clarity, originality and depth of its perceptions of a more comprehensive reality' (Cook 1998: 145). However, following these debates, Albert Hunt identified *Scum* as an example of the way in which ostensibly radical plays, 'consciously committed to challenging "official reality"', fail for precisely such formal reasons. Although Minton's 'version of "reality" is clearly very different from the official version', both he 'and the school of "social realist" playwrights of which he's typical' confirm 'one of the central lessons of TV's hidden curriculum – if you see it on the box, it must be true' (Hunt 1981: 31). From this standpoint, radical television practitioners, as John Tulloch

(1990: 10) summarised, 'are not agents of change at all, but dupes of myth and the "visual epistemology" of empiricism'.

This brief discussion of the critical climate of the 1970s has served to illustrate some of the ideological tensions which exist in Clarke's style, and to provide a background for his work in the 1980s. From *Made in Britain* onwards, Clarke's style explores the space between these forms of naturalism and those forms which were held up against it, particularly the brand of critical realism defined by Georg Lukács. Certainly, as Susanna Capon and Barry Hanson observed, Clarke was fascinated, even 'obsessed' by Brecht; as has been well documented, the influence of Brecht's 'theatre of alienation and the ideological base' was pervasive on radical theatre between the mid-1950s and late 1970s (Kelly 1998: 15, 137; see also Eyre and Wright 2001). One of the most important tensions in Clarke's later style results from his exploration of narrative space and of the relationship between objectivity and subjectivity in the moving image. As we have seen, these terms were invoked both in academic debate and in justifications of the banning of *Scum*; although it would be as undesirable as it would be impossible to claim this as a direct response to the critical moment of the late 1970s, Clarke's work fundamentally broadens after *Scum*, attaining precisely the ideological complexity for which critics had been calling. His work demonstrates a restless experimentation and formal dynamism which addresses these issues as part of a wider questioning of the 'visual epistemology' of state and media discourses.

It is unlikely that Clarke would have appreciated the neatness with which I have described *Scum* as a turning point. This was a troubled period; in an interview with Cas Cassidy he laconically nominated himself for *The Guinness Book of Records* as Most Banned Director (Cassidy 1979). In 1979, as he told Cassidy and Jennifer Selway respectively, a *Play for Today* collaboration with Tony Parker 'concerning the life of a female psychopath was banned by the BBC before I even got past planning', a play which 'was also concerned with the law – a story about a relationship between an ex-prisoner and a policewoman'. Clarke had earlier completed a documentary on Russian dissident Vladimir Bukovsky, but this was also the subject of a private screening (which Bukovsky himself attended). *The Times* found its failure to gain transmission odd since 'its "star", six months ago, was the most talked about man in Britain', and this 'politically potent and skilfully edited piece of work' was 'absolutely ideal for television' (Anonymous 1977c). Though David Markham (1978) compared it with *Scum* as a film which was banned without 'reason or explanation ... in spite of energetic protests by certain BBC staff members', BBC2 Controller Aubrey

Singer (1978) insisted that it was 'a private venture offered to BBC2' which was not 'purchased' because BBC2's *Man Alive* had duplicated material on Bukovsky for a feature of its own. With understandable delicacy given the *Scum* furore, Singer insisted that 'This is hardly a question of "banning" it'. Instead, Clarke encouraged Jehane Markham, whose parents campaigned for Bukovsky, to write a fictional play on the experiences of such dissidents in Britain, resulting in the brittle *Nina* (1978) (see Fenwick 1978). Though it would be hard not to read these suppressed dissidents, or the bawdy revolutionary silenced by puritanical Robespierre in the same year's *Danton's Death*, in terms of Clarke's recent experiences, he stressed his desire to move on: 'I don't want to become known as the bloke who makes marvellous prison movies' (Cassidy 1979). The film version of *Scum* had opened up new opportunities; Sandy Lieberson invited Clarke to Hollywood among a number of new directors developing projects at Twentieth Century Fox. The *Evening Standard* argued that, after 'ten years slogging away' on television, Clarke 'looks like the next British film-maker to hit the trail to America' (Anonymous 1979). Clarke's agent warned journalists not to 'jump to the conclusion that he's doing a film ... He's doing research, but the whole thing's rather vague.' After an abortive attempt to launch *Assassination on Embassy Row*, a political thriller on the American government's relationship with General Pinochet (see Kelly 1998), Clarke returned. He later recalled that 'the Hollywood people really liked [*Scum*] but said that there was no way they would have made it themselves'. Although Hollywood was 'very seductive', Clarke stressed that 'I wouldn't make a film with the edge written out' (Malcolm 1987). Television remained his first choice, and it provided him with the space to construct a truly distinguished body of work made in, and on, Britain. As David Hare told Richard Kelly (1998: 105), Clarke was 'a very, very good – you know, the best – television director' up until *Scum*, but after it 'he becomes something more ... it undoubtedly did deepen his work and gave it a sort of wildness that it didn't have before. He's quite a controlled artist up until then. Then basically anarchy breaks out and his attitude is "I'm going to smash the toys in the shop".'

In this chapter I discuss Clarke's work in the 1980s, addressing his themes and approaches and the ideological ramifications of his style and experimentation with narrative. The first section covers various productions in the period between *Beloved Enemy* and *Road*, the second section looks at his plays on terrorism and Northern Ireland, *Psy-Warriors*, *Contact* and *Elephant*, and the third section focuses on his final production, *The Firm*. Throughout, I draw attention to the way that Clarke dissected the political climate of the 1980s, particularly the discourses of Thatcherism. Indeed, as John Hill (1999: xi) argued of British cinema, given the pervasive influence of the Thatcherite project, it becomes 'impossible' to discuss British television drama in the 1980s 'without taking some account of how it was engaged in an ongoing dialogue with Thatcherite ideas, meanings, and values'.

However, in the post-*Scum* television climate, maintaining such a 'dialogue' was becoming more difficult, as Bignell, Lacey and Mac-murraugh-Kavanagh (2000: 1) observed: 'it is no coincidence that the single play, the most radical form of television drama, disappeared from the schedules during the oppressively reactionary 1980s. Implying dissent in every aspect of its dramatic agenda, "licensed" to give an opinion, the single television play asked for trouble and got it.' Clarke, paradoxically, thrived in this climate. Andrew Clifford (1991) argued that his early work was 'socially engaged but not strident, as though Clarke didn't need to stress his points when so many similar plays were being made by his colleagues', but once he found himself 'without colleagues to offer support' (with the BBC shifting from single plays to film production, and many of his contemporaries moving into cinema), Clarke was 'isolated' but also 'at his most vivid, vital and vigorous'. Engaging with Thatcherism with remarkable consistency and passion, Clarke's work is politically and aesthetically radical and impressively wide-ranging, exploring such diverse yet related themes as unemployment (*Road*), drug abuse (*Christine*), multinational corporations (*Beloved Enemy*), football hooliganism (*The Firm*) and Britain's role in Northern Ireland and its relationship with terrorism (*Psy-Warriors, Contact* and *Elephant*). It is also marked by the distinctive personal vision of an auteur, and a complex style which marks, as Michael Walsh (2000: 297) argued of *Elephant*, 'a terminus for British social realism'.

'Going round in circles' – themes and approaches in the 1980s

This section examines several of Clarke's productions from the 1980s, exploring how his crucial themes – including the gap between personal narratives and state discourses, repetition and the restriction of movement – are employed in his questioning of Thatcherite values. Thatcher radically altered the foundations upon which political consensus had been based, reducing inflation and taxation for the rich through a broadly monetarist economic policy which was predicated upon deliberately increasing unemployment, whilst privatising national industries and weakening trade unions. Despite the social dislocation caused by these policies, Thatcher cultivated a new consensus, maintaining that profit for the few was in the national interest, and that self-reliant individuals could participate in this enterprise culture (see Hall 1988). As we shall see, Clarke explores these themes in terms of both content and form, particularly in his signature use of Steadicam, whose effects demonstrate a symbiotic relationship between style and ideology. He develops crucial motifs, juxtaposing movement, in the Steadicam walks attached kinetically to individuated protagonists, with structural repetition.

The shift which occurs in his technique at the start of the decade can be illustrated by a comparison between *Beloved Enemy, Baal* and *Made in Britain*. Although Clarke stressed to Jennifer Selway in 1979 that he would not simply replicate *Scum*, and would 'just take on whatever interests me most', he suggested that his typical future project would similarly be 'a documentary drama based on the same kind of straight facts of establishment life'. This is an excellent description of *Beloved Enemy* (1981). Clarke was 'staggered' by Charles Levinson's investigations into the relationship between governments and multinational corporations, and testified to Levinson's lasting influence. Levinson's theses became 'part of my life', affecting 'Everything I look at around me, economically, politically' (Nightingale 1981). Clarke first aired Levinson's views with his functional documentary *Vodka Cola* (1980), whose title was derived from the deal brokered by Richard Nixon which allowed Pepsi Cola (who funded Nixon's 1968 presidential campaign) to build plants in the Soviet Union in exchange for selling vodka in the American market. In *Beloved Enemy*, Clarke and Leland dramatise Levinson's research to depict a typical trade deal involving a British-based multinational seeking to locate a tyre factory in the Soviet Union. Blake (Tony Doyle) states that 'nationalism and patriotism mean nothing' to multinationals, and that governments are not important because, in a dark echo of *Penda's Fen*, 'the company outlives them all'. The deal hinges upon laser technology, which in turn demonstrates the role of multinational arms corporations in Ronald Reagan's Star Wars programme. 'You've got to have an enemy' to justify trading, particularly when taxpayers' money subsidises wealthy multinationals, and the Cold War provided that mythologised enemy. The domestic status quo is maintained as a by-product, as dissidents and unionised workers in both East and West become unemployed in favour of workers who 'keep their traps shut'.

Beloved Enemy is in Clarke's established register, using a restrained style to articulate an institutional space. With a characteristic paring-down of narrative, Clarke removed a framing personal story about a head of a multinational and his daughter, which had been added after the rejection of a version designed just to show people 'sitting at a table discussing deals'. David Leland observed that Clarke surreptitiously restored this structure and removed narrative embellishment, then shot the play on very long lenses, giving 'a sense of standing back from it, a certain element of spying' as if 'with the right lens you could be very close to it' (Kelly 1998: 134). Clarke told Benedict Nightingale (1981) that he aimed to 'present a deal with the Russians without commenting on it. We opened the door on the overworld of multinationals, went in with a camera, showed the business relationships, and hoped it would be sufficient.' This rhetoric of objectivity could be applied to much of his work up to this point, and resembles Emile Zola's description of the naturalistic novel: 'It no longer interests itself in the ingenuity of a well-invented story, developed according to certain rules... You start from the point of view that nature is sufficient, that you must accept it as it is, without modification or pruning ... The work becomes a report, nothing more' (Zola 1964: 123–4). The style which Leland described was indeed a 'visceral ... choice' (Kelly 1998: 134). Some discussions take place in scenes featuring characters walking repetitively. The contrast between the camera's lack of movement and the mobility of the characters reinforces our distance from, and powerlessness to intervene in, this sphere of influence, and lends a distinct artificiality to the characters' awkward pacing up and down the same few feet of garden or poolside concrete. Nancy Banks-Smith (1981) observed that this 'bare, uncluttered' play was 'a beautifully done exercise in human chess: intellectually exhilarating if you can follow the moves, physically low on action ... Never have so many paced up and down to add a modicum of movement to dialogue.'

These scenes are comparable with the distanciation achieved in Clarke's studio staging of Brecht's *Baal* (1982). Here, he shot characters on similarly repetitive walks, statically recording their marching towards the camera before mixing to them walking over the same part of a featureless set, with captions or artificial location detail displayed on the other side of a split screen. In his detailed memoir of the play's production, John Willett (1998: 263–79) argued that, although *Baal* lacked the 'austere toughness' of Clarke's 'starker and simpler' and more obviously Brechtian initial conception, the play achieved 'Brecht's intended effects without affectation'. This was achieved not only through 'the "alienating" division of the episodes by the split-screen presentation of titles', but also by Clarke's continued exploration of formally theatrical composition. With little camera movement, 'the prevailing view would be of the set seen square-on right across the whole length or width of the studio', providing 'a slightly formal, remote view of the naturalistic scenes' (see also Fenwick 1982). *Baal* prefigures Clarke's subsequent work in its episodic depiction of an anti-hero repetitively striding through landscape, and in its use of movement to blur the boundaries between the objective and subjective positions taken by the camera.

The presence of these elements in *Beloved Enemy* demonstrates that the play bridges Clarke's 1970s and 1980s approaches: alongside its pared-down stillness is a more confidently formal matching of style to content. It ends with Clarke's camera amongst the news cameras at a press conference. Our knowledge of the detail of the deal, and of the multinational cadences brushed over in the press conference's conventional trade rhetoric, lends this change in position a distancing effect which exposes the level of contradiction beneath these 'straight facts of establishment life' and implicates the observing media, which was earlier described as a dog the company had trained to bark, in this misleading state discourse. This positioning could also be said to implicate Clarke's own camera. However, it was not until *Made in Britain* that Clarke fully integrated the relationship between objectivity and subjectivity, and his established motif of walking, into his camera style. The international scale of *Beloved Enemy* sheds light on some of the political causes of the unemployment and social dislocation explored in *Made in Britain* and *Road*. Blake's prediction that 'life on this planet is not going to get any better, except for the few' was borne out by the economic policies of Margaret Thatcher, whose prioritisation of market forces over welfare and open redistribution of wealth from poorer to richer opened a chasm between 'two nations' (see Jessop *et al.* 1988). Thatcher's insistence that she was creating 'one nation' acted less as a justification of policy than as a discursive denial of the validity of those who suffered its effects. Clarke subsequently explores the consequences for those excluded from discourse.

Made in Britain focuses on Trevor (Tim Roth), an intelligent and articulate sixteen-year-old who is also a neo-Nazi skinhead. Its scheduling as the last of four plays by David Leland on the education system (with different directors), under the banner *Tales Out of School*, makes Trevor the end product of that system. In *Birth of a Nation*, a teacher confronts apathetic pupils at a crumbling comprehensive who anticipate only unemployment, while in *Flying into the Wind* (subsequently the first film set for O-level English Literature), parents attempt to teach their children at home. *RHINO* ('Really Here In Name Only') and *Made in Britain* study two persistent truants, the former a fifteen-year-old West Indian girl caring for her abandoned nephew. Though she was presented passively, according to Peter Davalle (1983), as 'the pathetic victim of a totalitarian, albeit well-intentioned society, that makes no provision for youngsters who genuinely believe they can survive outside the system', in *Made in Britain*, neither Trevor nor the style which Clarke adopts to channel his character can be described as passive.

Sent to an assessment centre after repeated shoplifting, car thefts and racist attacks, Trevor confronts the social workers who attempt to reform him. His violent behaviour ultimately results in the imprisonment they predicted. The first shot of Trevor is a close-up which, in keeping with the recurring box/cage motif of Clarke's previous plays on incarceration, serves to confine him. However, within seconds it gives way to another crucial motif. Holding on a medium close-up, the camera stays with Trevor and walks with him from a waiting room into the magistrates' court. This marks the start of Clarke's use of Steadicam, a camera with the portability and intimacy of the hand-held camera, but which is strapped to its operator to assist smooth movement. Often the use of a hand-held camera on location, with largely natural sound and lighting, creates the documentary aesthetic which has long been associated with realism. Like the Italian neo-realists and the British New Wave before them, this generation of television practitioners embraced new technology to 'document' new subject matter, making the Steadicam part of an ongoing search for 'transparent technique' (Paget 1998a: 87). However, although *Made in Britain* 'confines itself to following' Trevor, reflecting Bazin's description of Rossellini's style in

Chapter 2, it does so with a more subjective effect, particularly in this opening sequence, in which movement, mise-en-scène, Roth's demeanour and the use of The Exploited's song *UK82* as a theme so economically establish Trevor's character. There is, as we shall see, a tension between the Steadicam's apparent subjectivity and the possibility of making an 'impartial report' implied by its residual rhetoric of immediacy. Harnessing his camera to Trevor, Clarke was saying to both camera and viewer, according to Roth, 'This is your man, go with him' (Kelly 1998: 147). This results in long, kinetic walking shots which became Clarke's central motif, as Andrew Clifford (1991) observed:

> The camera tracks a figure pacing with almost sadistic inspiration down a wasted street. We see legs pounding. The camera's wide-angle lens spoons the figure round a corner into another street. The figure's clothes and hair are ordinary, but there is something heightened about that ordinariness, as though the intensity in the eyes and the mouth are signs of a struggle against it ... the Steadicam keeps pace with them, as they beat against the pavement with the enthusiasm of violence. Who is this figure? He is the king football hooligan in *The Firm* ... the perfect skin-head of ... *Made in Britain*. She is Sue or Rita ... one of the silent terrorist assassins in *Elephant*. In short, this figure is the unhero or unheroine so prominent in ... Clarke's work throughout the Eighties. Culturally disenfranchised, mistaken, helpless – attacking the street, he or she liberates an internal world of anger, imagination, and unbearable honesty.

Notwithstanding the cinematic antecedents of this walking motif, from the weary tread of father and son in *Bicycle Thieves* to the languid wandering in Antonioni's work, Clarke's version is hugely distinctive and fundamentally ideological. David Thomson argued that 'No one has ever grasped the central metaphor of cramped existence in walking as well as Alan Clarke', who became 'a poet for all those beasts who pace and measure the limits of their cages' (Thomson 1995: 133). These 'heroic nihilists' are 'bursting with words, gesture, movement', and 'walk to avoid inertia'. Clarke 'loves them, without ever believing he can understand or tame them' (Thomson 1993: 79–80).

Made in Britain is the culmination of Clarke's study of movement and its restriction by authority, in terms of its stylistic execution and its ideological connotations. Both of these are foregrounded in the opening sequence. As I have noted, we are attached to Trevor's arrogant swagger. However, once he reaches his fixed position in the courtroom, the camera movement stops, as does his musical theme. We are detached from Trevor as the policeman reads society's interpretation of Trevor's actions from his notebook. Like the judge at the start of *A Life Is For Ever*, the magistrate dismisses his story with the official state story. Perhaps like Bill Cotton viewing *Scum*, the magistrate is appalled by this 'long, depressing list'. The notebook is an authored representation of his life, like the captions 'Made in Britain' and 'by David Leland' which interrupt the court scene. Although Clarke tended to use plain captions at the beginning of his productions, here the captions intervene, foregrounding authorial intervention. This sequence acts as a microcosm of *Made in Britain*'s structure: outside the centre, both Steadicam and audience 'go with' Trevor as he steals cars and smashes windows or walks the streets; however, this flow is halted by a twenty-minute scene in an interrogation room. Leland had used restricted movement as his starting point, envisaging 'a camera screwed to the ground and this figure stalking in and out of the space, locked in a room, and talking to the camera', to which Clarke replied: 'He's got all this energy, it's no good shooting off a static camera ... We want to take him all the way down the street ... into the dark, out into the light. We've got this fast film, we can push the stock.' According to Leland, Clarke 'thought about it until it came alive in his head as a piece of film-making, then the subject matter came alive for him too' (Kelly 1998: 142).

Placed in the middle of *Made in Britain*, the scene acts as an interruption to Trevor's mobility, a formal restriction of his movement related to the discourses of the state. Trevor has his background and future mapped out in diagrammatic form on a blackboard which, like the policeman's notebook, is one of *Made in Britain*'s devices for the institutional recording of transgression. Others include Trevor's file (the magistrate's 'list'), the log book which delays Trevor's entry into the assessment centre, and the social contract that Trevor refuses to sign. Like Foucault's prisoners, Trevor is treated as the object of information rather than a subject for communication; as Simon Shepherd (1994: 30) argued, 'Law is the crucial institution because it is seen to address individuals from outside them, to turn subjects into objects by inventing narratives about them'. Trevor resists these narratives, explaining that he won't keep 'watching my p's and q's because some mingy little fucker like you's gonna write it down on a piece of paper'. He is told to get a job, but when a visit to the Job Centre reveals the reality of the labour market, he takes cards down from the display, then throws a paving stone through the window. He partly disrupts another narrative by hanging around with a black youth, Errol. Together they break into the assessment records room, take out their own files, which they have not been allowed to read, and piss and shit on them. In keeping with the 'grotesque realism' associated with Mikhail Bakhtin, Trevor expresses his individualism through transgressive behaviour associated with the body: bodily functions, violence, sniffing glue and, in one of Clarke's most iconic shots, striding tribally semi-naked down the Blackwall Tunnel. This resembles the way in which Irvine Welsh's *Trainspotting* (1993, film 1996), according to Robert A. Morace (2001: 34–5), 'draws attention to the material body, emphasizing in Rabelaisian fashion its sheer physicality as distinct from the abstractions of politicians, liberal humanists, and, one might add, postmodern theorists'. Errol also reclaims terminology imposed upon him, shouting to the Pakistani victims of his and Trevor's attack: 'You baboons! Get back to the jungle!' Trevor's hateful racist comments were understandably controversial, although Tim Roth, sensing a Thatcherite 'crush the critic' mentality, wondered whether racism 'doesn't exist ... if you don't make any films about it' (*Tim Roth: Made in Britain*) Suppressing race as an issue rather than racism – after all, the system continues to fail Errol – the social workers according to Trevor 'lock up anything that frightens you'.

The ending of *Made in Britain* finds Trevor in a police cell. After annoying a constable with his knowledge of the procedures they have flouted, he is told that 'We got you now' and hit with a truncheon. The very last shot is a confining close-up, freeze-frame, on Trevor's defiant smile, an ambiguous ending reminiscent of François Truffaut's *Les quatre cents coups* (*The 400 Blows*, 1959), as Robert Chilcott (2001: 57) observed: this 'misunderstood youth, like Antoine Doinel, knows what is in store for him and sees no possibility or desire for escape'. Its similarity to the opening shot also gives the film a recursive, deterministic quality. However, this was not intended as the final scene. Leland (1986: 47) wrote an ending set in a detention centre, in which Trevor, enthusiastically digging the ground, says: 'fucking great. This is how they train the crème de la crème. Bleeding storm troopers. SS. SAS. Brick shithouses. Doors off hinges ... We've got the buggers on the run. It's our fucking turn!' The scene as written draws together some of the play's recurring imagery. 'Doors off hinges' recalls several doors which are locked, opened or kicked down and smashed windows, broken homes and liminal thresholds which simultaneously enclose Trevor and show a barred escape route. Nevertheless, *Made in Britain* gains from the ambiguity of the chosen ending. To a certain extent Trevor is a victim, like Derek Bentley in *To Encourage the Others*, who was hanged as a scapegoat for youth delinquency as much as for PC Miles's murder. Just as the state punished Bentley for seeking the affluence central to 1950s Britain, it punishes Trevor for asserting the aggressive individualism central to 1980s Britain, epitomising Thatcher's self-reliant 'individual protecting his sphere of freedom' (Jessop *et al.* 1988: 43–4).

However, the ending can also be read as a kind of victory. The attempt to impose narratives upon Trevor represents an expression of the Foucauldian disciplines of bio-power which seek, according to Jana Sawicki (1992: 136), to attach 'individuals to specific identities' and establish 'norms against which they police themselves'. Trevor resists this process, and so has to be policed. By cutting through the rhetoric of rehabilitation, Trevor exposes the agenda which underpins it, revealing education to be among the mechanisms which maintain support for the dominant ideology, which Louis Althusser (1971) described as the 'ideological state apparatus', and the policing forces upon which they can fall back, or the 'repressive state apparatus'. Describing the background to *Made in Britain*, Leland (1986: 5) contrasted the erosion of community schools by financial cutbacks with the prison system's plans for '2,000 additional cells for young people'. In an echo of *Beloved Enemy*, government and police investment in 'instruments of oppression', such as water cannons and plastic bullets, represented an 'economic boom' for their manufacturers. As indicated by the first line of *Made in Britain*, The Exploited's 'Violence starts upon the street and Thatcher wonders why', some argued that it was the inherent divisiveness of social policy that led to riots across Britain, including Brixton and Toxteth. Trevor absolves himself of the individual guilt constructed by the state. Social workers condemn his choices, or tell him 'It's your shit, you roll in it', but he refuses to accept the blame: 'you got decisions to make about my life, you get on with it – it's got bugger all to do with me'.

He has rejected 'the repeated emphasis on individual power and choice' which, as John Tulloch (1990: 63) observed, 'is central to myth's naturalizing function as ideology'. When social workers play to Trevor's intelligence, telling him that 'you could do well', Trevor replies, 'What do you expect me to be, thick in the head the way you want me?' Observing that many are dishonest but play by the rules, Trevor identifies that he cannot 'be honest' in a language which is not his own; faced at school with the subtext 'be the best, otherwise forget it', the only way he can speak is to 'be a fucking parrot'. This discussion reflects the description of working-class education by Herbert Spencer, quoted by Richard Hoggart (1957: 247) in his study of scholarship boys: 'The established systems of education ... encourage *submissive receptivity* instead of *independent activity*'. At one point, Trevor stops in front of a shop window which contains an image of normal family life demonstrating such submissive receptivity, with mannequins gathered around a television set in a living room display, in which each item is conspicuously marked with price tags. Like the protagonist of *Trainspotting* who refuses to 'choose life' and its consumerist trappings, Trevor runs away shouting 'Bollocks!'

Trevor turns the social workers' statements back on them by asking 'what are we going to do about *you?*' and insisting, despite their questioning of how he got himself incarcerated, that 'I hate you for putting me in here'. He has enacted a 'tactical reversal' in order to articulate what Foucault (1980: 81) described as 'subjugated knowledges'. Enacting 'subjugated knowledges' was the defining principle of Clarke's 1980s productions. However, notwithstanding the validity of Trevor's reversal, the nature of the identity to which he is clinging remains ambiguous. Describing the mannequins as 'the perfect English family', Howard Schuman (1998: 20) observed that they echo 'the "sick mother and father" of *Penda's Fen*, offering a parallel between Trevor's and Stephen's perverted views of Englishness'. Stephen Franklin's national identity interacted with his sense of family, and the same could be said of Trevor, whose family, indeed community, is absent. Trevor's xeno-phobic exclusion of outside influence is not far from the aggressively misdirected patriotism of Thatcherite rhetoric. Stephen ultimately grasped that nationality was mutable, but Trevor holds on to the language by which he defines himself. Geoffrey Nowell-Smith (1981: 233) observed that Jacques Lacan, in his writing on the transcendent ego, 'showed that the subject is constructed in and through language ... language incarnates meaning in the form of the series of positions it offers for the subject from which to group itself and its relations with the real'. Trevor's view of nationality is itself a constructed language, and unlike Stephen he cannot reconcile the contradictions inherent in this 'series of positions', contradictions which are arguably inherent in the cultural, political and social frameworks of Thatcherism. These ideas coalesce in Trevor's only comment on his family: when asked if he can return home, he replies, 'What home?'

When Trevor smashes the windows of an Asian family, we are positioned directly behind his throwing arm, implicated as either voyeurs or participants. Though Peter Ackroyd (1983) criticised *Tales Out of School's* 'conflation of documentary techniques with a melo-dramatic theme', exhuming drama-documentary debate by arguing that its 'sensationalism' undermined 'the truth' implied by its 'tone of moral outrage', Clarke moves away from the apparent passivity of observa-tional technique to the participatory rhetoric of Steadicam, a shift which brings to mind the distinction which Georg Lukács (1973) made in literature between 'naturalism' and 'critical realism'. Lukács compared the depictions of horse races by Tolstoy and Zola to argue that naturalism describes events from the standpoint of an observer – the experimental naturalism of Zola which, as I have argued, compares with the methodology of Loach's and Clarke's earlier work – whilst critical realism narrates events from the standpoint of a participant. Rather than observing with the objective rhetoric of the distanced documentary camera, Clarke drives Chris Menges's Steadicam, and the viewer, into the thick of the action, developing a style nearer to the critical realism of Tolstoy. His camera both positions the viewer as participant and places the character's story within wider society.

However, describing this technique as 'critical realism' risks underplaying the way his use of Steadicam oscillates between participation and observation. His approach is, according to Howard Schuman (1998: 20), 'unsettling not because of the violence, which is mainly verbal or mental, but because of the swings from attachment to detachment, proximity to distance, kinetic energy to static debate'. It is unsettling also because the camera's association with Trevor is as entrapping as it is freeing. Its claustrophobic intensity subjects Trevor to a form of permanent visibility, akin to the 'panopticism' described by Michel Foucault. Derived from Jeremy Bentham's model of the panopticon, a tower in prison from which warders could permanently watch prisoners' every movement, this institutional gaze ultimately altered the behaviour of prisoners, ensuring 'the automatic functioning of power', and has become a feature of wider society (Foucault 1991: 201). In Foucault's description of cells under the panoptical gaze lies an eerie echo of Clarke's Steadicam style: 'They are like so many cages, so many small theatres, in which each actor is alone, perfectly individualised and constantly visible' (1991: 200).

I cited Geoffrey Nowell-Smith's invocation of Lacan with reference to the 'author' director, rather than citing Lacan himself, because *Made in Britain* parallels two sets of languages: those which Trevor employs, rejects and is ultimately constructed by, and Clarke's own discursive practice, with which he facilitates Trevor's attempts to articulate his own language, but whose position is complicated by Clarke's simultaneously observational and self-announcing use of Steadicam. The institution itself utilises a rhetoric of objectivity, which is reflected in alterations in Clarke's style in crucial scenes of institutional discourse, as in the court and interrogation room, in which he moves away from a kinetic, subjective positioning with Trevor towards an objective, more distanced style, demonstrating a rigid 'discipline' akin to that preached to Trevor. As Clarke's style therefore demonstrates, the institution's own truth claim is based upon discursive practice, which was described by Foucault (1997: 297) as a 'set of procedures that lead to a certain result' validated or invalidated 'on the basis of its principles and rules of procedures', forming 'games of truth'. Trevor's individualism, and the camera's rhetoric of being subjectively attached to him, are problematised if subjectivity is itself socially conditioned as Foucault proposes. As defined by Danaher, Schirato and Webb (2000: xv), subjectivity presents 'individual identity as the product of discourses, ideologies and institutional practices'.

Made in Britain had a sustained impact, contributing, alongside the other *Tales Out of School* productions, to debates on the purpose of education. Sue Barker, of Central's Community Programme, recalled Central's efforts to liaise with viewers. Some Independent Local Radio stations opened their phone lines, with phone-ins on Radio Trent, LBC and Severn Sound 'jammed with callers of all ages and persuasions'; Severn's *Club 388* featured a discussion with Leland after *RHINO*, and contributions from 'punk rockers' after *Made in Britain* (Barker 1983). *TV Times* held a survey into the state of education, and Central provided information packs on key issues, including glue-sniffing and care proceedings. Despite tabloid reports of a 'storm over TV violence', there were relatively few complaints: Central's duty officer took nineteen calls 'complaining that the play contained scenes of racial abuse, violence and four letter language', and LWT took a similar number, many 'about the glue-sniffing scene' (Anonymous 1983). Although its reviews were not unanimously positive, *Made in Britain* went on to win the Prix Italia.

The chalk diagram with which the Superintendent maps out Trevor's future, forming a loop with the words 'no job', 'dole', 'thieving' and 'prison', articulates the crucial Clarke motif of circularity. 'Round and round you go', Trevor is told, resembling 'Exercise Yard', a composition by one of Tony Parker's prison interviewees in which the words 'round and round' were arranged in an everlasting hexagon (Parker 1973: 111). This motif is followed up in Clarke's final studio play, *Stars of the Roller State Disco* (1984), nominated for the Prix Futura. Here, unemployed youths have to skate pointlessly round and round a rink, constantly observed by cameras, subject to panoptical 'permanent visibility'. In one of many Orwellian dramas in 1984, they are bombarded with messages from video screens, and are doomed to tranquilisers and, as Jim Hiley (1984) put it, 'going round in circles'. A stylised exploration of the effects of youth unemployment and the casualisation of labour, the play centres on Carly (Perry Benson), a qualified carpenter who turns down shoddy work because 'I'm a bleedin' craftsman!' Its writer, Michael Hastings, told Hiley that society was 'in danger of inventing a new kind of person, who will be unemployed for half their life. You can smell this happening on the streets. Apart from nuclear weapons, it's the most important issue in this country.' For the rest of the decade Clarke further explored the social dislocation caused by Thatcherism. In three loosely connected productions from 1987, *Rita, Sue and Bob Too*,

Christine and *Road*, Clarke follows characters around desolated communities, personal and social spaces which are often re-gendered.

Rita, Sue and Bob Too, one of Clarke's two cinema films for Film on Four, focuses on the bored schoolgirls Rita (Siobhan Finneran) and Sue (Michelle Holmes). One night, married Bob (George Costigan), for whom they babysit, drives them out to Baildon moor for sex in his car, and they're keen for him to 'get stuck in there' on a regular basis. The opening sequence establishes a connection between the film's gender politics and Clarke's Steadicam style. The camera follows Sue's pissed-up dad returning from the pub; as he passes his daughter, it leaves him and follows her across the estate. Therefore Sue, according to John Hill (1999: 175), 'appropriates the public space from him (the impotent patriarch)'. In contrast with the association of landscape with young working-class males in British New Wave films such as *Saturday Night and Sunday Morning* (1960), in these shots 'women are the dominant presence'. Clarke made a similar distinction, arguing that films such as *Room at the Top* (1959) 'were all about working class angst, but at least all the characters had jobs. You couldn't make a film like that now' (Hutchinson 1987). In deindustrialised Britain, Sue's dad returns not from work but from enforced leisure, and, in an inversion of New Wave gender politics, is restricted to private/domestic spaces while his daughter occupies the public/work spaces. Men are left to spectate, like Bob's neighbour, who conveniently waters his garden at inopportune moments, or the men who comment on the hilarious scene in which Bob's wife faces up to Sue's mother. One comments that it's 'better than *Match of the Day*', referring to a male-gendered activity of which they are spectators rather than participants, while Bob and Sue's dad impotently circle each other. This conflation of class and gender politics was indelicately expressed in the film's tagline: 'Thatcher's Britain With Her Knickers Down'. Furthermore, with politically motivated attacks on welfare spending focusing on the easy target of single mothers, the sexual morality of the poor became a political issue, as is demonstrated by the controversy which surrounded the film's portrayal of Rita and Sue's forthright sexuality.

The film features, according to Adrian Wootton (1987: 282), 'a noticeable, if contradictory, feminist perspective'. Though Rita and Sue desire Bob, 'neither harbours any illusions about him, or any other male, in terms of personal relationships ... it is only the lack of economic alternatives which drives them to try to live with one man'. They refuse to be defined by their relationship to men, even as daughters. In her relationship with Aslam, Sue refuses the role of wife, as is reflected in the long tracking shot in which we first see Aslam's sister: she is an interruption, conspicuously placed between Sue and Aslam, representing the sort of womanhood which Sue does not want, as she pushes a pram, preaches domesticity and has her words spoken for her (translated) by a man. Clarke identified 'the film's strength' in 'the portrayal of that friendship' between Rita and Sue (Hutchinson 1987) and, as the title suggests, Bob is a disposable addition to that friendship. Their problems start when definitions change, as Rita moves in with him and conceives an ultimately miscarried child.

Many of the film's British reviews were negative, and neglected the film's underlying points, because of its juxtaposition of grim detail with bawdy comedy, although the latter importantly provides a sense of Rita and Sue's untapped vitality, which Clarke described to Derek Malcolm (1987) as 'life-enhancing but also very sad'. The film's sex-comedy ending, in which Bob dives back into bed with both Rita and Sue, is different from Andrea Dunbar's original theatre play, in which Bob marries Rita, and which ends with Sue's mother telling Bob's wife that 'All fellas do the dirty on you ... let them come on your conditions and stick to them. Don't let them mess you around' (Dunbar 2000: 82). As John Hill (1999: 184) observed, the film removes the play's 'feminine perspective' and 'distance from Bob's actions'. In contrast with his more complex television work, *Rita, Sue and Bob Too* seems to demonstrate a compromising of Clarke's voice by genre and the commercial pressures of cinema, resulting in a film which is arguably best described as 'hilarious yet lightweight' (Chilcott 2001: 57). However, those personal signatures which remain are themselves problematic; although Clarke sought to let 'the girls speak for themselves', and to 'match' their 'energy' whilst striving 'not to put myself in front of it' (Malcolm 1987), Hill (1999: 184) argued that there is in Clarke's 'formal inventiveness' and 'foregrounding of technique' a 'refusal ... to engage seriously' with the film's core issues. Katy Limmer (2003) responded that Dunbar retained 'authority' as author of the screenplay (which she drew from both the play of the same name and *The Arbor*). The difference between the two versions, Limmer stressed, was 'due to far more complex factors than simply a male auteur's perspective overwhelming that of the female author'. Indeed, in this flawed collaboration Dunbar's voice is as compromised as Clarke's. This was particularly keenly felt given that the script was, as Clarke told Malcolm, 'about her and her mates'. Brought up in poverty on the Buttershaw Estate in Bradford seen in the film, she had her first play, *The Arbor*, accepted for the Royal Court's Young Writer's Festival when she was a seventeen-year-old single mother living in a battered women's refuge. *Rita, Sue and Bob Too* was the second of only three completed plays in her turbulent life: she died of a brain haemorrhage in December 1990, in the Beacon (seen in the film), aged just twenty-nine.

Clarke's 'formal inventiveness' and 'foregrounding of technique' were employed more relentlessly, and with more success, back at the BBC. For the *Screenplay* strand, Clarke filmed two of his finest pieces, *Christine* and *Road*, in overlapping filming sessions between 18 May and 5 June 1987. Clarke continued to thrive in television's 'studio system', as *Screenplay* combined traditional video plays with experimental low-budget film productions akin to independent cinema: as David M. Thompson, one of the strand's originating producers, suggested in interview, *Screenplay*'s films were 'like a guerrilla operation'. Alongside *Screen Two* and with BBC1's populist *Screen One* in development, *Screenplay* was commissioned, Thompson recalled, to 'do drama of a different kind', at a 'lower cost', with new talent and 'different methods'. Head of Drama Peter Goodchild stated that, without being 'self-consciously ... avant garde', BBC Drama was 'prepared to fall flat on our faces' in trying something inventive 'to get as far away as possible from the rather static feel of TV plays' (Thomas 1987a).

Christine depicts a teenage heroin user and supplier. Reacting to the suggestion by Angela Thomas (1987b) that the BBC was 'preparing itself' for likely 'controversy', producer Brenda Reid replied that she and Clarke, both 'parents of teenage children', wanted to make 'a film that was as dire a warning as possible' about drug use. In collaboration with Arthur Ellis, Clarke stripped the portrayal of addiction down to, in Ellis's phrase, 'its absolutely irreducible minimum', resulting in a 'walking film' which portrays the monotony of addiction by matching minimalist narrative to a repetitious structure (*Director*). Films about drugs tend to be structured as cautionary tales of descent into addiction, as in Uli Eler's *Christiane F* (1981), one of *Christine*'s major influences. Reviewing *Requiem for a Dream* (2000), Mark Honigsbaum (2001) argued that a typical film about drugs 'starts on a high and ends on a cautionary low'. However, *Christine* does not feature this narrative pattern. Clarke's Steadicam follows Christine as she walks to a house, observes the taking of drugs, and then, after a characteristically elliptical cut, follows her walking to another house in which the same thing happens. The sequences of Christine (Vicky Murdock) walking, 'her demeanour downcast in the patented manner of the Bressonian heroine' (Kelly 1998: xxiii), become so numbing that they recall comments in Clarke's and Stuart Griffiths's translation of Georg Büchner's *Danton's Death*: 'We are all sleep walkers and our actions dream actions ... How tedious it is to get out of bed every morning and start setting one foot in front of the other ... millions more will go through the same motions.'

David Leland observed that 'a spareness of style dominates Alan's later work – he knocked away the conventional supports, cutting back on anything extraneous' (*Director*). His work becomes so minimalistic that the eponymous protagonist of *Baal* could be speaking for Clarke when he says: 'Everything there is to say about life on this planet could be expressed in a single sentence of average length.' His paring down to essences in *Christine* and *Elephant* resembles minimalist art, the effects of which can be equally ambivalent, risking alienation from aestheticised images. Although praised for his *Disasters* series, in which he replicated images to stress the repetitiveness of tragedy, Andy Warhol noted that 'when you see a gruesome picture over and over again, it doesn't really have any effect' (Hopkins 2000: 117). However, this minimalism was not a new development in Clarke's career. In interview, Peter Whelan recalled a rehearsal at Questors Theatre in the 1960s in which Clarke asked the cast to 'render each speech you had into one word'. Although spectators were bemused by people 'saying "Preoccupation!", "Liberty!", or looking at each other for a long time and saying "Downcast!"', Whelan added that this 'ritualistic' side to Clarke showed 'his deep worry about words, that he needed to be a film-maker, he needed to do *Elephant*'. On the subject of repetition, Whelan recalled Clarke's staging of *Hecabe*, in which the chorus had to simultaneously beat the stage fifty times with long poles, which required terrific concentration 'because at the fiftieth bang you had to stop, and if one person went on it would bring the house down ... you get mesmerised when you're doing this, and you think, God, was that 33 or was that 34?'

Christine also resists conventional narrative causality, and draws attention to that resistance in its use of aborted narratives. A car accident is mentioned but, uninterestingly, nobody was hurt. When a character injecting in another room cries out, he turns out to just be annoyed at missing a vein and wasting money. The nearest *Christine* gets to a plot is a party that is planned but never happens. People take heroin, repetitively, until we become desensitised, as Clarke, as in *A Life Is For Ever*, invites boredom. Also, *Christine*, like much of Clarke's work, resists state-sponsored 'explanations' of social problems in favour of a more complex motivational ambiguity: although the government advertisements warning that 'heroin really screws you up' showed addicts in deprived settings, the addicts of *Christine* are, as Robert Chilcott (2001: 58) noted, more affluent youths 'who choose to live like this'. Christine cleans up after herself, washing out needles in clean sinks in fitted kitchens. She is a good consumer; the play ends with her staring blankly at a television, another lifestyle choice based upon continuous consumption, as unmoving as the living-room mannequins of *Made in Britain*. In its sparse mise-en-scène and repetitious structure, *Christine* is the twin of *Elephant*, estranging its audience through a self-consciously episodic plot, unsympathetic protagonists and self-reflexive camerawork. In the first drug-taking scene, the camera moves in for close-ups of needles entering arms, an uncharacteristically voyeuristic movement in which the camera announces its own presence. The camera walks with Christine but its identification with her is never complete. Despite the subjective connotations of the camera's positioning, Clarke's refusal of identification encourages an objective viewing position, heightened by a nagging awareness of the cameraman's presence. As a result, *Christine* offers, according to Amy Taubin (1994: 62), 'a powerful contact high that makes you feel as if you're simultaneously inside the film and watching it from a great distance'.

Clarke's second *Screenplay* production, *Road*, powerfully depicts the human cost of Thatcherite economics. Despite its uncharacteristically poetic dialogue and recurring use of pop songs, its distillation of his thematic and stylistic signatures makes it a cornerstone of his work. His most stunning evocation of the relationship between character and environment, *Road* episodically introduces a variety of characters in a desolate Northern town, on a night out during which Brink and Eddie (Neil Dudgeon and William Armstrong) meet Louise and Carol (Jane Horrocks and Mossie Smith), and encourage each other into greater articulacy. Although based on Jim Cartwright's play, first staged at the Royal Court's Theatre Upstairs in March 1986, this production was, according to W. Stephen Gilbert (1990), 'reshaped' by Clarke into 'something that owed nothing to the stage', a film 'reconceived' with a Steadicam. After a strike saved Clarke from having to make *Road* on video on a studio set (see Kelly 1998), he took the opportunity to pare down the original, remove the narrator Scullery and other characters, and open up the play, following characters around the streets near Easington Colliery, a community in decay since the Colliery's closure after the Miners' Strike. However, alongside his dominant signatures, it is important to note David M. Thompson's observation in interview that Clarke remained 'a real collaborator', with Cartwright 'very very involved' and both producers made to 'go through the whole thing all over again every time he took three minutes out – we must have seen it literally dozens of times'.

Road was filmed with Clarke's new cameraman, John Ward, in what David Leland described in his introduction to *Road*'s 1991 repeat as a 'significant and rewarding collaboration'. Ward, who brought a similarly kinetic Steadicam style to Stanley Kubrick's *Full Metal Jacket* (1987), worked on Clarke's last three productions, this, *Elephant* and *The Firm*, which are arguably the peak of Clarke's individual vision. Clarke's camera replaces the play's narrator and promenade staging, which served to 'plunge' the theatre audience 'into the centre of the community' (Gore Langton 1986: 85). The attachment of Steadicam to characters, particularly those who speak directly to it, 'confers a kind of *privilege* on the audience' (Paget 1998b: 123) and on the actors, who respond with some of the most unflinching performances in Clarke's career. The camera's constant scrutiny was welcomed by Clarke's actors; earlier in the decade, Tim Roth felt freed by camera and lighting strategies which provided a '360 degree space in which I could operate' (*Tim Roth: Made in Britain*). However, that scrutiny also represented a paradox according to Stephen Frears because, although it meant that 'performances have to be very, very real', it was also 'theatrical ... because there's no montage' (Kelly 1998: 142).

These tensions are most clear in the extraordinary monologue delivered by Valerie (Lesley Sharp) in an unbroken four-minute walking shot. Maintaining *Rita, Sue and Bob Too*'s inversion of New Wave gender politics, Valerie walks public space, describing her unemployed husband's imprisonment in the domestic space, a 'poor beast in the wrong world', a 'wounded animal' in whose hands the vacuum cleaner looks like 'a toy'. Although the 'sustained figurative language' and 'rhythmic resonances' of the dialogue 'run beyond the limits of the conventional social realistic play' (Paget 1998b: 114–15) and signpost an innate theatricality, Clarke does not simply film a performance, but allies technique to its rhythms and underlying themes. When Valerie describes her husband 'telling me I should do more about the place, eating whatever's in the house, pissing and missing the bog, squeezing the kids too hard, shouting then sulking', there is a juxtaposition between her husband's enforced inactivity and the activity expressed in the repetition of verbs ('telling ... eating ... squeezing' and so on). Crucially, this is in turn reinforced by the juxtaposition between movement and stasis in Clarke's style. Clarke captures the wasted energy of unemployment by portraying working-class characters walking nowhere through deserted communities – reflecting the paradoxically static 'road' of Cartwright's title – and, in the subjective rhetoric of Steadicam attachment, queries the myth of individual participation propagated by Thatcherite rhetoric. These effects are rooted in the mediation of the experiential, recalling Raymond Williams's (1979) concept of 'structures of feeling', as Steadicam places us within the characters' lived experience, as they walk 'their' streets, demonstrating a fragmented but, in Williams's term, 'knowable community'. However, as Williams accepted, experience cannot emerge in a text untainted by ideology. In his late

1980s work, Clarke acknowledges the mediation of ideology in the formality of the sequential and episodic structure which acts to give the 'feeling' a 'structure' rooted in political process. These walks often fall back on themselves through Clarke's use of repetition and circularity, which act as a structural denial of progress, a lack of forward movement which is juxtaposed with the progressive rhetoric of Thatcherism captured in the camera's relentless motion.

This style is far removed from the rhetoric of objectivity which drew such institutional and critical hostility around the time of *Scum*. John Hill noted that *Road*, like *Rita, Sue and Bob Too*, contains some residual visual and thematic 'signifiers' of Northern realism, and recalls, in its unbroken takes, Bazin's writing on the way 'the long take preserved temporal and spatial unities'. It also carries 'connotations of documentary' with its 'elimination of reverse-field cutting and point-of-view shots' (Hill 1999: 175; 2000: 58). However, he added that Clarke makes use of 'highly stylised shots' which 'exceed the requirements of narrative exposition'. Indeed, separating writer and director, critic Nick Smurthwaite (1987) wondered whether 'such technical flair should have played any part in Cartwright's harrowing social document'. Derek Paget (1998b: 116) placed both versions of *Road* in the context of Mass Observation, the British documentary film movement and the Royal Court Theatre, in their attempts to depict the North 'by simultaneously *observing* and *aestheticising* it'. These highly appropriate comparisons attest to Clarke's ability to portray, in the lineage of Humphrey Jennings, the poetry of the everyday, and reaffirm the ideological dangers of claiming a truly 'objective' representational position. In his discussion of character positioning and 'documentary drama' (see Chapter 2), John Caughie argued that television had 'a metonymic relationship to reality rather than a metaphoric one', as the 'objectivity' of its camera disposed it 'towards the observation of the real rather than the participation in it which the subjective camera gives to cinema'. Therefore, in ideological terms 'the rhetoric of the documentary, the fixed and fixing look', constituted the 'object', for instance the working-class, as 'simply there, unproblematic', as if 'the object of a gaze ... filmed "for their own good"' (Caughie 2000a: 122, 112). In its system of gazes, the possibility of 'reversibility' in its protagonists' confrontation of the camera, and the multiplicity of discourses, namely the tension between Clarke's style, documentary-realist tradition and theatricality, *Road* resists and brings into question the 'fixed and fixing look' and the connotations of the integration of documentary and drama which could 'only be achieved by *failing* to dramatize' its subject matter.

The querying of 'realist' rhetoric is keenly felt in *Road*'s use of locations, which serve various functions simultaneously: a documentary reporting of conditions, a metaphoric representation of socio-political discourse, an expressionistic and surrealistic reflection of the feelings of its protagonists, and a theatrical site for drama. As W. Stephen Gilbert observed, in these streets devoid of passers-by 'there's this piece of drama going on – it's not the real world, it's drama, with protagonists – and there's no real world behind it' (*Director*). Speaking on *Open Air* in 1987, Clarke established the connection between location and characters which is *Road*'s defining triumph, arguing that 'the actuality of the real environment ... in its semi-derelict form' was 'an expression of how they felt internally'. This approach is reminiscent of the studio sets built for *Billy the Kid and the Green Baize Vampire* (1986), which Clarke described in that film's publicity material: 'it isn't a recognisable world of a council estate ... It's grubby, it's seedy, it's mean, but the characters within it have theatricalised the environment in which they live'. The bare, distressed interiors of *Road* were real locations but were redressed and ripped out at will by designer Stuart Walker because they were due for demolition, and the results, further distorted by Clarke's experimentation with lenses, constitute an ideal enactment of Bertolt Brecht's pronouncement that 'If the set represents a town it must look like a town that has been built to last precisely two hours ... A place need only have the credibility of a place glimpsed in a dream' (Brecht 1978: 233). Similarly, the Millstone pub features, according to Derek Paget (1998b: 124), an 'eloquent poverty of design' which 'blows away the tidy referential codes of social realism, re-siting the scene beyond humour and beyond reality'; indeed, with its fire-eater and assorted characters, the Millstone's carnivalesque surrealism surpasses even the Hogarthian final pub scenes of *Boys from the Blackstuff*.

One of *Road*'s key strategies in addressing Northern England's fate under Thatcherism in the 1980s is, paradoxically, to dislocate its sense of time and place. Although it uses songs from 1987, like the appropriately titled *Living in a Box*, its evocation of loss takes place in an almost expressionistic limbo devoid of its old signifiers of identity, just as the stage set featured a 'broken road sign' whose 'name part has been ripped off' and apparently forgotten, leaving 'only the word "Road"' (Cartwright 1986: 3). *Road* opens with Brink, dressed in a suit more reminiscent of the status symbols worn by working-class males at leisure a generation earlier, striding timeless streets, with Gene Vincent's *Be-Bop-A-Lula* on the soundtrack. Even before Jerry (Alan David) addresses the camera with his inability to 'get over the past' and his descriptions of National Service and work, there is in these cultural signifiers a sense of Clarke's own youth, an association which was reinforced by the song's use in the documentary *His Own Man*. The song's year of release was 1956, a year which John Caughie (2000a: 69–70) described as a catalyst for social change and the climate which fostered radical television drama. To the usual signifiers – Suez, Khrushchev's denunciation of Stalin, *Look Back in Anger* and the first staging of Brecht in Britain – Caughie added the British premiere of *Rock Around the Clock*, as rock'n'roll's soundtrack for youth was another factor in 'the Left's engagement with popular culture'. Therefore, although *Road* lacks the relentlessly repetitious structuring of Clarke's other work in the period, there is inbuilt in its cultural topography a potent manifestation of repetition: in the scarred desolation of the mise-en-scène reminiscent of the bombsites of postwar Britain, there lies a negation of the cultural and political agenda which emerged from it. In this void, notions of full employment, community, the Welfare State, or even public service broadcasting, not only have lapsed but have been rendered so meaningless that they almost never existed.

Written in the wake of the 1984–85 Miners' Strike, *Road* depicts, as Derek Paget (1998b: 108) argued, 'a day in which the organised working-class were widely perceived to have been defeated by the new, militant conservatism'. Therefore, *Road* 'can be seen partly as an "End of History" text'. Here, as in Tony Blair's Britain, 'the grand ideological battles of the twentieth century are over', because 'inequity based on class and wealth' is so naturalised that it is no longer a subject for discussion (Pilger 1999: 5, 8). This 'class war waged at a distance by the technocrats of the new cold war' renders non-consumers as non-people, struggling against a discourse of 'history without memory' (Pilger 1999: 61). Questions pick at *Road*'s discursive limbo, refusing, in their yearning for 'ago', to accept the end of history, even as its meanings lose definition: 'I can't see how that time could turn into this time ... Who's spoiling life?'; 'Can we not have before again? Can we not?' *Road* ends with a cathartic outpouring of buried articulacy and reaffirmation of identity, as Brink, Eddie, Carol and Louise draw inspiration from Otis Redding's *Try a Little Tenderness* and fight the limits on their voices. Louise declares that 'I never spoke such a speech in my life', and the four agree that 'If I keep shouting somehow a somehow I might escape'.

Road won the Golden Nymph at the Monte Carlo International Television Festival in 1987. In the process of developing a platform for characters to discover their voices, Clarke had underlined his own distinctive voice. He was now working at the top of his form.

'Bandit country': Northern Ireland and terrorism in *Psy-Warriors* (1981), *Contact* (1985) and *Elephant* (1989)

Pressures on the representation of Britain's military presence in Northern Ireland came to a head in the Thatcher years, but the subject had already proved to be the greatest test of the putative radicalism of the British television single play. In 1980, Richard Hoggart argued that radical drama was 'too important not to engage with the most serious internal problem in Great Britain', lamenting the fact that in twelve years since the 'Troubles' began, there had been only nineteen plays or series episodes on the subject, and that, with rare exceptions such as Colin Welland's *Your Man from Six Counties* (1978), most failed to reflect its complexity. This point remains valid, despite the relatively high number of dramas on Northern Ireland since Hoggart's protestations – Edward Braun (2000: 110) estimated seventy plays and series episodes since 1980. Alongside overt censorship, Hoggart argued that writers operated a form of self-censorship, avoiding the issue because it was seen as a 'switch-off subject' and because its political sensitivity left their work open to such intense scrutiny. In a seminar on the television play in 1980, Kenith Trodd, producer of another of Hoggart's exceptions, *Shadows on our Skin* (1980), agreed that 'Northern Ireland is one of the few areas where this form can test its mettle'. He affirmed that the play could have been made only within this system, with 'the institutional force of the BBC behind us, against all the political forces ranged against us' (Morgan 1980: 11).

In their discussion of media representations of terrorism, Schlesinger, Murdock and Elliott distinguished between programmes which were 'closed' in their approach – news bulletins and action-adventure series such as *The Professionals* (1977–83), which operated 'within the terms of reference set by the official perspective' – and single plays as an example of 'relatively open' texts which provided 'spaces in which the assumptions of the official perspective can be interrogated and contested and in which other perspectives can be presented and examined' (1983: 32). However, the single play's freedom to create such spaces was being eroded; to add to the list of banned and censored dramas in Chapter 2, *The Legion Hall Bombing*, a 1978 play on the judicial treatment of terrorist suspects in Northern Ireland, was delayed and altered without the involvement of writer Caryl Churchill or director Roland Joffé, who subsequently removed their credits (Anonymous 1978g). Elements of the British press have reacted angrily to productions which engage with the issues, including Neil Jordan's *Michael Collins* (1996), Paul Greengrass's *Bloody Sunday* (2002), Jimmy McGovern's *Sunday* (2002) and

Ken Loach's *Hidden Agenda* (1990), the latter of which won at Cannes despite the protests of British journalists. The opposition to Loach's film convinced Roy Greenslade (2000: 78) that the press had become 'a propaganda arm of the British state' seeking to enact 'a form of cultural censorship'. Contextualising debates on representations of Northern Ireland, Trevor Griffiths related the failings of drama to 'the deficiencies of other forms of television coverage' (Morgan 1980: 7–8). According to John Pilger (1999: 519), it was left to films such as *Hidden Agenda* to 'play a role forsaken by journalism'.

Given their interrogation of the official perspective on the 'Troubles', it is important to place *Psy-Warriors, Contact* and *Elephant* in the wider context of media representations and political responses to them. In 1971, two years after the Provisional IRA were formed, backbenchers lobbied for the imposition of 'patriotic censorship' on the media and, as Liz Curtis (1984: 10) observed, Home Secretary Reginald Maudling met the Chairmen of the BBC and ITA. The BBC ran into trouble in the same year over *The Question of Ulster*, a discussion programme formated as a mock tribunal which was ultimately transmitted the following year, boycotted by government and major Unionists. In 1973, Kenneth Griffiths's more 'authored' monologue *Hang Up Your Brightest Colours: The Life and Death of Michael Collins* was shelved by ATV. In 1977, the Secretary of State for Northern Ireland attacked the BBC for supporting terrorists, citing an interview with a Republican who called for British troops to go home in coffins. Two years later, Margaret Thatcher attacked the BBC for interviewing a spokesman for the Irish National Liberation Army after they had killed Airey Neave; within weeks, the BBC reconsidered their standpoint when Lord Mountbatten was killed. Then came an incident in which a news crew observed the staged takeover of Carrickmore by Provisional gunmen, intended to show the inadequacy of British claims that they were in control of the border. Thatcher felt that 'it is time the BBC put its own house in order' (Leapman 1987: 96–9, 107). The situation deteriorated in the 1980s, with Thatcher determined to 'remove the various voices of the Irish Republican Army (IRA) from television screens' (Paget 1998a: 54). In 1985, the BBC's Governors yielded to the Home Secretary's disapproval of *At the Edge of the Union*, and withdrew it (like Griffiths's monologue, it was finally shown on BBC2, with changes, in 1994).

It was also in 1985 that Thatcher responded to the publicity given to Arab hijackers with the statement: 'We must try to find ways to starve the terrorists of the oxygen of publicity on which they depend' (Leapman 1987: 297). At a time when the government's 'tough line on terrorism' included 'refusing to grant "political" status to republican prisoners in

Northern Ireland or to bow to hunger strikers' (Hill 1999: 9), this became the defining principle of responses to British rule in Northern Ireland. In 1988, Thames and the IBA resisted government attempts to suppress *Death on the Rock*, which investigated the killing of three IRA members in Gibraltar by the SAS. Later that year (with *Elephant* still awaiting a slot), restrictions were introduced forbidding broadcasters from using the voices of terrorists, leading to their ludicrous dubbing with actors' voices, deliberately out-of-synch. According to Michael Mansfield QC (1994: 7), in this 'extraordinary climate of fear and censorship perpetrated by the British government', various 'statutes and court actions have all but done away with freedom of speech', with this Broadcasting Ban accompanying the Prevention of Terrorism Act, the Police and Criminal Evidence Act and the Official Secrets Act. Mansfield listed 'a monstrous regiment of filmic narratives that have faced re-editing, delay or non-transmission', including *Shoot to Kill*, *Suspect Community* and *Mother Ireland*. The emasculation of investigative journalism on the subject had a knock-on effect because the best 'television plays ride on the back of these front-line troops, spurring them on, but immobile without them' (Morgan 1980: 9). As projects such as *To Encourage the Others* and *Scum* demonstrate, Clarke's work was often motivated by this kind of interaction.

Viewed in this context, *Psy-Warriors*, *Contact* and *Elephant* are among the most politically radical productions ever made on Northern Ireland. *Psy-Warriors* places terrorism in the context of the state, while *Contact* and *Elephant* employ various strategies to reflect the gaps and silences in broadcasting and state discourses. Furthermore, all three utilise form to question the discursive strategies imbued in media representations. If much of Clarke's work portrays characters trying to escape the political imposition of narratives at the level of content, his Northern Ireland productions explore the imposition of narrative at the level of form. Stripping away narrative to create minimalist and alienating forms which reject context, he addresses the failure of fictional and non-fictional forms to directly confront the role of the British in Ulster.

In its articulation of the psychology of terrorism, *Psy-Warriors* provides a context from which to judge the contrasting refusal of motivational detail in *Contact* and *Elephant*. Three people (Rosalind Ayres, John Duttine and Derrick O'Connor) are taken to a military installation under suspicion of planting a bomb in a pub frequented by British soldiers. Deprived of legal and human rights as suspected terrorists, the three are separated and subjected to varying psychological disorientation and physical humiliation in the name of interrogation. According to Colin Roy Munro (1979: 156), similar content motivated the banning of *Article Five* (see Chapter 2), whose title referred to the clause concerning torture in the Universal Declaration of Human Rights and whose message was that 'British taxpayers have condoned torture, by supporting an army which has used torture or methods approaching it'. Given state discourses in the wake of '9/11', and revelations of American atrocities in Iraqi detention centres, *Psy-Warriors* remains a highly relevant production, in which David Leland poses the question: 'how far can we torture and degrade prisoners in the name of democracy and freedom?' (Anonymous 1981).

In his most stunning piece of studio direction, Clarke allies his technique to an analysis of power rooted in the gaze. The act of looking is constantly signified in all three of these productions, which connects with Foucault's extension of the panoptical gaze, in which the acquiring of knowledge became associated with 'visual metaphors, such as insight and vision, so that the idea of looking (or gazing) is associated with power, knowledge and value' (Danaher *et al.* 2000: 57). Clarke foregrounds 'looking' through various characteristic strategies, including a highly formal and problematically theatrical use of long-shot compositions from side-on, the querying of space through close-ups shot on long lenses, a mediating foregrounding of the bars of cages, disorienting alterations in framing and a contrasting of harsh lighting and thermal shots of sensory deprivation. As well as mirroring the protagonists' claustrophobia, these strategies reaffirm the association between looking, knowledge and power, as they are associated with the Chief Interrogator (Colin Blakely), the play's privileged source of knowledge.

The play's twist necessitates a further perceptual shift, as it is revealed that the three detainees are themselves soldiers undergoing a test. In the most disturbing manifestation of Clarke's interest in institutionalised violence, they have been brutalised to ascertain their ability to withstand such techniques and, in turn, to brutalise terrorist suspects in Northern Ireland. Part of the play's 'alternative perspective', according to Schlesinger, Murdock and Elliott (1983: 106), was its suggestion that the security services were 'less interested in defending democracy than in extending their reach and power'. Had the pub bomb exploded, the Interrogator explains, it would have been attributed to the IRA, maintaining a 'symbiotic relationship' as 'we help keep the terrorist cause in the public eye and the terrorist helps us justify the need for greater security'. The subject matter was so controversial that the play was shown in a later timeslot than normal for *Play for Today*, although its transmission on the night that the hunger striker Bobby Sands died meant that, as its writer David Leland recalled, 'the switchboards were jammed, saying "This is IRA propaganda"' (Kelly 1998: 136).

Although only playing devil's advocate with Turner, the Interrogator's discussion of the psychology of Palestinian terrorists represents an 'oppositional perspective', to employ the most radical of Schlesinger, Murdock and Elliott's categories of terrorist representations, which 'justifies the use of violence in the pursuit of political ends' (1983: 27). The Interrogator argues that 'we learn nothing' about the Palestinians: not only do we 'know nothing of life in the camps of the Palestians', we 'choose not to know'. Since Black September, the Palestinians 'have become the enemy', committed to violence as 'their last line of defence'. Forced 'to answer violence with violence', terrorists 'use their bullets to subdue the violence of the people who exploit them ... They kill to breathe.' Although Turner insists that she would not have sent her child to be trained by the Palestinians, as Ulrike Meinhof had done, and that terrorism is 'wrong' and 'fanatical' and 'cannot be justified', she cannot respond to the Interrogator's questioning of how she would act if she had 'no rights' and was 'persona non grata according to international law ... regarded as though you were not really a person at all'. This conversation establishes discursive positions which *Contact* and *Elephant* go on to radically integrate into their form: terrorism as 'fanatical', colonised person as 'not really a person at all' and a recursive epistemological position based on choosing 'not to know'.

After years trying to get the project off the ground, Clarke filmed *Contact* between 6 and 29 August 1984. It was first screened in January 1985, the first production in BBC2's single-film slot *Screen Two*. It epitomises the strand's remit, combining the radical subject matter of the single play with a distinctive visual style. *Contact* won First Prize at the Locarno Film Festival, which Clarke described as a 'high spot' of his career, 'absolutely great' (*Billy the Kid and the Green Baize Vampire* publicity material). The script was derived from *Midnight Blues*, the memoir of A. F. N. Clarke (no relation), a captain in the Parachute Regiment who led border patrols near Crossmaglen in South Armagh. In an initially close collaboration, he developed a detailed and semi-autobiographical script around a Platoon Commander's breakdown. However, the director pared the script down, removing plot exposition and much dialogue, until *Contact* conformed to his own vision, becoming, as lead actor Sean Chapman observed, a 'set of sequences, describing army operations' (Kelly 1998: 153). In its treatment of these operations, *Contact* addresses the discourses of British rule.

Contact opens with a lengthy establishing shot of a country road. Its framing in the foreground acts to mediate the lush greens of rural Ireland in the background, a shot which demonstrates an incursion by urban space. After a prolonged silence, a car speeds into view. Several

British soldiers emerge from outside the frame and block the road. The image establishes a contrast between the natural green of the country-side, a pure green with connotations of Ireland and Irish nationalism, and the camouflage uniforms of the soldiers, here first seen against the grey of the road. There is a similar contrast between their uniforms and the organic greens and browns worn by an apparently innocent Irish-man they later interrogate. These shots reinforce the idea that the soldiers cannot assimilate themselves fully into their surroundings. As the scene develops, our first view of 'contact' between the soldiers and the Irish is based upon the British exercising their power. One man is shot dead, the other lies on the ground while the unspeaking Comman-der pushes a gun into his face. Throughout this scene, and for most of *Contact*, the Irish are silent. Described simply as 'gun-runners', they represent an administrative problem for British rule, which is deaf to, or actively silences, the subaltern culture of the indigenous people. This colonial reading is reinforced by the description of Northern Ireland in *Psy-Warriors* as Britain's 'last colonial battlefield ... the rear end of the cruelty and exploitation of over thirty colonial wars'. In an image which anticipates the circularity of *Elephant*, the Interrogator compares it to a 'dog devouring its own tail'. The political reading implicit in this scene is reinforced by its virtual replication later, when the soldiers shoot gun-runners and the Commander again forces his gun into the mouth of a captive. Reflecting the Interrogator's 'symbiotic' rhetoric, the guns are being transported to locals to fight the British soldiers, so the repetitious skirmishes continue because the soldiers remain present; their first appearance blocks both the frame and the road, obstructing the movement of the Irish and our view of them. Drama stems from the soldiers' misreading of signs. They find danger in gun magazines left on the grass, a couple emerging from a derelict building, and a group of young children out camping. The crisis point is always, as the title implies, at the point of contact between the soldiers and the Irish.

As in *Psy-Warriors*, elements of Clarke's style reflect the limited view of the soldiers, in the process exposing the power inscribed in the act of looking. Largely, Clarke uses a hand-held camera to react to events with an 'unmediated' rhetoric reminiscent of documentary. There are very few of Clarke's trademark shots in which a camera walks 'with' characters. The effect is to link the observational camera with the distanced state. In the soldiers' operations in what they describe as 'bandit country', the Irish are the unelaborated 'Other', an unseen presence of which we become aware only when British soldiers come under attack. At those points the camera reacts, lurching and zooming in a vain search for the gunmen. In addition to the two shades of green mentioned earlier, in the night sequences Clarke uses infra-red cameras, which emphasises that this is, as Brian McIlroy (2001: 127) observed, 'a society predicated upon clandestine surveillance'. Furthermore, the night camera has the disorienting effect of filling the screen with overwhelming greens. Nancy Banks-Smith (1985) observed that the platoon is 'bathed in a thin, liquid green light like aliens'. The title *Contact* reinforces this notion of the platoon trespassing in an alien landscape. Furthermore, as Howard Schuman (1998: 20) proposed, the infra-red could turn 'us into alien observers; the viewer is therefore both comrade and enemy, victim and aggressor'. Clarke again resists the editorialising use of music and non-diegetic sound, leaving only distant bird call or the rustling of trees. As a result, in Banks-Smith's phrase, the viewer's ears 'grow points and prick forward with the aching acuteness of the hunter and the hunted'.

The rural soundtrack is displaced by scenes in Army quarters underscored by the unnatural humming of a power source. The sounds of the countryside are replicated by artificial echoes, such as the showers which clean the soldiers after wading through rivers, or blocked out altogether by the personal stereos with which the young troops relax on their bunks. This location, therefore, becomes a limbo in which the British are further distanced from their surroundings. This is reflected in the camera's own distance from the Commander, which makes it appear 'as if the camera approaches him with extreme wariness' (Hiley 1985), and in army psychology, as the Corporal tells the Commander, 'Don't get involved, boss. Bad for the brain.' The close-ups were shot on long lenses, to the extent that Chapman was often unaware that he was in close-up, with the effect of making Ireland a hazy and indistinct background, as Clarke 'framed these soldiers as figures in a landscape where they have no mission, no prayer and no place' (Kelly 1998: xix). *Contact*, therefore, becomes a post-colonial war film, in which Clarke's strategies both demonstrate the landscape's refusal to be easily defined and locate the act of looking within the discursive frameworks of colonialism.

This is reflected in its minimalist narrative. The absence of defined mission aims or understanding on the part of the British results in repetitive searches and pointless death. *Contact* borrows the modes of the 'tour of duty' war film, but, contrary to our expectations of that genre, we are not led to sympathise with the soldiers. Indeed, Clarke told Chapman that 'I'm not fuckin' interested in the army, it's full of idiots' (Kelly 1998: 154). Through its sparse characterisation, *Contact*, according to David Leland in his introduction to its tribute repeat screening, 'breaks the mould of the soldiers-at-war film. There's no chirpy Cockney or dour Scot and nobody takes the piss out of a character called Taff.' Contrary to the iconography of the war film, there is no narrative causality or resolution. As a non-discursive war film focusing on the problems of leadership, *Contact* has some correlations with the films of Samuel Fuller, who often 'excludes as much as possible in the way of context and films the internal pressures' on an unsympathetic leader and the men he leads, who do not know why they are fighting (Hardy 1970: 48). *The Steel Helmet* (1951) follows a patrol behind enemy lines, whose protagonists are deceived and confused by the native land, and 'enter a limbo of their own. In a slow pan across their faces, Fuller shows them staring blankly ahead' as madness is 'the only form of impassivity ... available to men at war' (Hardy 1970: 104). Fuller also made use of a walking motif. As another leader says in *Merrill's Marauders* (1962), 'When you come to the end of your rope, all you have to do is put one foot in front of the other, just take the next step – that's all there is to it'. David Thomson (1993: 80–1) compared *Contact* with Anthony Mann's 'abstract study of an infantry patrol lost in Korea', *Men in War* (1957). Mann, Thomson argued, 'has never had an equal at the depiction of landscape, immensely extended spatial relationships, and the dramatics of distance'. Though 'Clarke's style is not as classical as Mann's', *Contact*'s strategies also employ physical movement to convey 'the animal in people ... dwarfed by eternity and the tranquility of the land'. Clarke's avoidance of conventional narrative strategies made *Contact*, according to Amy Taubin (1994), 'a rare thing – a truly antiwar movie'. According to V. F. Perkins (1972: 149), the effect of such conventional strategies on David Lean's *The Bridge on the River Kwai* (1957) was to undermine its proclamation of 'the futility of war', with 'emotional dynamics' which 'invited us to share in the excitements, tensions and triumphs offered by the action'. Therefore, in Lean's film, 'War was said to be futile and experienced as glorious, victory was said to be empty and felt magnificent'.

   Contact's soldiers resemble *Scum*'s trainees, which could be read as a deliberate paralleling of institutionalised youth, given that *Scum* was intended as part of a trilogy including a play about youths entering the army (see Chapter 2). In the regimented, imprisoning headquarters, the young men, led by *Scum*'s 'daddy' John Blundell, eat and wash communally before retiring to their cell-like rooms. The soldiers' youthful vulnerability is emphasised by a scene in which they discover a group of children out camping. The Commander seems troubled by one child staring up in fear at the platoon, a reflection of the mysterious armed confrontations suffered by his own young charges, and a foreshadowing of his own guilt. In such sequences, Clarke, as Brian McIlroy (2001:

128) observed, explores the 'tension' implicit in the position of the soldier who 'follows orders and tries not to get killed in the process', and depicts routine 'with his almost mathematical precision'. However, McIlroy underestimated *Contact*'s radicalism when he added that this focus on 'day-to-day operations' meant that the lack of 'support from the local populace should not be overinterpreted'. Although *Contact* resists overt signposting, it often captures Chapman's character in 'quite terrifying moments of mental absence' which demonstrate an analysis of 'illegitimate authority' (Kelly 1998: xix). This leaves, according to Howard Schuman (1998: 20), the 'unstated question – why are the English in Ireland? ... to which there is no clear answer, only a lament for wasted lives'. Clarke's refusal to flesh out the Commander's character supports the play's rhetoric of absence, and his breakdown, though never made entirely explicit, forms an existential distanciation with wider metaphorical significance. *Contact* ends with the Commander looking broken, in a mid-shot against a brick wall. This shot is a variation on the ending of *Made in Britain*, connecting the two. Indeed, Tim Roth was initially offered the part of the Commander (Kelly 1998: 153).

Clarke's subsequent move from the rural spaces of *Contact* to the urban spaces of *Elephant* partly supports the observation by Michael Walsh (2000: 294) that films tend to feature a 'polarisation of images of Ulster' of 'city centre versus country, especially border country'. On one level, Clarke operates in the 'same binary', because the countryside of *Contact*, whether a wilderness imbued with 'Otherness' or a historical Ireland resisting its colonisers, contrasts with the urban space as controlled area of production captured in the machine-like structure of *Elephant*. However, this binary soon collapses, because both spaces are ontological rather than geographical, not so much Irish views as views *of* Ireland.

Taking the structures of *Christine* even further, *Elephant* juxtaposes a narrative stripped of motivational detail with a numbingly repetitive structure, resulting in his most 'hypnotic, sickening, ritualistic, and alienating' production (Thomson 1993: 83). Its minimalism borders on the expressionistic: over its thirty-seven minutes, *Elephant* features eighteen sequences, each depicting a sectarian killing. In each sequence, the Steadicam follows a walker, observes him killing or being killed, and often walks away with the killer, before Clarke cuts to a lingering shot of the victim's body. Apart from one brief moment, there is no dialogue. At no point is any contextual information given about the killers' identity, motivations, religion or which groups they represent (if any). Although contemporary viewers were forewarned by extra-textual detail – for instance, press coverage and *Elephant*'s scheduling in a series of plays from BBC Northern Ireland – the text itself features little information about setting, other than a glimpsed street name and the title's reference to Bernard McLaverty's description of the Troubles as being like having an elephant in your living room. The 'disjunction' between title and content, according to Brian McIlroy (2001: 128), 'provokes the viewer' and forces 'a more energised' questioning of the subject matter.

Clarke was approached by BBC Northern Ireland producer Danny Boyle to direct an orthodox script set around the relationship of someone in the IRA. However, as Clarke's daughter Molly recalled, Clarke and Boyle felt that, as 'two English people', they did not 'have the right to do it' (*Own Man*). Clarke told *Open Air* in 1989 that he and Boyle risked being 'a couple of Englishmen visiting Ireland, doing a kind of pseudo-important drama and getting out of there'. In 'awe' of the violence and moved by the fact that 'over the last twenty years there's been two thousand sectarian killings', many of them not reported in Britain, Clarke sought to 'throw that information back visually at the mainland'. This desensitising presentation of killing after killing, without narrative footholds, leaves the viewer, according to Simon Hattenstone (1998: 4), 'appalled by the killings, then bored', as Clarke attempted 'to show how inured we have become to murder'. As a result, as David Thomson (1993: 81) argued, 'The most outrageous thing about *Elephant* is that we are not invited to be angry, to protest'.

The relentlessness of Clarke's presentation was understandably controversial. Though filmed between 28 November and 10 December 1987, its transmission was delayed before it finally aired in January 1989. Several critics felt that *Elephant* portrayed the 'Troubles' as a hopeless sectarian conflict which failed to address the role of the British. Peter Lennon (1989a) argued that Clarke's 'misconceived' treatment only 'reinforced the impression created by brief news reports that sectarian killings in Northern Ireland have no context and are carried out by automata'. He added that 'you cannot make a statement of any value about Northern Ireland if the context of vested interests, political and religious, is not acknowledged'. Bemoaning the 'arid cleverness' of Clarke's idea, Mark Lawson (1989) similarly wrote that, 'If writers and directors have any business in this jungle at all, it is in telling you how the elephant got there and how it might be removed'. *Elephant* could be said to contain, within its remorseless avoidance of narrative, a degree of evasion. It was 'attractive to the BBC' for that very reason, according to Danny Boyle, because they 'didn't have the usual consideration of "Are the terrorists going to speak?"' (Kelly 1998: 193) In the climate of the time, such evasions were understandable; as a point of contrast, in

Nineteen 96 (1989), G. F. Newman wrote about the security service's shoot-to-kill policy with its 'action transferred to Wales seven years into the future' (Cornell *et al.* 1996: 405). Perhaps, as one critic wrote of *The Firm, Elephant* portrays 'a world where the most extreme fanaticism carries the greatest prestige and the cause to which it is dedicated has long since been forgotten' (Anonymous 1989a). It could support a right-wing analysis, with its self-perpetuating circularity reflecting Norman Podhoretz's statement that 'the cause of terrorism is terrorists' (Schlesinger *et al.* 1983: 5). A few weeks after its transmission, Anne Karpf (1989: 8), reviewing a programme about the Baader-Meinhof gang, wrote that 'Governments prefer their terrorists demotic, and terrorism seen as the incarnation of Evil, to be vanquished by the national Good'.

However, critics such as Lawson failed to engage with the complex effects of *Elephant*'s resistance of context. In *Elephant*, as in *Christine*, 'the repetitions create a sense of disparity, between the banality of the visual surface and the submerged bulk of its awful implications' (Kelly 1998: xxii). Viewed in the context of Clarke's responses to Thatcherism, *Elephant* deserves its description by Howard Schuman as 'probably the single most radical television film ever made, both politically and aesthetically' (*Own Man*). Lennon's comparison of *Elephant* with 'news reports' is entirely valid, but I would argue that this is its ideological strength. As W. Stephen Gilbert (1989) wrote, by 'explaining and contextualising nothing', *Elephant* implies that it is 'no different from any other image' of the 'Troubles'. It is in a formal analysis of these images as discourse that its radicalism lies. In its repetitively deadly silences can be found the consequences of the discursive climate fostered by the British government: a refusal to 'talk' to terrorists, a depoliticising and dehistoricising denial of individuals' motivations and the centuries of history underlying them, all united in a discourse of indiscriminate and unthinking 'fanaticism'. Rather than arguing that the killings have no motive or context, *Elephant* foregrounds the discourses by which those contexts are presented, or more often not presented, to the mainland; an epistemology based upon, in the language of *Psy-Warriors*, a choosing 'not to know'. *Elephant* is, therefore, central to an understanding of the ideology of Clarke's films, just as the 'definition of "terrorism" – indeed the entire way in which the concept is represented through images, explanations, evidence – is central to the exercise of ideological power and influence in our society' (Schlesinger *et al.* 1983: 1).

Each sequence begins with Clarke's Steadicam engaged in walks with an unidentified figure. Brian McIlroy observed that the camera's focalisation around the killers 'promotes an affinity' with them (2001: 90), but it also, as Michael Walsh observed, constitutes 'Clarke's attempt to disturb the viewer', who is made to 'look through the eyes of the killer', a 'tactic of disorientation familiar in slasher films' (2000: 297). Indeed, Clarke's style draws attention to the way that the grammar of classic realism is constructed around identification with a character (see Chapter 2). *Elephant's* study of desensitisation and the ideology of representation is, therefore, even more wide-ranging; in its desensitising screen violence and its self-announcing style, it 'must make anyone interested in film notice how his or her sense of murder is dependent on movies' (Thomson 1993: 81). As well as reflecting the discursive absences of news reports on Northern Ireland, Clarke's attempts to throw information back 'visually at the mainland' related ideological effects to conventional film style. He told *Open Air* in 1989 that he and Boyle did not want to 'exploit' the situation in Northern Ireland 'for dramatic purposes, or for narrative purposes, or for emotional purposes, and put music under it'. Danny Boyle reaffirmed their intention to avoid making a 'moody thriller ... out of people's tragedies' (Kelly 1998: 198); according to Derek Paget (1998b: 122), this 'conscientious attempt to press the ordinariness of modern murder onto its audience' avoided 'the intertextual knowingness' of subsequent films on media representations of violence such as *Natural Born Killers* (1994). Writing on 'the "I" of the camera' in the films of Alfred Hitchcock, William Rothman (1988: 85) argued that 'the camera can "nominate" a human subject as an exemplar of evil only by revealing at the same time that this figure's villainy is inseparable from the camera's bond with him or her – that is, only by nominating *itself* as well, and thereby implicating the film's creators and viewers'. To an extent, the camera's focalisation places the absence of the killers' motivation with the viewer. Once the repetitive structure becomes clear, the prolonged scrutiny of each walking shot invites a search for clues as to whether each figure is victim or killer, but the lack of signifiers reinforces this cognitive void.

At the point of contact between killer and victim, Clarke's style shifts from the problematically subjective following shot to the equally problematically objective use of conventional film narration: shot of killer, reverse-shot of victim, close-up of gun, shot of impact. In these highly formal moments of pure montage, *Elephant* draws attention to editing as a formal discourse, demonstrating the form's construction of space in almost geometric terms, making 'elegant, eccentric diagrams of the space in which killer and killed meet, the crossing of paths and executed intersections'. There is indeed 'something unsettling in having slaughter made the pretext for geometry' (Thomson 1993: 83). After reinforcing circularity by framing killers walking away in sometimes identical shots to those in which they arrived, Clarke ends each sequence with a long static shot of the victim's body, capturing the aesthetic of photo-reportage. For the British public, this would be the start of the story, a newspaper photograph of a nameless corpse somewhere in Ireland. The issues of circularity, unknowability and repetition which are central to *Elephant* have since become core aesthetic approaches in photographic representations of the 'Troubles' by artists in Northern Ireland, who incorporate images without annotation which foreground the spectator's preconceived interpretative position (Murphy 2003). These sequences are the ultimate example of Clarke's movement from attachment to detachment, from subjective to objective positioning, as Clarke achieved a Brechtian 'estrangement effect', in terms of 'making you part of the character and then suddenly throwing you out' through self-announcing montage and aestheticised still-life compositions, 'making you judge what was happening' (Schuman, *Memories of Elephant*).

This is reinforced by *Elephant*'s approach to narrative. Its refusal of plot and characterisation represents the culmination of Clarke's questioning of narrative, which, as I argued in Chapter 2, was built upon elliptical structuring and a refusal of embellishment which evaded the causality of mainstream narrative cinema. Not since the experimental narrative films of Chantal Akerman – Amy Taubin (1994) compared *Christine* with *Jeanne Dielman, 23 Quai du Commerce* (1975) – has a director so rigorously explored narrative through ritual and minimalism. Edward Branigan (1992: 3) defined narrative as 'a perceptual activity' which organises data into a 'pattern which represents and explains experience', organising 'spatial and temporal data into a cause-effect chain of events with a beginning, middle, and end that embodies a judgement about the nature of events'. It also 'demonstrates how it is possible to know, and hence to narrate, the events'. By confronting the way in which structure 'represents' *and* 'explains' content, and claims to 'know' and 'judge' events within a 'cause-effect chain', *Elephant* serves to foreground the ideological mediation of the narrative process.

The radicalism of this combination of form and narrative can be explored through reference to Loach's *Hidden Agenda*, which approached Britain's alleged shoot-to-kill policy through an investigative structure resembling a political thriller. John Hill (1997b: 131) located complaints about this structuring alongside the 'Costa-Gavras debate', which tied in with debates on the 'classic realist text' (see Chapter 2) by questioning 'the possibility of making a radical film employing conventional cinematic norms'. Whereas Jean-Luc Godard's work from *La Chinoise*

(1967) onwards sought to ally 'revolutionary messages (or content)' with 'an appropriately revolutionary form' which abandoned 'the traditional Hollywood conventions of linear narrative, individual, psychologically-rounded characters, and a convincing dramatic illusion (or "classic realism")', the films of Constantin Costa-Gavras sought to 'bend mainstream Hollywood conventions to radical political ends' and thereby 'sugar the pill' to reach a wider audience.

Elephant differs markedly from this approach, which is epitomised by *Hidden Agenda*'s structure, although *Michael Collins* went further by incorporating a relationship with a character played by Hollywood star Julia Roberts. One of the dangers of employing mainstream conventions to discuss such issues is that, because they function as 'agents' of classical cinema's narrative 'causality', any film which adheres to its conventions encourages 'explanations of social realities in individual and psychological terms, rather than economic and political ones' (Hill 1986: 56; 1997b: 132). Clarke often resisted such effects, from the Bazinian observation and evasion of causality of *A Life Is For Ever* and *Diane* to the removal of an interpretative character from *Beloved Enemy*. In *Elephant*'s series of events lies the ultimate example of Zavattini's argument that 'a stone is a stone, not a stepping stone to something else'. This contrasts with the way that Alfred Hitchcock's films, or most contemporary blockbusters, move from set piece to set piece, narratively motivated or morally justified by scenes of dialogue. It would be fascinating to conduct a Kuleshov-type experiment, and study the reaction of audiences to each of *Elephant*'s sequences if scenes were cut in with the backstory of each victim and killer.

For critics of political thrillers in the style of Costa-Gavras, form itself 'inevitably diluted' their radicalism, as their conventions 'encourage certain types of political perspectives and discourage others' (Hill 1997b: 131–2). John Hill argued that there was an implicit sense of 'problem-solving' in the conventional narrative structure identified by Tzvetan Todorov (1977) as 'the passage from one equilibrium to another'. Films begin with 'a stable situation which is disturbed by some power or force', resulting in 'a state of disequilibrium', until 'the action of a force directed in the opposite direction' restores the equilibrium, albeit of a different kind to the initial equilibrium. According to Hill (1986: 55), there is in this movement 'a presumption, built into the very conventions of narrative that these "problems" can be overcome'. Therefore, in 'social problem' films, 'the articulation of the film's "social problem" into the problem-solving structure of narrative necessarily implies that it too is capable of resolution'. In its resistance of this structure, *Elephant* offers the kind of 'alternative account of social problems' proposed by Hill, replacing this innate conservatism with an emphasis on 'their intractability, their inability to be resolved, at least within the confines of the present social order'. Each repetition serves as a rejection of resolution, whilst the bookending of most of its sequences with similar walking shots provides a disturbing impression of the restoration of 'equilibrium'.

In its use of cyclical structure, *Elephant* confronts a myth articulated by John Pilger (1999: 4), 'the myth that we now live in an "information age" – when, in fact, we live in a media age, in which the available information is repetitive, "safe" and limited by invisible boundaries'. Like the Zapruder footage of the assassination of President Kennedy, the same image of violence is constantly replayed and viewed from different angles, as if the image contains its own inherent meaning, but it reveals nothing. Hayden White (1996: 23, 21) discussed the amateur footage of the attack on Rodney King by Los Angeles police in similar terms, questioning 'the power of the media to represent events in such a way as to render them, not only impervious to any effort to explain them but also resistant to any attempt to render them in story form'. Indeed, the replaying of such images, for instance the King assault or the exploding space shuttle *Challenger*, 'had the effect of making this seemingly unambiguously documented event virtually unintelligible *as an event*'. In *Elephant*, as in White's thesis, events 'do not lend themselves to explanation in terms of the categories underwritten by traditional humanist historiography, in which human "agents" are conceived to be ... conscious and morally responsible for their actions'. Blurring the 'distinction between facts and meanings', which is 'a basis for historical relativism', *Elephant* foregrounds the ideologically interpretative role of narrative; in formalist terms, it presents a chronological series of events, akin to the 'fabula' described by Victor Shklovsky, but resists the sense of causal logic by which the viewer constructs the 'syuzhet', or plot, from that data.

Moreover, viewed in terms of debates on narratology in historical writing, it brings into question the ideological mediation of historical representation. Hayden White (1981: 2) argued that historians narrativise their subject matter, placing events within narratives which attempt to give them 'the coherence, integrity, fullness and closure of an image of life that is and can only be imaginary'. White was not arguing that the historical event has no fixed meaning, but that the 'discursive turn' imposes a subjective order upon them. Historical narratives, White (1998: 16) contended, were 'verbal fictions, the contents of which are as much *invented* as *found*'. Radical texts which impose their own order upon the subject risk failing to reclaim that subject matter from the narratives imposed by the state – *Elephant* avoids the strategies of other films on the subject, for instance their narrativisation as a structural problem for the British (indeed, the 'hidden agenda' of Loach's film is purely domestic). Of this 'imaginary' coherence of narrativity, White (1981: 2–3) asked, 'Does the world really present itself to perception in the form of well-made stories, proper beginnings, middles and ends' or 'as mere sequence without beginning or end?' Clarke's structuring of *Elephant* allows the issues to occur as 'mere sequence without beginning or end', and creates a form of realism which almost denarrativises the events it portrays, by dislocating them in temporal and spatial ellipses and foregrounding his, and the viewer's, inadequate attempts to 'author' meanings upon them.

In its repetitive and prolonged walks around swimming pools, warehouses, streets and corridors, Clarke's Steadicam aesthetic is at its most problematic: self-announcing in its skirting of objective and subjective positions, it operates in the gap between the camera's surface documentary elements (portable camera, natural sound and lighting, diegetic sound) and its rhetoric of attachment to protagonists. It is also highly stylised and, as David Thomson observed, 'mercilessly beautiful' (1993: 83). There is a painterly effect to the repetitions, long takes and still-frames, which encourages a Bazinian scrutiny of the mise-en-scène, noting textual details of colour and composition, the angles of fallen bodies, the 'long corridors filmed like bodily canals, endless viscera' (Tessé 2003). W. B. Yeats's poem on the events of Easter 1916 springs to mind: 'A terrible beauty is born' (Yeats 1990: 93). Although Thomson (1993: 83) added that it was not 'pictorial or spectacular in the sense of David Lean', for him 'Clarke has the rigour of a Fritz Lang' because 'the camera is like fate'. As in *Road*, its sparse mise-en-scène creates multiple effects; alongside its sense of absence and discursive void there is also a spatial critique of Thatcherite economics which provides, according to Michael Walsh (2000: 296), 'a kind of answer to the question the film's action leaves open ... dramatising the region's deindustrialisation in the very ease with which it finds empty factories and commercial spaces in which to shoot'.

A decade on from debates on the visual epistemology of realism (see Chapter 2), Clarke, in his juxtaposition of highly expressive effects, narrative experimentation and a problematising of documentary elements, evolved an ideological form which foregrounded 'the camera's misleading faculty of being able to record the real' (Rotha 1949: 88) and represented a 'terminus for British social realism' (Walsh 2000: 297). Like *Road*, *Elephant* is rooted in a landscape of 'history without memory' (Pilger 1999: 8), articulated within a cyclical structure which is the embodiment of Brecht's belief that 'Today's catastrophes do not progress in a straight line but in cyclical crises' (Brecht 1978: 30). Reclaiming Brecht from the formalists, Clarke adapts his techniques for the political purposes Brecht envisaged, developing a political form built upon 'discovering the causal complexes of society' and 'unmasking the prevailing view of things as the view of those who are in power' (Bloch *et al.* 1977: 82). The alienating effects which Clarke achieves in the movements from attachment to detachment in *Elephant* are not a postmodern wink to the audience about his films' constructedness but a dialectical process rooted in 'contradiction'. His displacement of narratives and experimentation with form reflects what Colin MacCabe (1974) called 'the contradiction between the dominant discourse of the text and the dominant ideological discourse of the time'. The term 'dominant ideological discourse' could almost have been invented to describe Thatcherism.

Elephant is, as David Hare (1990) observed, a 'characteristically personal way of trying to get people to look afresh at life in Northern Ireland'. In Chapter 1, I quoted François Truffaut's argument that the auteur 'transforms the material into an expression of his own personality' rather than 'transferring someone else's work faithfully' (Buscombe 1973: 76). Although David Hare observed that 'throwing out the script on *Elephant* was incredibly painful' to Clarke, he had become an auteur 'in the sense of only thinking of the script as a beginning' (*Own Man*). In its distillation of Clarke's dominant themes and approaches, *Elephant* constitutes, as Robert Chilcott (2001: 58) observed, 'the culmination of Clarke's style, pure cinema, the bleakest, most uncompromising of all his work, and the cementing of Clarke the auteur'. Tragically, he had only one more production in which to assert that distinctive voice.

The Firm (1989)

The Firm was Alan Clarke's last production, and, for many, his greatest. It has been called 'one of the best dramas ever shown on television' by Andrew Clifford (1991), 'a crackling entertainment ... possibly Clarke's funniest film' by David Thomson (1993: 81) and 'one of the few authentic television masterpieces' by David Hare (1990). It is tempting to see *The Firm* as a fitting ending to Clarke's career, given its summation of his themes, but this would be to contrive a neat ending from the viciously arbitrary coincidence of his premature death. Dennis Potter wrote *Karaoke* (1996) and *Cold Lazarus* (1996) in 1994 under the 'matter-of-fact death sentence' of terminal cancer, consciously conceiving them as his 'memorial ... testament both to my character and my career' (Potter 1994: 28; 1996: vii, xv), but Clarke did not, as he was unaware of the cancer that would kill him barely eighteen months after *The Firm*'s transmission. This production should have marked the ending of just one phase of his career, as he became (in the auteur-critic sense) the complete director: it encapsulates and deepens Clarke's vision, trading upon the collision of attachment, detachment and ideology created by his use of Steadicam. With the 1980s and Margaret Thatcher's premiership nearing their respective ends, *The Firm* under-lines his responses to the ideological narratives of Thatcherism. Charac-teristically, this involves his most contentious attempt to give voice to a demonised social group: football hooligans. It remains the definitive statement on hooliganism, as is clear from the number of reviewers who described *The Football Factory* (2004) as 'not a patch on Alan Clarke's far tougher' and more insightful treatment (Lawrenson 2004).

As ever, to talk of Clarke's 'vision' is not to dismiss the contribution of his collaborators. Even at this late stage in the history of the single play, writer Al Hunter was privileged in most reviews as *The Firm*'s author. It slots neatly alongside Hunter's previous radio play on hooliganism, and his subsequent television plays, *Safe* (1993) on teenage homelessness, and *Alive and Kicking* (1991), about a football team of recovering drug addicts. However, by this point in his career Clarke's more auteurist approach resulted in his most acrimonious relationship with a writer since *Diane*. Hunter researched the film for a year, and after completing a script underwent months of rewriting to meet Clarke's specifications. Clarke again pared down a script, in this case from a two-hour original, as Adam Sweeting (1989) reported. An established actor, Hunter wanted the part of Brummie thug Oboe, but Clarke refused and then, as Hunter told Hugh Hebert (1994), 'he said you can't come to rehearsal, and I don't want you to come to the filming, and I said "Bollocks", it's like throwing a party and not going to it'. When Hunter ignored the producer's warning and turned up, Clarke stopped the rehearsal and sent the actors away. The result of this painful process is that *The Firm* is ultimately Clarke's film, the (inadvertently) final chapter in a body of work in which his was now the dominant authorial voice.

Clive 'Bex' Bissell (Gary Oldman) is an intelligent, successful estate agent, and, in his spare time, a football hooligan. The leader of 'Inter City Crew' or 'ICC', Bex attempts to put together a national firm, under his leadership, to follow England to the 1988 European Championships in Germany to take on rival hooligans. To achieve this leadership he must prove himself 'top boy' by beating the firms of his two rivals, albino

'Yeti' (Philip Davis) from the South London firm 'the Buccaneers' and the Birmingham-based 'Oboe' (Andrew Wilde). Both fixtures are played away from home. The first takes place in Birmingham. After being deprived of reinforcements who are petrol-bombed by Yeti at a motorway service station, Bex's firm is routed by Oboe's superior numbers. Oboe corners young Yusef and slashes his face, in retaliation for which Bex viciously attacks Oboe at his home. Later, Bex's son cuts his mouth on Bex's Stanley knife. When Bex refuses an ultimatum from his wife Sue (Lesley Manville) to stop fighting, they argue and he leaves home. Sharing her concern over Bex's obsession with Yeti, some of his colleagues back out. When the ICC fails to arrive for an arranged fixture, Yeti's crew celebrate in a pub, but it is here that Bex leads an apparently suicidal surprise attack. His small firm routs Yeti's mob, and Bex mutilates Yeti outside. However, Yeti pulls out a gun and shoots him dead. Later, interviewed by a documentary crew, the joint firms, united in Bex's memory, state their intent to go into Europe.

Filmed between 26 April and 25 May 1988, *The Firm* was first transmitted in February 1989 in BBC2's *Screen Two* slot. Appearing just a month after *Elephant*, *The Firm* seems an entirely different type of film, replacing *Elephant*'s stylised structure and austere silences with vibrant performances, hilarious dialogue and relentless narrative drive. However, it shares with *Elephant* a concern with violence as a self-perpetuating, ritualistic act. Hugh Hebert (1989) reported that the writer aimed 'to tell people something about the roots of hooligan violence without glamorising the subject or being titillating', but the charismatic characterisation lent empathy to scenes of violence, an approach which is often as morally unsettling as *Elephant*'s refusal of such associations. Maintaining his central visual trope, Clarke tracks Bex's exhilarating journey step-for-step with John Ward's Steadicam. Hunter, an admirer of Clarke's direction, observed that this was 'a very important part of the film. You go in there with the same adrenalin running as the gang themselves' (Sweeting 1989). As in *Elephant*, the moments in which attachment gives way to the camera's (and the viewer's) disengagement from the action have a devastating impact.

Far from wanting to glamorise football hooligans, Clarke – according to John Ward – thought them 'the scum of the earth' (Kelly 1998: 202). He felt they were ruining the game he loved, and refused Hunter's request to meet the hooligans he had used for research. And yet, Clarke resists moralising, instead granting his characters the charismatic articulacy that his films often lend those not usually allowed to articulate themselves. He was congratulated by David Hare (1990) for having the 'skill and moral certainty to bring off' Oldman's 'knife-edge performance'. Although Clarke claimed that he wanted Bex to be 'not merely unsympathetic' but 'despicable', he gave Oldman the freedom to develop the character, who becomes, as Simon Hattenstone (1998) noted, 'as witty and sexy as he is grotesque', helping us to 'empathise with ... even, almost, to admire' him as Clarke used the form 'to make us confront our demons'. However, Clarke also gives the hooligans enough rope to hang themselves, providing, as Peter Lennon (1989b) argued, 'no alibi', 'no tender sociological concern', 'no pity for the dispossessed' and no 'excuse of severe psychological disturbance'. This removal of socio-logical arguments also, according to Minette Martin (1990), 'forces the audience to think and feel about the nature of evil'.

A lifelong Everton supporter, Clarke disappointed critics who were looking for a connection with 'the ritualised battle on the field, football itself' (Hebert 1989). On *The Late Show*, he seized upon an improvised line by Steve McFadden – 'stop the rucks at football, we go boxing, we go snooker, we go darts' – as 'the main point of the film': 'We didn't say "Let's make a violent film". The characteristics of these particular guys is that they behave violently on certain days of the week in a ritualistic kind of way, which has nothing to do with football.' The hooligans employ football terminology, talking of 'pre-match tension' or taking a 'team photo', but Clarke emphasises their separation from the game. Only a few seconds of *The Firm* takes place inside a football ground, when Yeti looks for his rivals in the crowd, and he keeps his back to the game. Even when the boys play football, Clarke frames his shots to show the players but exclude the ball. Their playing of football is connected with the vandalism of a car elsewhere, by the ironic use of Dean Martin's *That's Amore* over both sequences. Their distance from the game is most clearly satirised later, when Yusef points to a huge facial scar inflicted by a knife and says: 'That's football.'

Clarke was keen to establish that he did not set out to 'make a violent film' because, like so many of his previous productions, *The Firm* was discussed largely in terms of 'Clarke's flair for directing violence' (Sweeting 1989). In the censorious climate of the late 1980s, the representation of violence was interpreted as an act of glorification regardless of context. Therefore, some described *The Firm* as a laddish tale of football violence: Peter Paterson (1989) saw it as a 'wasted opportunity' which neglected 'the well-springs of soccer violence' to show 'the violence itself in sadistic and foul-mouthed detail'. Al Hunter himself felt that Clarke and his crew had 'got off so much on this violence at the end, they lost control' (Hebert 1994). Reports indicated that *The Firm* received over a hundred complaints from viewers, largely for violence and bad language (Dickson 1989). Brian Scovell (1989) reported that Crystal Palace's chairman, Ron Noades, threatened legal action over the use of the club's Selhurst Park ground after being assured that 'it had nothing to do with football hooliganism'. As with the film version of *Scum*, *The Firm*'s notoriety spread while it was still in production. In a piece for *The Sun* predicting a 'Storm As BBC Plan Soccer Yob TV Shocker', Garry Bushell (1988) took the opportunity to attack the BBC, raging at scenes which are unrecognisable from the finished play, including the mob 'arming themselves with guns, machetes and acid for a revenge mission to Germany', and the murder of Bex by 'West German hooligans'. Although his report that 'six stuntmen have already been injured' was an exaggeration, there were moments in rehearsal and filming in which cast members almost lost control, particularly in the scene in which rival firms meet, because, as John Ward recalled, 'Alan had got everybody up so far, just like the murderball scene in *Scum*' (Kelly 1998: 206). Producer David M. Thompson felt isolated from the 'level of latent violence on set' (Kelly 1998: 205), which included a scene in which Charles Lawson (as Trigg) spontaneously punches out a ceiling panel. Such notoriety has affected *The Firm*'s reception; the cover of its video and DVD releases appeal to the perceived market for a 'brutal' film 'from the director of *Scum*'. Thompson maintained that, although some actors may have got carried away, 'I don't think that was the case with Alan. I don't think any part of Alan celebrated violence' (*Director*). Far from exploiting violence, Clarke showed a quality that surprised Hugh Hebert (1989): 'Restraint is possibly the last thing you expect to get in a television play about soccer hooligans directed by Alan Clarke'.

Jack Bell (1989) accurately predicted that *The Firm* would lead to 'a punch-up with TV watchdogs'. Mary Whitehouse wrote to the BBC's Governors to complain that *The Firm* had instantly 'made a nonsense' of the BBC's much-publicised new guidelines on violence (Dickson 1989). Meanwhile, William Rees-Mogg was drawing up new guidelines for the Broadcasting Standards Council, which criticised 'the display of weapons ... particularly when knives readily available in the home are involved', and theorised that the presence of violence 'may be a sign that the writer and director lack sufficient confidence in other aspects of their work and are using violence to sustain the audience's interest' (Brooks 1989). *The Firm* could 'mount a strong "developing understanding" defence' against such complaints, John Dugdale (1989) argued, adding that, after *Elephant*, 'Two "Mogg Alerts" for a single director within a month is pretty good going'. Some critics stepped back from the media frenzy to proclaim *The Firm*'s 'truth' and 'integrity', and to question the underlying suggestion that viewers were 'so dim that you only have to show a Stanley knife on TV for the Great British Unwashed to think, "Oh, I'll go out and buy me one of those to cut people's faces with"' (Anonymous 1989b). However, others maintained that *The Firm* contained 'some of the most horrifying scenes ever seen on the small screen' (Bell 1989). Tabloid newspapers, media watchdogs and MPs had called for it to be banned, and there was a point at which, with *Scum* still banned and *Elephant* delayed, Clarke was prepared, according to John Ward, for 'his trilogy of banned movies' (Kelly 1998: 194). In interview, producer David M. Thompson suggested that he had been 'over-cautious' in his approach to some of the cuts made to *The Firm*. Clarke 'regretted the way we slightly toned down the violence, particularly in the sound effects', and Thompson noted that 'it now looks rather tame'.

The cuts also affected elements of characterisation. Whilst Oldman, Clarke and Hunter constructed a morally ambiguous character whose actions were left for the audience to judge, certain cuts encouraged greater empathy with Bex. For example, in a set of scenes which mirror *Elephant* in their portrayal of the circularity of violence, Yusef (referred to as an 'under-five' as a young hooligan) is slashed across the face by Oboe; Bex carries out a revenge slashing of Oboe; then Clarke cuts to Bex's child (a real under-five), who will become a victim, firstly by chewing his father's Stanley knife, and ultimately by being orphaned. However, Bex's attack on Oboe was edited to remove the close-up of his Stanley knife slashing Oboe's eyeball (shades of Luis Buñuel's *Un chien Andalou* (*An Andalusian Dog*, 1928)), reducing the impact of the cut to Bex's baby. Instead, the attack on Oboe features a discreet cut to long-shot from outside the house akin to the withdrawal from horror by Alfred Hitchcock's camera in *Frenzy* (1972). Thompson recalled in interview that the eyeball shot was 'completely disgusting' and 'unnecessary', but its removal seems to undermine the sequence's attempt at, as Thompson told Richard Brooks (1989), 'a conscious depiction of the consequences of violence'. Since the audience is exposed to the horror of Oboe slashing Yusef, but spared the horrific reality of Bex's attack, Oboe is signposted as villain to Bex's hero. What is lost is the fact that Bex's attack is not simply as cowardly as Oboe's – both feature two men overpowering and slashing an unarmed man – but is much more vicious, and conducted in Oboe's own home, away from the agreed terms of engagement.

The furore obscured the fact that *The Firm* is one of Clarke's most political films. After documenting the effects of Thatcherite economic policy on the dispossessed, Clarke now portrays the thought processes of those who shared their world-view, making *The Firm* his most overt allegory of popular Toryism. This reading was grasped on the set: Philip Davis argued that the hooligans were 'the result of Thatcher's Britain ... they weren't kicking against the system or the bosses, they were kicking against each other', adding that 'it really sums up the 1980s'. David Hare went further, calling it 'the best' of 'the great implicitly anti-Thatcherite films of the 1980s' (Kelly 1998: 201). The opening sequence establishes the connection between Thatcherite economics and football hooliganism. Bex strides towards an expensive house with prospective purchasers, the latent aggression of his walk mirrored in his confident sales patter, as he jokes about it suffering from damp because it doesn't need 'the hard sell'. He strides away in another characteristic Steadicam shot, from which John Strickland's consummate editing takes us to the violence of Yeti's attack on Bex's car, and on to Bex's firm playing football. There are echoes of the style and structure of *Elephant*, as we follow Bex to the house with his victims, then follow him as he strides away, having made a metaphorical killing, leaving the victims inside. This is reinforced in the next scene, Yeti's attack on ICC property, which ends like an *Elephant* sequence, with a near-still frame of a urinal, although here it is not blood but the legend 'Buccaneers' that is sprayed on the wall. The juxtaposition between affluence and violence is repeated later, with a swift cut from Bex practising an attack on Yeti to Bex in his estate agency office.

Bex's affluence is partly a literal reflection of real-life trends; in his sociological study of Sheffield United's 'Blades' firm, Gary Armstrong noted that hooligans from London were considered to be 'rich in appearance with expensive, casual, pastel-coloured clothing supplemented by gold jewellery and distinctive hairstyles', aided by their 'high proportion of "old" lads i.e. from their late twenties onwards' (Armstrong 1998: 243). However, his job also has a political resonance. Like their real-life counterparts, Bex, Yeti and Oboe thrived under Thatcherism, their affluence providing a stark contrast with the conditions suffered in the Northern settings of *Rita, Sue and Bob Too* and *Road*. Mimicking the name and catchphrase of Harry Enfield's satirical character, one member of the firm waves his wad and boasts of having 'loadsamoney'. They are an extension of the establishment, their acronym ICC mirroring that of the world cricket elite, just as real-life firms used acronyms like BBC. It is therefore highly appropriate that Bex lives at Number 11, an address identified in Britain with the Chancellor of the Exchequer; cinematic numerologists may also note that Trevor in *Made in Britain* drives a (Tory blue) old banger which features the number 10, Margaret Thatcher's address. Like Trevor, the hooligans' violence is condemned although they are responding to the socio-economic conditions around them; unlike Trevor, they have accepted these conditions unquestion-ingly. This is a 'dog eat dog' world in which 'you don't let people treat you like shit'. Their aggression is the work-hard-play-hard yuppie creed of series like *Capital City* (1989–90) or films like *Wall Street* (1987), their competitiveness that of the floor of the Stock Exchange or the post-City squash game. As Amy Taubin (1994: 60) argued, Bex's violent behaviour 'is both socialized and natural. It's the logical by-product of the dog-eat-dog market economy, and it is also the root impulse behind that economy.'

Bex is the core of *The Firm*'s Thatcherite allegory. Like Thatcher, he has trouble from within his firm from 'wets' who doubt his vicious tactics, particularly his treatment of poorer citizens as expendable means to an end. The battle for power involves three parties, who at one point meet in a hotel room, in a scene that alludes to parliamentary debate in the House of Commons. The respective leaders stand in almost formal opposition in the framing, trading insults to the jeering approval of their supporters, who are arranged equally formally behind them. On the soundtrack as Yeti arrives at a hotel near Tower Bridge, the chimes of Big Ben can be heard in the distance. The smaller third party have their delusions of grandeur cruelly exposed by Bex and his Stanley knife, leaving a basic opposition between two fundamentally similar parties. Also like Thatcher, Bex is ultimately brought down by in-fighting over 'going into Europe'. His attempt to get everyone behind him, and beat a rival who accuses him of 'running scared', means that Bex, like the Thatcher government, faces a situation summar-ised by a headline among his West Ham cuttings: 'Now for Britain's greatest European challenge.' Also, just as Thatcher was confronted with terrorist attacks on the British mainland, Bex has to deal with strategic attacks on his firm around London by Yeti. This enemy, like that of *Contact*, rarely comes out into the open, being an 'other' marked out tribally, living in the South, a 'manor' on which Bex leads an assault.

The Firm also refers to a specific plank of Thatcherite class rhetoric employed in her condemnation of hooligans. Hooliganism receives coverage out of proportion with the relatively small threat it poses to society beyond its own practitioners – as one convicted hooligan stated, in court 'they make out it's us, the animals, smacking old women with flasks of tea', when in fact 'it's lads exactly the same as us underneath another banner' (*Hooligan '96*). Given this, some commentators have found other meanings. The regulation of football hooliganism is rooted in the desire, recurrent in political and literary discourse, to control working-class collectives. Gary Armstrong (1998: 6) observed that 'as far back as 1314 football was banned in London in an attempt to preserve public tranquillity, for it was feared the tumult and disorder surrounding these games might well give occasion to the forces of sedition and treason'. Similarly, Thatcher, who demonised collectivisation as part of her emasculation of trade unions, arguing that 'true solidarity' for workers was putting 'their country first' (1989: 163), made a class reading of hooliganism, proposing that they would be deterred by huge price increases because, in the words of Gary Oldman, 'she imagined that it was fifteen- and sixteen-year old kids on the dole who had nothing better to do' (Kelly 1998: 200). This reading formed a core part of academic studies on the subject, including a major study financed by the Football Trust, whose authors sought to explain the phenomenon by devoting a chapter to 'the structure of "problem" housing estates' (Murphy *et al.* 1990: 136).

Less than two months after *The Firm* was transmitted, ninety-six Liverpool fans were crushed to death at an FA Cup semi-final held at Hillsborough on 15 April 1989. The cause was not hooligan activity but South Yorkshire police wrongly opening a gate and ushering thousands of people into an already packed terrace. *The Sun* enthusiastically supported the discourse through which the police attempted to cover their actions. Its editor Kelvin Mackenzie oversaw the notorious front page on 19 April 1989: claiming to tell 'THE TRUTH', *The Sun* falsely stated that fans molested a dead girl, 'picked pockets of victims', 'urinated on the brave cops' and 'beat up PC giving kiss of life' (see Pilger 1999 on the subsequent fallout). The political implications of a supposedly working-class newspaper slandering working-class 'animals' against the police, so soon after 'picking sides' in the Miners' Strike, can not be overstated. Jimmy McGovern has argued, through the character of Alby in the 1994 *Cracker* serial *To Be a Somebody*, and through his drama-documentary *Hillsborough* (1996), that the disaster was the culmination of a concerted effort by the Thatcher government after the Miners' Strike to belittle and animalise working-class culture. The disaster was worsened by the high metal fences which Hillsborough, like most football grounds, was required to have to cage in the 'animal' hooligan elements. *The Firm*, therefore, could be said to be about much more than football hooliganism.

In keeping with much of Clarke's work, *The Firm* addresses the discourses through which the state, sociologists and the police describe hooligan activity. Gary Armstrong (1998: 126) wrote that the police extended 'panoptical' CCTV surveillance culture on the back of their reading of hooliganism, which became the norm because 'it was written down in a document disseminated by their professional hierarchy'.

Policing hooliganism 'was a political thing', according to hooligan Bill Gardner, who argued that 'Thatcher wanted it to be part of her law-and-order campaign' (Pennant 2002: 61). Neatly subverting this intrusion into civil liberties, *The Firm* demonstrates the inadequacy of the Thatcher government's identity card scheme through its sites of action: none of the violence takes place within a football ground. This was transmitted, with what Martin Cropper (1989) described as 'suspiciously cute timing', a day after Colin Moynihan MP memorably explained the scheme on the BBC's children's programme *Going Live!*

Like the diagrammatic representation of Trevor's 'choices' in *Made in Britain* or the rhetoric of rehabilitation in *Scum*, *The Firm* consistently problematises its own 'search for meaning'. For instance, Bex prevents a youth from quitting by warning him that he will lose face, as 'this is your manor, you've got to walk up and down the street every fucking night'. However, he then deconstructs his own motivation, noting that 'that's peer group pressure, that is. It's a real bastard.' With his A-level in Sociology, Bex is aware of the 'study of social problems', and resists being studied himself. Director Richard Jobson (2004) cited this awareness as one of his reasons for loving *The Firm*, recalling that the 'football-related gang' he was once part of 'weren't stupid ... they understood how people perceived them'. At one point, the firm watch a television sociologist attempting to explain hooliganism. He describes it as 'a search for meaning' and status. This fits in with the traditional view that '"core" football hooligans are engaged in a quest for status and excitement or emotional arousal', which is their 'central source of meaning and gratification in life' (Murphy *et al.* 1990: 87).

In one of many recent football hooligan memoirs, Shaun Tordoff (2002: 5) summed up the common response to 'middle class psychologists', asking that they 'don't bother analysing us ... FOR THOSE WHO HAVE BEEN INVOLVED, NO EXPLANATION IS NECESSARY. FOR THOSE WHO HAVEN'T, NO EXPLANATION IS POSSIBLE.' This response, reminiscent of Clarke's approach since collaborating with Tony Parker, lends resonance to Nunk's response to the on-screen sociologist: 'Why don't 'e just tell 'em we like 'itting people?' They chant about the sociologist's onanistic tendencies, an act of spectator participation which ironically parallels the sociologist with a football match: the lads are sitting around the television, drinking and chanting. The scene may even reflect Clarke's position: the sociologist's presence was partly a response to producer David M. Thompson's request that, as he recalled in interview, 'there should be more meaning ... more explanation about what this "buzz" was'. The boys show a newcomer their ICC tattoos, and Bex takes out his Stanley knife to gouge a similar tattoo into his arm. The scene is building to an unpleasant climax when the lads suddenly rub off their supposed 'tattoos' which were actually written in pen, and laugh at the relieved youth. By enacting and then dismantling the motifs of tribalism, the scene shows the instability of the sociologist's reading, even if previous quotes and the film's structure suggest that Clarke's own reading was inherently 'ritualistic'.

Bex's walks around areas of London marked out by regional and class boundaries, and his skirmishes with other firms, serve as a marking out of territory akin to that of 'home' and 'away' ends in football grounds. This tribal aspect is politicised by the way Bex is located so firmly within the landscape that made him: Britain, and, more problematically, 'British-ness'. Despite endemic hooliganism in South America, the Netherlands and Italy, journalists often call it the 'English disease'. The 1988 European Championships are crucial to the plot because this was the first European football tournament involving England's national side since English club sides were banned from Europe following the 1985 Heysel stadium disaster (the 1986 World Cup had been safely distant, in Mexico). At a time when English clubs were among the most successful in Europe, this ban, allied to the comparative scarcity of overseas players, exacerbated supporters' feelings of insularity, and made the European Championships a major signifier of national identity. Football researcher John Williams argued that, because of 'historical baggage' and media coverage, 'what happens to the team and how the team performs somehow signifies the fate of the nation', attempting to compensate for 'our decline and loss of influence and power' (*Hooligan '96*). However, if Philip Davis's film *I.D.* (1996) portrayed hooliganism as a means of asserting regional and masculine identity (its plot turning on an undercover policeman becoming dangerously assimilated into the group identity), in *The Firm* individual and regional identities merge with national identity. Bex's call to unite against Europe reflects both the Right wing's virulent anti-Europeanism and its recourse to rhetoric rooted in the two World Wars, emptily employing patriotism as an insular device by repeating that 'someone's got to fly the flag'. *The Firm* ends with the hooligans preparing to do battle in a European conflict (the European Championships) being held in Germany, which they hail by singing that Britain won 'two World Wars and one World Cup'. In one preview, Barry Norman wondered whether 'young men need wars to work off their natural aggression'. However, this aggression is as socially conditioned as it is 'natural'; one real-life hooligan observed the parallel between the average crew's desire to 'take that as ours', which he described as 'a sense of empire', with Britain's military action in the

Falklands in 1982, 'an example of football hooliganism on a grand scale' (*Hooligan '96*).

The firms' notion of Britishness is clearly localised. One of the characters brandishes a hat with the Union Flag on it, but across its centre is written 'London'. At this point, London hooligans had a ferocious reputation; Gary Armstrong (1998: 243) reported that Sheffield United hooligans saw this as 'a product of living in London, a place many Blades considered "weird" and "violent"'. Inter City Crew like to travel, as their name suggests – like the East London club West Ham's notorious Inter City Firm, who named themselves after their pioneering tactic of catching normal Inter City trains in small groups rather than arriving en masse in club colours – but, in Clarke's allegory of centralization, London is where the real battles for power are fought. Confronting the marginalized third party from the Midlands, who complain that Cockneys 'always think you've got the right to run things', Bex asserts London's right to rule the provinces. On the Birmingham trip, Yusef is slapped for wearing a hat with the name of Glasgow club Celtic, and asked, 'What have we got to do with Scotland, son?' In keeping with the construction of Britishness propagated by the *Sun*, this is very much a film about London.

Clarke's representation of London is so potent that, as John Orr argued, *The Firm* has influenced the city's subsequent portrayal across British film and television drama. During Bex's visits to members of his firm, Clarke's 'sweeping Steadicam shots' become, according to Orr (2000: 142), 'bold brush strokes which journey from Thamesmead into the heart of the city', from leafy suburbia to decaying tower block, revealing often 'imperceptible gradations of status'. Wealthier hooligans can walk away but, in an implicit class reading, characters' options narrow further down the social scale. Hailing from the City of London, the firms wield economic power against the weak as effectively as monetarist economic policy. Before *The Firm*'s only terrestrial repeat broadcast in 1991, David Leland described the hooligans as 'a well-heeled bunch, no victims of society ... the kind of chaps who throw pound coins as missiles at the less prosperous supporters of Northern clubs'. This image of coins as missiles recurs throughout the film, as the tools of violence are used alongside the hooligans' materialistic status symbols. The story's initial catalyst is the defacement of Bex's car, and the ICC's designer underwear, by the elaborately coiffured Yeti, who later destroys morale by torching Aitch's car. Yeti drives his VW Golf through Bex's firm's football match, encapsulating *The Firm*'s central rhetoric of the intrusion of self-aggrandising designer masculinity into football. In keeping with the stereotyped psychological link between men and their cars (Sue at one point berates Bex for 'making love to the car'), the idolatrous pleasures of possessions are inextricably linked with masculine identity.

The Firm's reading of hooliganism also questions changing gender roles. The major hooligans have office jobs lacking the masculinity asserted by their weekend violence. In one scene, Bex receives some new weaponry, which he takes to his parents' house, and stands in his childhood bedroom, learning how to use an extendable stick, with phallic connotations. He even lends the Stanley knife its maker's name as a male label: 'I give you ... Stanley.' Alan Coren (1989) argued that the film explored the impact of 'screen fiction and screen fact' in the characters' actions, as 'observed violence had bred imitation; you saw it in the strut, the language ... the outcrop of every range-war and shoot-out ever filmed'. *Billy the Kid and the Green Baize Vampire* also shared this use of mythological figures in the construction of male identity, whilst one of *Road*'s protagonists wanted to 'walk like Robert Mitchum'. However, *The Firm*'s association of violence solely with masculinity is a simplification enforced by the removal of a contentious scene in which Bex's wife gained pleasure from his sexual violence soon after his attack on Oboe. In their arguments, their sexuality, and Sue's response to their child's accident, there is a mutual level of aggression, which undermines the idea that hooliganism acts as a masculine distraction from his family role.

Bex's problems intensify when he fails in the role of father, endangering the lives of both his son and his surrogate family. Like the Commander in *Contact*, Bex assumes paternal control of a group for military purposes, to the detriment of the real children with whom they are juxtaposed: the children in the woods in *Contact* and, in *The Firm*, the real 'under-five' who receives similar injuries to the 'under-five' Yusef. Ultimately, loyalty to this family and to the 'buzz' leads to separation from Sue, which is paralleled by Aitch's decision to opt out of escalating violence. After following Bex to his taxi in his traditional Steadicam style, Clarke then follows Aitch back to his house, the only time that this character receives this visual treatment. Clarke had previously attached his camera problematically to characters, notably in *Elephant* but also in *Fast Hands*, following Prince after the bout he had arranged led to a boxer's brain damage. As well as arguably showing Aitch turning his back on his friend, the shot establishes a conscious opposition between Bex's extremism and the view of a character with whom we are suddenly empathically attached.

The major complicating factor in the film's attitude to masculinity is Yeti. Just as the post-industrial economy has rendered traditional male pursuits obsolete, so Yeti favours not the traditional confrontational fisticuffs mourned by Bex's dad but 'sniper' attacks on property. Bex becomes obsessed with Yeti, repeating almost as a mantra, 'I have got to have him', signposting the kind of homosocial narrative common to Hollywood action films, in which obsession with a male rival in effect replaces desire for wives and lovers. In *The Firm*, women are rarely engaged with: Trigg interrupts an intimate moment between Bex and Sue, Aitch claims to have refused a one-night stand because the girl was 'a dog', while strippers are chanted at as if, like footballers, they are for watching rather than participating with, and a belly-dancer has drinks thrown over her. The central narrative follows Bex's pursuit of a blonde, but this blonde is Yeti. At the start Yeti marks Bex's underwear with paint, after which Bex threatens to 'engrave my name all over your arse' with his Stanley knife, a phallic and sado-masochistic echo of lovers carving their names into trees. This reading was originally made more forcefully, but a shot of Bex slashing Yeti's buttocks was removed. Throughout the film, characters mime sexual acts with each other, talk of orgies, threaten a 'spanking' and refer to each other as 'she' and 'her' and 'top girl', but their awareness of this discourse makes this another largely (although not unproblematically) subverted reading.

The film's narrative is predicated upon the collision between these two figures, from the opening five minutes in which both are introduced with kinetic Steadicam shots, to the ending, in which Bex gets his man, only for Yeti to provide the fatal twist. When Yeti pulls out the gun, Bex smiles, 'Oh, come on', as if this threat cannot be taken seriously because it contravenes the game's rules. Researchers into hooliganism insist that such weapons are unacceptable for most hooligans and the writer and cast were concerned about the change to the script (see Kelly 1998). However, it is an almost inevitable ending given the narrative's logic of escalation, and was such a memorable twist that it appeared in one magazine's list of 'the 50 greatest TV moments of all time' (Anonymous 1998). Far more satisfying is the jarring use of a second ending, entirely Clarke's invention, which is radically different from everything that has preceded it. The united firms are interviewed by a documentary crew, and 'explain' hooliganism. In this scene, largely improvised by the actors, suggestions include 'the buzz', masculinity, Britishness, and Yusef's declaration that his facial injury means 'football'. As David Bordwell (1982) argued, in film the use of a second ending or coda usually 'functions to achieve the final stability achieved by the narrative'. However, this coda has precisely the opposite effect. The characters propose various 'meanings' which are untrustworthy because they have either not been factors or have been satirised by the characters citing them.

In stark contrast with this static television screen, Bex is filmed with Clarke's characteristically dynamic 'participatory' Steadicam style. Some critics had picked up on the technique: Christopher Petit (1989) described it as 'Clarke's directorial signature', while Peter Lennon (1989b) connected *The Firm* with *Elephant* in its use of 'urgent, purposeful walking as the sign of true aggression'. In one shot following Yusef, medical staff and a policeman down a hospital corridor, Clarke recalls not only the harshly lit interior spaces of *Elephant* but also *Funny Farm*, one of the productions in which he developed the device. His rhetoric of involvement, described by David Hare as the 'democratic camera', is as disturbing as it is powerfully inclusive, and in *The Firm* Clarke 'refined the style to an incredible degree' (Kelly 1998: 200). According to John Orr (2002: 106), with its dynamic 'proximity', Clarke's Steadicam, like Derek Jarman's Super 8, represented 'a new closeness of attention, at times limpet-like in clinging to the figure or the face in movement', which provided 'an echo of a changing society whose anxieties have speed and dislocation as their core focus'. In one of very few academic attempts to read this simultaneously objective and sub-jective rhetoric, Orr briefly added that this was a 'traductive realism for a new age'. This traducing, combining 'transforming and transgressing', was 'a maligning of the subject by the image, often with the subject's complicity', 'social abjection crossed with aesthetic deformation'. The viewer lives 'with the figure whose face dominates the screen, but without easy empathy', encountering 'non-identity' through 'the affective fragment'. In this 'liminal process', 'identity' is both lost and found (Orr 2002: 108). Certainly Clarke's style is both attached to character and aware of the ideological construct of the camera's gaze; indeed, at a time when CCTV cameras began to arrive at football grounds, Clarke's camera is simultaneously within the group and observing it.

This relates to two themes which have recurred throughout this book and which need only be briefly recapitulated here. Firstly, the participatory rhetoric of Clarke's style moves beyond the naturalistic aesthetics prevalent in many 'political' television plays with reflexive moments that expose the dramatic and documentary 'looks' as ideological constructs. Secondly, this technique becomes a process by which these ideological constructs are disrupted, revealing ideology to be in 'contradiction'. To return to Georg Lukács's comparison of horse races in *Anna Karenina* and *Nana*, he argued that Zola wrote the latter from the point of view of an observer because he lived in conditions of 'fully constituted, fully achieved capitalist society' (1973: 115), whereas Tolstoy's writing reflected the transformations of society around him.

Clarke's style contains a sense of historical transformation, a sense that purportedly normative ideological structures, contrary to the myths of their cultural dissemination, are in the process of being constructed. In Bex's case, this goes beyond the subversion of ideologically imposed 'meanings'; like characters in *Christine* and *Road* connected to their environments through Clarke's employment of 'structures of feeling', Bex's walks both place him within his society and configure him as a dynamic catalyst within it. Clarke's participatory rhetoric is all the more ideological when attached to hooliganism, the policing of which was rooted, in Armstrong's terms, in an attempt to prevent their 'unscripted participation', along with clubs' attempts to generate passive consumption. Our alliance with the hooligans' creative acts of participation contrasts with the alienation engendered by the passive spectatorship and consumption of *Christine*.

This sense of attachment is crucial to Clarke's style. Defending his involvement with hooligans as part of his sociological methodology, Gary Armstrong (1998: xiii) quoted a phrase from Jean Baudrillard which, I believe, also expresses the essence of Clarke's technique: 'The point is not to write the sociology or the psychology of the car, the point is to drive. That way you can learn more about this society than all academics could ever tell you.' However, the final shot represents one of Clarke's most unsettling movements back from attachment to detachment. He moves the dramatic camera, which has been implicated with the hooligans throughout, behind the unrepresentative documentary camera crew. In its own way the shot resembles the memorably ambiguous closing shot of Robert Bresson's career, the ending of *L'Argent* (1983), as a crowd of bystanders gaze beyond the arrest of an axe murderer's arrest, and continue to stare after he has left the frame. Like *L'Argent*, the scene queries spectators' attachment to evil and the equivocal nature of measuring 'ethical responsibility for human beings' actions' (Reader 2000: 151–2). However, as Keith Reader has said of Bresson's final shot, it is difficult to 'attribute a single sense or value' to a shot which becomes 'less a closure than a perpetual opening, or even a Möbius-like looping back into a body of work'. It could read as an unconvincing attempt on Clarke's part to disassociate himself from the violence he has portrayed, although interpreting the camera position so literally ignores the fact that the camera is positioned behind Yeti when he shoots Bex. Indeed, Richard Last (1989) was disturbed to feel 'a stab of pleasure' as Yeti shot Bex, taking this as proof that 'screen violence tends to deprave and corrupt'. As in the similar final shot of *Beloved Enemy*, the camera's movement behind the news crew foregrounds the construction of a representation of characters about whom the audience is much better informed. In the most profound legacy of the banning of *Scum*, Clarke revealed in his 1980s work a mistrust of the visual epistemology of cinematic and state discourses, and in this one sequence implicates himself and dramatic form in the processes of misrepresentation. It is all the more disturbing that this was the final shot of Clarke's life.

In hindsight, it is striking that *The Firm*'s ending is so consciously elegiac. The tributes to Bex were to be echoed in Clarke's own obituaries: 'you had to come in on it, because it was visionary'. *The Firm* cemented Clarke's reputation, particularly abroad, winning the Prix Europa and, at the Golden Prague Festival, both the Critics' Prize and the Best Director's Prize. However, the scale of the controversy surrounding it reinforces the sense of many critics that *The Firm* was 'the last gasp of honest, political drama' (Chilcott 2001: 59). Christopher Petit (1989) noted that 'twenty years ago his sort of attack and bite were quite common', but he was now 'almost its sole representative'. Coming to the end of such a passionate, clever, sexy, funny, exhilarating ride, there is still a sense of much more to come, an urge to reach for the next tape in the pile only to remember that, grotesquely unfairly, there isn't one. It is a source of vicious irony that Clarke's initial cancer was located in the area that distinguished his life's work. The backbone.

Conclusion

Alan Clarke died on 24 July 1990. Many of his collaborators and admirers have argued that the radical single play died with him. Although welcoming the afterlife provided for Clarke's work in cinema seasons, David Thomson (2002) lamented: 'if only the season was playing where it ought to be, and where it is most needed – on the television screen'. In his introduction to the tribute repeat broadcast of *Road*, David Leland argued that this 'fine example of the uniqueness of British television' was part of 'a vanishing species', which was 'under threat from government policy of abandoning public service broadcasting to market forces'. In effect, the Thatcherite discourses which Clarke documented ultimately silenced the kind of drama with which he was associated; as David Hare (2002) wrote, the television play 'was first vandalised and then purposely eliminated by post-modernist hooligans at the BBC, who robbed public service television of ... the most effective argument it had for the licence fee'. Given the life-changing power of *Penda's Fen*, and the elegiac tone of critics' comments on it in Chapter 1, it is difficult not to accept at face value the process described by Arne – of 'entertainment barons' viewing the public not as people 'with eyes to see' but 'blind gaping holes at the end of a production line they're stuffing with trash'.

It is important to qualify such 'Golden Age' rhetoric with the observation that this kind of drama still occasionally appears, for instance in the work of Stephen Poliakoff, William Ivory and Jimmy McGovern, or the work of directors operating in the Clarke lineage, such as Paul Greengrass, with *Bloody Sunday* and *Omagh* (2004), or Danny Boyle, whose collaboration with Jim Cartwright on *Vacuuming Completely Nude in Paradise* (2001) resulted in a modern classic. It is also possible to romanticise the past, as David M. Thompson warned in interview: 'People only ever remember *Cathy Come Home*, they don't remember all the dross.' However, there is little doubt that the kind of broadcasting structures which I have outlined in this book have been eroded, leaving the conspicuous absence in contemporary television of the regular institutional space within which writers and directors could develop their own voices, or at least test themselves on a variety of projects. As W. Stephen Gilbert (1990) noted, 'No director now building a television career can hope to enjoy the opportunities that Clarke's generation took for granted. And for that reason (but not only for that reason), television will never again be rewarded with the engagement and the courage of an Alan Clarke.'

This situation seems paradoxical, because, in the period covered by this book, television drama's hierarchies changed. Directors gained more influence than writers as drama shifted to a more visual form of storytelling. In the mid-1970s, Dennis Potter accurately predicted that 'the days of the television play are numbered; it will soon all be done on film, and it'll be a director's medium like the cinema. It only remains an author's medium at the moment because of British anachronisms' (Cushman 1976: 62). In the 1980s, the BBC and Channel Four moved increasingly towards cinema production. Film on Four under David Rose energised film production, combining attempts at popular cinema with a burgeoning arthouse scene in which the likes of Derek Jarman and Peter Greenaway received sustained funding. The unexpected success of Stephen Frears's and Hanif Kureishi's *My Beautiful Laundrette* (1985) bolstered Channel Four's shift to film, although the BBC's response was rather more gradual. In Channel Four's debut year, BBC Head of Plays Keith Williams stated: 'One has to be pleased, at a time when the cinema industry is ailing, that Channel Four is providing an extra outlet for film-makers, and our riposte could have been to match that number of films. But our commitment to studio is substantial, both in terms of building and equipment, and in the staff we have' (Anonymous 1982b). Far from being an aesthetically regressive step, this constituted the BBC's attempt 'to put new energy and imagination' into carrying drama forward. Celebrating Clarke's *Psy-Warriors* as an exploration of space which was quite distinct from studio drama's theatrical connotations, Williams added that 'the television play lies somewhere in that direction'. However, by the time Mark Shivas became the BBC's Head of Drama in 1988, he was able to restructure and rename BBC Plays as BBC Films, reflecting the fact that 'we make more films than plays' (Cook 1998: 247).

This change had contrasting effects for directors. Filmed strands such as *Screen Two* presented opportunities which Clarke grasped, articulating his personal vision on work such as *Contact* and *The Firm*. And yet, there were now fewer slots available because of costs, and increasing tendencies to minimise risk and underplay the specifically British and regional subject matter of the single play, particularly in projects which were dependent upon co-funding. The sheer number and breadth of projects associated with *Play for Today* became narrowed. Clarke's most distinctive work was made on film, but it was made for television, within the structures of the television play. The underlying reasons for the paradox outlined above – the lack of a space for individual directors despite drama's increasing orientation towards the visual – can be found in the rest of Potter's statement, in which he connected drama's shift towards becoming a 'director's medium' with the end of the 'days of the television play' (Cushman 1976: 82). The problem lay not in the simple convergence of *technical* forms through which 'anachronistic' studio plays were replaced by films in which the director was now the primary figure of creative authority, but in its challenge to the very existence of the radical play as a *cultural* form. Using the example of Ken Loach, John Caughie (2000a: 198) argued that:

> a very fundamental shift has occurred between *Cathy Come Home* and *Ladybird, Ladybird* ... the gain of a British art cinema may be at the expense of something quite valuable and immediate in a national television system ... the social anger of *Ladybird, Ladybird* circulates within an aesthetic and a cultural sphere which is given prestige (and economic viability) by international critics' awards, whereas *Cathy Come Home* circulated as a national event and functioned as documentary evidence within the political sphere.

It is this form which has all but disappeared, a form predicated upon the specificity of the national, and upon championing the individual voice, regardless of whether that voice is expressed by writers or directors, or on video or film (for more on convergence see Hill and McLoone 1996; for Film Four's debt to television drama see Saynor 1992).

This book has sought Clarke's 'voice' as a film-maker, and the 'voices' which his productions articulated. It has discussed Clarke's discourses, and the state and media discourses which his work interrogates. However, it has done so from within another discursive framework, namely that of academic writing. I want to end by acknowledging the extent to which these voices have been expressed through another voice, namely mine. Of course an element of selection is inevitable; for instance, word count led to the removal of a section on *Danton's Death*, whilst the remit of The Television Series justified the removal of *Billy the Kid and the Green Baize Vampire* and the reduction of the *Rita, Sue and Bob Too* section. However, my discursive strategies shaped the book more fundamentally than that. Take the section on *Elephant* – its socially oriented post-structuralist approach unpicks the play's complexities and pays tribute to Clarke's skill as a director, but goes much further in its interpretation of form than Clarke might have felt comfortable with, given that (according to Kelly's interviewees) he seemed to share the 'relentless' reading of Northern Ireland which I claim *Elephant* argues against.

The search for a voice is a major theme in *Road*, my personal favourite of all his work, a television play which I can now say, with the imposed discourse of hindsight, changed my life. However, it is to my shame that the enclosed section on *Road* gives no indication of this – indeed, it fails to address the final scene, which is my favourite scene ever shot, by any director, in any television play or film. This is because I do not feel comfortable writing in academic language about something which speaks to me so personally. The section on *Road* is part of an ideological analysis of Clarke's themes and approaches, and is therefore structured within a discursive strategy. That section provides a solid interpretation of a major television text, but *Road* is *not* a 'text', it is *part of my life*. When I started my Ph.D. on Clarke, *Road* more than any other production made me aware that I was grasping for my own voice, feeling restrained, unwilling to frame in academic language how I felt the first time that I saw *Road*, living in circumstances and feeling feelings which the play articulated so … indescribably. At the end, I was unsure whether I was supposed to turn off the television or the world outside. I am still unable to watch Louise's despairing, angry (and, most crushingly of all, hopeful) speech without crying. Previously so inarticulate, she seems surprised by the voice she has suddenly found, saying that 'I never spoke such a speech in my life'. In hindsight, on that night, her voice could have been speaking for me. When Valerie marches around the streets, raging at the pain caused by other people, by poverty, raging at everyone and no one, well, I know that feeling. I know the barren streets roamed by fighting dogs in *Rita, Sue and Bob Too*, the casual ease of drug dealing and use in *Christine*, the battle for a place in the violent hierarchies of *Scum* and *The Firm*. Clarke strives to represent these from within, and to anybody with any experience of their subject matter it is striking that he gets the feeling so consistently *right*.

But interpreting this through mise-en-scène or camerawork or performances or through theory, vitally important though these are, will never be good enough; the feeling is the heart and soul of it, and it's in my guts but not in my vocabulary. It's there in Trevor in *Made in Britain*, a collision of the articulate – funny, persuasive, belligerent – and the inarticulate – the frustration, the rage, the *not quite*. It's about the articulacy of inarticulacy ... but then, who made 'inarticulacy' such a long word? Though my research began when I was on the dole on the council estate I grew up on, it has been completed from within a higher education system whose very culture is shaped (despite the denial propagated by its pervasive normalisation) by the middle-class backgrounds of most of its participants; given that, how can I write about the *Road* of my understanding? I am more articulate than I was when I first saw *Road*, but it is a form of articulacy which renders a lot of those feelings inarticulable. As Trevor was all too aware, the kids who did best at school were those who saw that the 'clever' answer was the one in the teacher's head, framed in their language. Since I'm here to write this, that must apply to me. According to Albert Hunt (1981: 122), 'the way people are taught to think of language itself involves manipulation by an elite ... the very phrasing of the questions invites working-class pupils to try and write in a language that isn't their own ... since teaching right across the board is done in "their" language, this affects the chances of working-class children in almost every aspect of education'. Academic theses and books are to an extent initiation ceremonies, in which the author demonstrates that they have successfully assimilated the languages of their institutions. Without wishing to overempathise with some of Clarke's characters, I shared the dilemma of learning to speak in somebody else's language or becoming effectively excluded. Like the director, the academic faces the paradox of writing about radical subject matter within a form which is itself ideologically loaded. The 'political economy' of 'truth', according to Foucault (1984: 73), is 'produced and transmitted under the control' of 'a few great political and economic apparatuses', which include 'university, army, writing, media'. Clarke found a form through which to articulate these dilemmas; somehow I must do the same.

As much as possible, I have used the analytical tools at my disposal in the service of Clarke's work, to unpick his contribution to their style and form, and to attempt to understand their effects. I returned time and again to Tim Roth's recollection of the direction that Clarke gave him when he was playing Trevor: 'Make him speak. Make him really fucking speak' (Kelly 1998: 144). Where I have felt restricted by academic discourse, Clarke's own voice has surfaced, whether describing drama-documentary debates as 'rubbish' or saying 'bollocks' to a comparison with Bresson. On my wall as I write this, as a warning, is a copy of Clarke's yearbook entry at the Ryerson Institute (see Chapter 1). Because Clarke 'failed to submit his biography', the anonymous author apologises that his entry 'is being written by someone who knows nothing about him'. Where this book has failed to give a sense of

Clarke's personality away from work, I point the reader towards Richard Kelly's oral biography. However, I sincerely hope that this book has provided a thorough understanding of the man through its attentiveness to the work to which Clarke dedicated his life.

Appendix: television programmes directed by Alan Clarke

The listing shows the television programmes and three cinema films directed by Alan Clarke between 1967 and 1989. Information is given about the play strand or series in which each production appeared, the production company which made it and the broadcaster which transmitted (tx) it. To reflect the television climate of the time, ITV regional transmissions are included. I have excluded repeat transmissions for reasons of space (although the bibliography contains information on BBC2's tribute season). Writers (w.) are indicated, as are producers (prod.). Because this book is about a director, this listing differs from others in the series: script editors are not listed, but cast members are, as are designers (des.) and (only in productions made entirely on film) film cameramen or directors of photography (DoP), who play a crucial role in the realisation of a director's vision. I have indicated commercial availability, and where recordings are known to be lost from the archives. Corrections are welcomed for any future edition.

Half Hour Story: Shelter, 1967, 26 min.

(w. Alun Owen, prod. Stella Richman, des. David Catley)
Cast: Wendy Craig (The Girl), Colin Blakely (The Man)
Associated Rediffusion for ITV, Tx: 15 May, 10.05pm (Border, Channel Islands, Southern, Ulster)
Regional variations: 16 May, 9.55pm (Granada), 10.10pm (Tyne Tees), 11.05pm (Midlands), 19 May, 9.10pm (Associated Rediffusion), 10.39pm (Anglia), 22 May, 10.05pm (Grampian), 8 July, 9.25pm (Teledu Cymru); Not transmitted in Scotland or Television Wales and West (TWW)

Half Hour Story: A Man Inside, 1967, 26 min.

(w. Pauline Macaulay, prod. Stella Richman, des. Michael Yates)
Cast: Freddie Jones (Walter Bishop), Yvonne Antrobus (Cynthia Smith),

Nicholas Evans (Harvey), Darryl Read (Delivery boy)
Associated Rediffusion for ITV, Tx: 22 May, 10.05pm (Border, Channel Isles, Southern, Ulster)
Regional variations: 23 May, 9.55pm (Granada), 10.10pm (Tyne Tees), 11.10pm (Midlands), 26 May, 9.10pm (Associated Rediffusion), 11.10pm (Anglia), 29 May, 9.10pm (Grampian), 15 July, 9.25pm (Teledu Cymru), 24 August, 10.30pm (Scotland); Not transmitted in TWW
* No recording exists

Half Hour Story: The Gentleman Caller, 1967, 26 min.

(w. Roy Minton, prod. Stella Richman, des. Andrew Drummond)
Cast: George Cole (Hicks), Tony Selby (Ged), Mike Pratt (Clack)
Associated Rediffusion for ITV, Tx: 12 June, 10.05pm (Border, Channel Isles, Granada, Southern, Ulster)
Regional variations: 13 June, 10.10pm (Tyne Tees), 10.55pm (Midlands), 16 June, 9.10pm (Associated Rediffusion), 10.39pm (Anglia), 19 June, 10.05pm (Grampian), 5 August, 9.25pm (Teledu Cymru), 7 September, 10.30pm (Scotland); Not in TWW
* No recording exists

Half Hour Story: Which of These Two Ladies Is He Married To?, 1967, 26 min.

(w. Edna O'Brien, prod. Stella Richman, des. John Emery)
Cast: Glenda Jackson (Claire Foley), Sheila Raynor (Norah Foley), William Squire (Alex Sandford)
Associated Rediffusion for ITV, Tx: 12 July, 9.00pm (Anglia, Associated Rediffusion, Border, Channel Isles, Grampian, Granada, Midlands, Scotland, Southern, Tyne Tees, Ulster)
Regional variation: 9 September, 9.25pm (Teledu Cymru)
* No recording exists

Half Hour Story: George's Room, 1967, 26 min.

(w. Alun Owen, prod. Stella Richman, des. Fred Pusey)
Cast: Geraldine Moffatt (the woman), John Neville (the man)
Associated Rediffusion for ITV, Tx: 30 August, 9.00pm (London)
Originally scheduled for 20 September, George's Room replaced the scheduled play Quick on the Takeover in the London region; I have been unable to confirm regional transmissions
* Only a 12-minute extract exists

The Informer: *Sleeping Dogs Lie*, 1967, 53 min.

(w. Richard Harris, prod. John Whitney, executive prod. Stella Richman, des. Barbara Bates)

Cast: Ian Hendry (Alex Lambert), Heather Sears (Janet Lambert), Neil Hallett (Detective Sergeant Piper), George Murcell (Willie Cluff), Terence Rigby (Lomax), Raymond Smith (Anker), Stan Simmons (Mason), Redmond Bailey (Charlie (barman)), Terry Duggan (The Man with the paperback), David Brook (policeman)

Associated Rediffusion for ITV, Tx: 27 November, 10.30pm (Grampian, Midlands, Tyne Tees)

Regional variations: 29 November, 8.00pm (Anglia, Associated Rediffusion, Channel Isles, Granada, Teledu Cymru, TWW, Ulster), 30 November, 9.00pm (Southern), 27 December, 8.00pm (Border, Scotland)

* No recording exists

A Man of Our Times: *Sally Go Round the Moon*, 1968, 53 min.

(w. Julian Bond, prod. Richard Bates, executive prod. Stella Richman, des. Frank Nerini)

Cast: George Cole (Max Osborne), Jennifer Wilson (Muriel), Jean Harvey (Sally), Norman Eshley (Simon), Margaret Boyd (Edie), Lucy Appleby (Clare), Christopher Witty (Michael), Michael Hall (head waiter)

Associated Rediffusion for ITV, Tx: 15 January, 10.30pm (Grampian, Midlands, Teledu Cymru, TWW, Tyne Tees)

Regional variations: 16 January, 10.30pm (Granada), 18 January, 9.00pm (Anglia, Associated Rediffusion, Border, Channel Isles, Southern), 11.20pm (Scotland)

A Man of Our Times: *Got Yourself Sorted Out at All?*, 1968, 53 min.

(w. Julian Bond, prod. Richard Bates, executive prod. Stella Richman, des. Barbara Bates)

Cast: George Cole (Max Osborne), Jennifer Wilson (Muriel), Jean Harvey (Sally), Charles Tingwell (David Somes), Clive Morton (Henry Somes), Maxine Audley (Mrs Alcon), Maurice Hedley (Prentic), Nora Swinburne (Mrs Prentic), Diana Beevers (Gwen), Gabrielle Blunt (Shirley), Penny Durrell, Athene Fielding (Secretaries), Richard Cornish (Young Man)

Associated Rediffusion for ITV, Tx: 22 January, 10.30pm (Grampian, Midlands, Teledu Cymru, TWW, Tyne Tees)

Regional variations: 23 January, 10.30pm (Granada), 25 January, 9.00pm (Anglia, Associated Rediffusion, Border, Channel Isles, Southern), 11.20pm (Scotland)

* No recording exists

Half Hour Story: Goodnight Albert, 1968, 26 min.

(w. Roy Minton, prod. Stella Richman, des. John Clarke)
Cast: Victor Henry (Albert), Gwen Nelson (Mrs Parker)
Associated Rediffusion for ITV, Tx: 6 February, 7.30pm (Anglia, Associated Rediffusion, Tyne Tees)
Regional variations: 7 February, 10.30pm (Channel Isles), 8 February, 10.30pm (Scotland, Southern), 12 March, 8.30pm (Grampian), 19 March, 8.35pm (Granada), 3 April, 9.10pm (Midlands), 26 April, 8.00pm (Channel Ten, Teledu Cymru); Not in Border or Ulster

A Man of Our Times: Never Mind How We Got Here – Where Are We?, 1968, 53 min.

(w. Julian Bond, prod. Richard Bates, executive prod. Stella Richman, des. Barbara Bates)
Cast: George Cole (Max Osborne), Jean Harvey (Sally), Peter Barkworth (Roberts), Basil Henson (Oliver Manson), Shelagh Fraser (Mrs Manson), Christopher Witty (Michael), Lucy Appleby (Clare), Bruce Robinson (Rex Manson), Reg Peters (Waiter), Ralph Ball (Lomax)
Associated Rediffusion for ITV, Tx: 11 March, 10.30pm (Channel Ten, Grampian, Midlands, Teledu Cymru, Tyne Tees)
Regional variations: 12 March, 10.30pm (Granada), 14 March, 9.00pm (Anglia, Associated Rediffusion, Border, Channel Isles, Southern), 11.20pm (Scotland)
* No recording exists

Half Hour Story: Stella, 1968, 26 min.

(w. Alun Owen, prod. Stella Richman, des. Bernard Goodwin)
Cast: Geraldine Moffatt (Stella), Ray Smith (the man)
Associated Rediffusion for ITV, Tx: 18 June, 10.30 (Channel Isles)
Regional variations: 19 June, 9.00pm (Associated Rediffusion, Border, Grampian, Midlands, Tyne Tees, Ulster), 10.30pm (Granada), 20 June, 10.30pm (Scotland, Southern); Not Anglia, Harlech, Teledu Cymru

Half Hour Story: The Fifty-Seventh Saturday, 1968, 26 min.

(w. William Trevor, prod. Stella Richman, des. John Clements)
Cast: Frances White (Mavie), Ronnie Fraser (McCarthy)
Associated Rediffusion for ITV, Tx: 2 July, 10.30pm (Channel Isles)
Regional variations: 3 July, 9.00pm (Associated Rediffusion, Border,

Grampian, Midlands, Tyne Tees, Ulster), 10.30pm (Granada), 4 July, 10.30pm (Scotland), 6 July, 10.45pm (Harlech, Teledu Cymru)

Half Hour Story: *Nothing's Ever Over*, 1968, 26 min.

(w. Edna O'Brien, prod. Stella Richman, des. Barbara Bates)
Cast: Michael Craig (Him), Eileen Atkins (Her), Bill Lyons (Her clerk), Desmond Newling (His clerk), Mischa de la Motte (Judge)
Associated Rediffusion for ITV, Tx: 16 July, 10.30pm (Channel Isles)
Regional variations: 17 July, 9.00pm (Associated Rediffusion, Border, Grampian, Midlands, Tyne Tees, Ulster), 10.30pm (Granada), 18 July, 10.30pm (Scotland), 19 July, 11.10pm (Southern), 20 July, 10.45pm (Harlech, Teledu Cymru); Not transmitted in Anglia

Half Hour Story: *Thief*, 1968, 26 min.

(w. Alun Owen, prod. Stella Richman, des. Fred Pusey)
Cast: Sian Phillips (A Girl), Alan Lake (A Man)
Associated Rediffusion for ITV, Tx: 23 July, 10.30pm (Channel Isles)
Regional variations: 24 July, 9.00pm (Associated Rediffusion, Border, Grampian, Midlands, Tyne Tees, Ulster), 10.30pm (Granada), 25 July, 10.30pm (Scotland, Southern); Not transmitted in Anglia, Harlech or Teledu Cymru
* No recording exists

Company of Five: *Stand by Your Screen*, 1968, 53 min.

(w. Roy Minton, prod. Stella Richman, des. Roger Hall)
Cast: John Neville (Chris Gritter), Gwen Watford (Ada Gritter), Ann Bell (Bess Hogg), Cyril Luckham (Norman Gritter), Patricia Lawrence (May Green)
London Weekend Television (LWT) for ITV, Tx: 7 December, 9.55pm (Midlands, Tyne Tees, Yorkshire)
Regional variations: 8 December, 10.20pm (Anglia, Border, Grampian, Granada, Harlech, Harlech Wales, LWT), 14 December, 9.55pm (Central Scotland, Channel Isles); Not transmitted in Southern (who showed only three of the six *Company of Five* plays)

Company of Five: Gareth, 1968, 53 min.

(w. Alun Owen, prod. Stella Richman, des. Frank Nerini)
Cast: John Neville (Gareth Owen), Gwen Watford (Megan Owen), Ann Bell (Anne Gordon), Ray Smith (Thomas Davies), Edward Evans (John Williams), 'Pant-Cymro'
LWT for ITV, Tx: 14 December, 9.55pm (Midlands, Tyne Tees, Yorkshire)
Regional variations: 15 December, 10.20pm (Anglia, Border, Grampian, Granada, Harlech, Harlech Wales, LWT), 21 December, 9.55pm (Central Scotland, Channel Isles); Not transmitted in Southern (see above)

Saturday Night Theatre: The Piano Tuner, 1969, 53 min.

(w. Julia Jones, prod. Kenith Trodd, des. John Clements)
Cast: Frank Finlay (Wilfred Tiley), Daphne Slater (Miss Delia), Shelagh Fraser (Daphne), Helen Lindsay (Blanche), Kenneth Keeling (Wally), Hazel Coppen (woman in pub), Patsy Crowther (second woman)
LWT for ITV, Tx: 8 March, 9.00pm (Grampian, London Weekend Television), 9.30pm (Anglia, Border, Central Scotland, Channel Isles, Granada, Harlech, Harlech Wales, Midlands, Southern, Tyne Tees, Westward), 11.40pm (Yorkshire)

The Gold Robbers: The Arrangement, 1969, 53 min.

(w. Eric Coltart, prod. John Hawkesworth, des. Colin Piggott)
Cast: Peter Vaughan (Detective Chief Superintendent Cradock), Arto Morris (Detective Sergeant Thomas), Donald Webster (Tilt), Johnny Wade (Eddie Makin), Maria Aitken (Val), Johnny Shannon (George Nechros), George Innes (Dillo), Ronald Clarke (Nobby Clarke), Coral Atkins (Arlene Makin), Eileen Way (The Dowager), Nicholas Ball (Terry Cradock), Peter Copley (Asst. Commd. Farr), David Webb (Constable Miles), Harry Hutchinson (snooker room attendant), Trevor Martin (Bernie Makin), Raymond Smith (Billy Sweet)
LWT for ITV, Tx: 25 July, 9.00pm (Anglia, Border, Central Scotland, Grampian, Granada, Harlech, Harlech Wales, LWT, Midlands, Southern, Tyne Tees)
Regional variation: 8 August, 9.00pm (Yorkshire)

Plays of Today: The Ladies: Doreen and *Joan*, 1969, 1 hr 32 min.

(w. Alun Owen, prod. Ronald Travers, des. Christopher Thompson)
Cast of *Doreen*: Alan Lake (John), Ray Smith (Eric), Juliette St David

(Emma), Geraldine Moffatt (Doreen)
Cast of *Joan*: Ann Bell (Joan), Peter Sallis (Mr Street), Angela Pleasance (Jackson), Maurice Quick (Stephen)
Tx: BBC2, 18 September, 9.10pm
* No recording exists

The Wednesday Play: The Last Train Through Harecastle Tunnel, 1969, 1 hr 16 min.

(w. Peter Terson, prod. Irene Shubik, des. Derek Dodd)
Cast: Richard O' Callaghan (Fowler), John Le Mesurier (Judge Grayson), Paul Brooke (Farquhar), Iain Reid (Smith), Robert Hartley (McCullow), John Owens (Corporal), Bill Lyons (Truculent), Laurie Asprey (Brian), John Gray (Blondie), Jonathan Burn (2nd Lt Florence), Noel Dyson (Mrs Dyson), Claire Davenport (Megs), Victor Platt (Mr Dyson), Joe Gladwin (Adam Coulson), Griffith Davis (Jackie Coulson), John Scott Martin (Ticket man), Angela Pleasence (Beatrice Grayson), Shelagh Fraser (Mrs Grayson), Anthony Kelly (The gardener), Eileen Way (Mrs Phillips), Toke Townley (Mr Phillips)
Tx: BBC1, Wednesday 1 October, 9.10pm

Saturday Night Theatre: The Comic, 1969, 53 min.

(w. John Hales, prod. Kenith Trodd, des. Andrew Drummond)
Cast: George Cole (Tod), Isabel Dean (Peggy), Renée Houston (Olive), Hilary Dwyer (Judy)
LWT for ITV, Tx: 29 November, 10.10/10.15pm (Anglia, Border, Central Scotland, Channel Isles, Grampian, Granada, Harlech, Harlech Wales, London Weekend Television, Midlands, Southern, Tyne Tees, Yorkshire, Westward)

The Wednesday Play: Sovereign's Company, 1970, 1 hr 20 min.

(w. Don Shaw, prod. Irene Shubik, des. Colin Pigott, DoP Peter Hall)
Cast: Roland Culver (General Cantfield), Gareth Forwood (Andrew Cant-field), James Cosmo (Senior Under Officer Patterson), Stephen Shepherd (Junior Under Officer Sanders), Clive Francis (Dexter), James Hazeldine (Dawkins), Oliver Cotton (Sender), Larry Dann (Hurt), David Rowlands (Dankworth-Lowe), John Wentworth (General Decamps), Laurence Hardy (Colonel Frayne), Moray Watson (Major Hacker), John Nettleton (Major Grace), Graham Lines (Captain Lawrence), Raymond Adamson (R.S.M.

Power), Lewis Wilson (C.S.M. Larch), Norman Mann (Sergeant Liman), Norman Mitchell (Mr Dawkins), Margaret Lang (Mrs Dawkins), Chris Cunningham (Chauffeur), Ron Conrad (Youth), Stephen Carter (Nigerian Cadet)
Tx: BBC1, 22 April, 9.15pm

Play for Today: *I Can't See My Little Willie*, 1970, 1 hr 14 min.

(w. Douglas Livingstone, prod. Irene Shubik, des. Derek Dodd)
Cast: Nigel Stock (Arthur), George A. Cooper (Frank), Avril Elgar (Christine), Jo Rowbottom (Val), Daphne Slater (Mary), Frank Gatliff (Phillips), Ronald Clarke (Johnny), Michael Graham Cox (David), John Scott Martin (Landlord), Patsy Smart (Woman in bar), Matthew Clarke (Janicee), Elaine Donnelly (Louise), Malcom McFee (Peter), Elaine Mitchell (Susan), Harold Goodwin (Dennis), Bert Palmer (Mr Jones), Colin Cunningham (Man in bar), Penny Dixon (Waitress), Alan Lawrance (Salvationist), Harry Davis (Ben), Eric Lindsay, Fred Hugh, Eddie Connor (Barmen), Reggie Cross (Organist)
Tx: BBC1, 19 November, 9.20pm

Play for Today: *The Hallelujah Handshake*, 1970, 1 hr 15 min.

(w. Colin Welland, prod. Graeme McDonald, des. Colin Pigott, DoP John Wyatt)
Cast: Tony Calvin (Henry), Jeremy Wilkin (Geoff), John Phillips (Rev. Howard Whithead), Lynn Farleigh (Anne), Howell Evans (Bob), June Watson (Wendy), Sheelagh Wilcocks (Mrs Atkinson), Ann Curthoys (Brenda), Harry Davis (Alf), Queenie Watts (Connie), Myles Hoyle (Jim), Michael McKevitt (Andrews), Janet Burnell (Mrs Wyndham), Ralph Ball (Scoutmaster), George Selway, Wesley Murphy, Laurence Terry (Workmen), David Webb (Probation Officer), Eric Longworth (Clerk of the Court), Alan Foss (Magistrate), Simon Barnes (Arresting Officer), John Roden (Police Sergeant), Dennis Castle (Prison Warder), Andrew Benson (Son), Tracey Peryman (Daughter), Nelly Griffiths (Old lady)
Tx: BBC1, 17 December, 9.20pm

Play for Today: *Everybody Say Cheese*, 1971, 1 hr 13 min.

(w. Douglas Livingstone, prod. Irene Shubik, des. John Cooper)
Cast: Roy Kinnear (Henry Hunter), Avis Bunnage (Hylda Cheatham), James Hazeldine (George Green), George Tovey (Frank Cheatham), Christine Ozanne (Janet Cheatham), Winifred Sabine (Mrs Cramp),

Margaret Brady (Barbara), Esta Charkham (Dianne), Basil Clarke (Mr Old), Horace James ('The Maid'), Queenie Watts (Mrs Brass), Sara-Jane Ladbrook (Linda), John Scott Martin (Man at exhibition)
Tx: BBC1, 3 June, 9.20pm
* No recording exists

Thirty Minute Theatre: Under the Age, 1972, 31 min.

(w. E. A. Whitehead, prod. David Rose, des. Margaret Peacock)
Cast: Paul Angelis (Susie), Michael Angelis (Mike), Stephen Bent (Jack), David Lincoln (The Boy), Rosalind Elliot (Alice), Sylvia Brayshay (Sandra)
BBC Birmingham, Tx: BBC2, 20 March, 10.40pm

Horace, 1972, 1 hr 30 min.

(w. Roy Minton, prod. Mark Shivas, des. Colin Pigott, DoP John Wyatt)
Cast: Barry Jackson (Horace), Stephen Tantum (Gordon), Christine Hargreaves (Ivy), Talfryn Thomas (Dick), Hazel Coppen (Mrs Radford), James Mellor (Sidney), Patricia Lawrence (Miss Bowler), Robert Hartley (Mr Scrimshaw), Howard Goorney (Mr Frankel), Ken Perry (Whitsun), Caleigh Simmons (Brenda), Daphne Heard (Mrs Beal), Eric Francis (Customer), Pamela Miles (Waitress), Jeffrey Gardiner (Jeffries)
Tx: BBC2, 21 March, 9.20pm
* A spin-off series, *Horace*, was made by Yorkshire for ITV, airing at 7.00pm Tuesdays and Thursdays between 13 April and 29 April 1982 (w. Roy Minton, prod. Keith Richardson, d. James Cellan Jones)

To Encourage the Others, 1972, 1 hr 44 min.

(w. David Yallop, prod. Mark Shivas, des. Daphne Shortman)
Cast: Charles Bolton (Bentley), Billy Hamon (Craig), Roland Culver (Lord Goddard), Philip Stone (Humphreys), Wensley Pithey (Cassels), John Ringham (Parris), Arthur Lovegrove (Mr Bentley), Carmel McSharry (Mrs Bentley), Michael Sheard (Fairfax), Barbara Hickmott (Iris Bentley), Derrick Slater (Harrison), Ken Halliwell (McDonald), Graham Lines (Bass), Maurice Quick (Stevens), Ronald Mayer (Mr Craig), Vyvian Hall (Albert Bentley), Christopher Coll (Miles), Denis Cleary (Close), Dennis Castle (Warder), Roshan Seth (Jazwon), Keith Campbell (Nickolls), John Beardmore (Clerk of Court), Guy Graham (Foreman of Jury), Philip Howard (Usher)
Tx: BBC2, 28 March, 9.20pm

***Play for Today: A Life Is For Ever*, 1972**, 1 hr 16 min.

(w. Tony Parker, prod. Irene Shubik, des. Richard Henry)
Cast: Maurice O' Connell (Johnson), Neil Seiler (Gibson), David Hargreaves
(Peters), Lorrimer (Roy Boyd), Antony Webb (Gemmill), Basil Clarke
(Andrews), Roger Hume (Stradley), Tony Meyer (McCallister), Rick James
(Williams), Arthur Skinner (Marlow), Terence Davies (Buchan), Dennis
Castle (Morton), Simon Castle (Henderson), Ralph Ball (Teacher), Eric
French, Peter Jolley, Crawford Lyall (Prison Officers).
Tx: BBC1, Monday 16 October, 9.25pm
Repeat tx: BBC1, 11 July 1974, 9.25pm
* Although the BBC have no copy in their archives, I understand that there
is a print in circulation.

***The Edwardians: Horatio Bottomley*, 1972**, 1 hr 19 min.

(w. Julian Bond, prod. Mark Shivas, des. Fanny Taylor)
Cast: Timothy West (Horatio Bottomley), Henry Woolf (Tommy Cox), John
Normington (Julius Elias), Basil Clarke (W. J. B. Odhams), John Welsh (Mr
Justice Hawkins), June Brown (Eliza Bottomley), Michael Gover (Reuben
Bigland), Anthony Webb (Willie Lotinga), George Merritt (Old man),
Christopher Banks (Mr Justice Salter), Norman Claridge (Sir Charles
Russell KC), Norman Barrington (Melvyn Hayes), Robert Hartley (Frank
Russell), Frederick Hall (Travers Humphreys), John Gatrell (O'Hagan),
Fred McNaughton (Jury foreman), Guy Graham (Shareholder), Peter Jolley
(Member of audience), Terry Francis (Cashier), Reg Matthews (Greaney),
Johnny Clayton (Hess), Simon Conrad (Boy from Odhams)
Tx: BBC2, 28 November, 9.25pm

***Achilles Heel*, 1973**, 56 min.

(w. Brian Clark, prod. Verity Lambert, des. Roger Hall)
Cast: Martin Shaw (Dave Irwin), Charlotte Howard (Mandy Irwin), Fred
Griffiths (Wilf), Alan Barry (Ted), Margaret Heald (Girl), Matthew
Guinness (Pete Colwyn), Norman Jones (Jerry Wilbur), Richard Steele
(Doctor), John Rae (Mr Bennett), Mike Kinsey (First barman), Ronald
Hackett (Les Dawson), Michael Earl (First pub customer), Craig McFarlane
(Small boy), Kenneth Cranham (Gordon), Karen Boyes (Fiona), Ken
Haward (Man in car), Dan Caulfield (Second barman), Richard Henry
(Second pub customer), Brian Moore (Commentator)
LWT for ITV, Tx: 18 March, 10.15pm

Play for Today: *Man Above Men*, 1973, 1 hr 13 min.

(w. David Hare, prod. Mark Shivas, des. Fanny Taylor)
Cast: Gwen Watford (Susan), Alexander Knox (the Judge), John Gatrell (First Prosecuting Counsel), John Moore (Benson), John Salthouse (Andrews), Nellie Griffiths (Old woman), Cheryl Hall (Ann), Lewis Wilson (Attendant), Elizabeth Bell (Barbra), Louise Nelson (Nurse), Myles Hoyle (Ian), Charles Kinross (Second Prosecuting Counsel), Maggie Flint (Mrs Andrews), Amelia Bayntun (Mrs Marshall), Oliver Maguire (Kelly)
Tx: BBC1, 19 March, 9.25pm
* No recording exists

Play of the Month: *The Love-Girl and the Innocent*, 1973, 2 hr 7 min.

(w. Alexander Solzhenitsyn, adapted by Nicholas Bethell, David Burg, prod. Cedric Messina, des. Richard Henry, Robert Berk)
Cast: David Leland (Nemov), Gabrielle Lloyd (Lyuba), Richard Durden (Khomich), Patrick Stewart (Gurvich), Allan Surtees (Brylor), Michael Poole (Yakhimchuk), Barry Jackson (Gai), John Kane (Chegenyov), Barbara Hickmott (Granya), Theresa Watson (Shurochka), Alan Gerrard (Kolodey), Terence Davies (Kostya), John Quarmby (Mereshchun), Jan Conrad (Munitsa), Forbes Collins (Chmuta), Reg Pritchard (Ovchukhov), Hal Jeayes (Dorofeyev), Malcolm Hayes (Solomon), James Ottoway (Belobotnikov), Arthur Whybrow (Goldtooth), Eric Mason (Georgie), James Coyle (Lennie), Edward Finn (Vitka), John Herrington (Fomin), George Comack (Gontoir), Len Maley (Kaplyuzhnikov), Peter Schofield (Visiting Warder), Jeffrey Chegwin (Dimka), Trevor Lawrence (Angel), Violet Lee Own (Bella), Robert Robinson (Aga Mirza), Vass Anderson (Pososhkov), Anthony Brothers (Escort Sergeant), William Ridoutt (Bath orderly), Michael Golden (Cook), Alexis Chesnakov (Musician), David Ellison (First bricklayer), Norman Ettlinger (First foreman), Carl Forgione (First man), Peter Geddis (First gangleader), Brian Grellis (Machineshop foreman), Reg Hogarth (Accordionist), Merelina Kendall (First woman), Lynne Preston (First student), Frank Seton (Goner), Ted Valentine (Smith foreman)
Tx: BBC1, 16 September, 8.15pm

Play for Today: *Penda's Fen*, 1974, 1 hr 29 min.

(w. David Rudkin, prod. David Rose, des. Michael Edwards, DoP Michael Williams)
Cast: Spencer Banks (Stephen), Georgina Anderson (Mrs Franklin), John Atkinson (Reverend Franklin), Ron Smerczak (Joel), John Richmond (Headmaster), Ian Hogg (Arne), Jennie Hesselwood (Mrs Arne), John Scott

(Nicholas Pole), Roy Preston (Brott), Ian Gemmell (Harry), Joyce Grundy (Mrs Gisbourne), Ivor Roberts (Cooke), Moray Black (Sixth-former), Christopher Douglas (Honeybone), Frank Veasey (Council workman), Elizabeth Reville (Nurse), Pat Bowker (Joel's girl), Graham Leaman (Sir Edward), Helen McCarthy (Mrs Kings), Joan Scott (The Lady), Roy Gatenby (The Man), Geoffrey Staines (King Penda), Geoffrey Pennells (Demon), Martin Reynolds (Angel)
BBC Birmingham, Tx: BBC1, 21 March, 9.25pm

Play for Today: A Follower for Emily, 1974, 1 hr 3 min.

(w. Brian Clark, prod. Graeme McDonald, des. Richard Henry)
Cast: Herbert Ramskill (Harry Lenton), Betty Woolfe (Emily Selby), Frederick Bennett (Bert Nichols), Ella Milne (Edie Branch), June Watson (Matron), Jumoke Debayo (Evelyn), Margaret Heald (Jean), Bart Allison (Mr Morgan), Vi Delma (Mrs Gadsby), Jeanne Doree (Mrs Brown), Richard Gregory (Mr Railton), Claudette Critchlow (Jane), Valerie Murray (Maria), Barbara New (Ann Johnson), William Ridoutt (John Nichols), John Dolan (Mr Taylor), Toby Lenon (Mr Brammall), Julie May, Jacqueline Blackmore (Domestics)
Tx: BBC1, 4 July, 9.25pm

Play for Today: Funny Farm, 1975, 1 hr 33 min.

(w. Roy Minton, prod. Mark Shivas, des. Richard Henry)
Cast: Tim Preece (Alan Welbeck), Gordon Christie (Jack), Michael Percival (John), Chris Sanders (Bill Spence), Allan Surtees (Arthur Rothwell), Bernard Severn (Ted Spinner), Michael Bilton (Sidney Charlton), Wally Thomas (Mr Chadd), Kenneth Scott (Jonathan), Anthony Langdon (Les Dewhurst), Donald Bisset (Mr Scully), Terence Davies (Walter), John Locke (Jeff West), Helena McCarthy (Joyce), Francis Mortimer (Graham), Arnold Diamond (James Ball), Dorothy Frere (Edna Ball), Patricia Moore (Miss Taylor)
Tx: BBC1, 27 February, 9.25pm

Diane, 1975, 1 hr 35 min.

(w. 'David Agnew' [Jonathan Hales], prod. Mark Shivas, des. Austen Spriggs, DoP David Whitson, Peter Hall)
Cast: Janine Drzewicki [Duvitksi] (Diane), Frank Mills (Weaver), Tim Preece (Terry), Paul Copley (Jim), Charles Bolton (Harry), Colin Higgins

(Kevin), Oliver Maguire (Rooney), Dee Anderson (Carol), Mario Renzullo (Dave), Peter Hugo Daly (Benny), Peter Newby (Brian), David Janson (Alan)
Tx: BBC2, 9 July, 9.00pm

Love for Lydia, 1976, untransmitted

(w. Julian Bond, prod. Richard Bates)
* See Chapter 2. Clarke's episodes were never shown, though both exist in the archives. The episodes were remade for the transmitted series, which ran from 9 September 1977 on ITV and is now available on DVD

Plays for Britain: Fast Hands, 1976, 48 min.

(w. Roy Minton, prod. Barry Hanson, des. Alex MacIntyre)
Cast: Bill Buffery (Jimmy), Ernie Claydon (Eggie), Peter Spraggon (Ray Prince), Stephen Bill (Geoff), Gillian Taylforth (Maureen), Maria Charles (Hilda), Frederick Radley (Harry), Chas Bryer (Peter), Paul Davis (Warboys), Bruce Wells (MC), George Howard (Referee), Joe Devitt, Ron Horn, Mort Jackson, Joe Willsher (Seconds), Brian Hawksley (Dr Brittain)
Thames for ITV, Tx: 4 May, 9.00pm

Bukovsky, 1977, untransmitted

(independent production, prod. David Markham)
* See Chapter 2

Play for Today: Scum, 1977 untransmitted/1991, 1 hr 14 min.

(w. Roy Minton, prod. Margaret Matheson, des. Tony Thorpe, DoP John Wyatt)
Cast: Trainees: Raymond Winstone (Carlin), David Threlfall (Archer), Martin Phillips (Davis), Davidson Knight (Angel), John Blundell (Banks), Phil Daniels (Richards), Ray Burdis (Eckersley), Patrick Murray (Dougan), Ian Sharrock (Rhodes), Tony London (Woods), Peter Kinley (Betts), Sheridan Earl Russell (Jackson), Colin Mayes (Sumner), Trevor Butler (Toyne), Philip Da Costa (Formby), Peter Francis (Baldy), Steven Butler, Michael Deeks, Mark Dunn, Christopher Gilbert, Simon Howe, Mike Mungaven, Reggae Ranjha, William Vanderpuye. Officers: Richard Butler (Governor), John Judd (Sands), Bay White (Matron), Peter Gordon (Goodyear), Stewart Harwood (Greaves), Robin Hopwood (Burton), Dennis Castle (Duke),

David Stockton (White), Julian Hudson (PT Instructor), George Lee (Chief Officer), Sean Hopwood, Ray Jewers, Joe Fordham (Block officers)
Tx: (Intended: BBC1 *Play for Today* 8 November 1977, untransmitted), BBC2 *Alan Clarke Season*, 27 July 1991, 11.53pm
* Available on DVD in UK and US

Play of the Month: Danton's Death, 1978, 1 hr 34 min.

(w. Georg Büchner, freely adapted by Stuart Griffiths, Alan Clarke, prod. David Jones, des. Stuart Walker)
Cast: Norman Rodway (Danton), Ian Richardson (Robespierre), Peter Gordon (Delegate from Lyons), Katherine Fahy (Julie), Felicity Gibson (Marchioness), Mandy Woodward (Eugenie), Shane Briant (Herault-Sechelles), Anthony Higgins (Camille), Emma Williams (Marion), James Aubrey (Lacroix), Carole Harrison (Rosalie), Nell Brennan (Adelaide), Roger Sloman (Barere), Michael Pennington (Saint-Just), William March (Young gentleman), Michael Bilton (First gentleman), Christopher Banks (Second gentleman), Zoe Wanamaker (Lucille), Michael Hughes (Legendre), Don Henderson (Mercier), John Woodnutt (Fouquier-Tinville), Seymour Matthews (Herman), Jonathan Adams (Collot d'Herbois), Michael Cronin (Billaud-Varennes), Nigel Lambert (Narrator)
Tx: BBC1, 23 April, 8.05pm

Play for Today: Nina, 1978, 1 hr 17 min.

(w. Jehane Markham, prod. Margaret Matheson, des. Dick Coles, DoP Peter Bartlett)
Cast: Eleanor Bron (Nina), Jack Shepherd (Yuri), Merelina Kendall (Nursing Sister), Jonathan David (Dr Ivanov), Paul Lockwood (Kolya), Helena McCarthy (Mother), James Woolley (Adrian), Brian Hawksley (Dr McEndrick), Keith Campbell (Dr Golding), Roger Brierley (Trevor), Linda Polan (Yvonne), Alan Foss (Dr Peter Stein), Jonathan Darvill (Phillip), Jane Wood (Pam), Colin Higgins (Nicky), Bruce Boa (Arthur Bates), Kate Binchy (Betty Bates), Derek Brechin (TV interviewer)
Tx: BBC1, 17 October, 9.25pm

Scum, 1979, 1 hr 37 min.

(w. Roy Minton, prod. Davina Belling, Clive Parsons, associate prod. Martin Campbell, executive prod. Michael Relph, Don Boyd, art director Michael Porter, DoP Phil Meheux)
Cast: Ray Winstone (Carlin), Mick Ford (Archer), Julian Firth (Davis), John

Blundell (Banks), Phil Daniels (Richards), John Fowler (Woods), Ray Burdis
(Eckersley), Patrick Murray (Dougan), Herbert Norville (Toyne), George
Winter (Rhodes), Alrick Riley (Angel), Peter Francis (Baldy), Philip Da
Costa (Jackson), Perry Benson (Formby), Alan Igbon (Meakin), Andrew
Paul (Betts), Sean Chapman (James), Ozzie Stevens (Smith), Ricky Wales
(Chambers), Peter Howell (Governor), John Judd (Sands), Jo Kendall
(Matron), John Grillo (Goodyear), Philip Jackson (Greaves), Bill Dean
(Duke), P. H. Moriarty (Hunt), Nigel Humphreys (Taylor), James Donnelly
(Whittle), Joe Fordham (Reg), Ray Jewers (Gym Instructor), Ian Liston
(White), Charles Rayford (Philpott), John Rogan (Escort)
Film released by GTO/Berwick Street Films, GB
First tx: Channel Four, 10 June 1983, 11.30pm
* Available on DVD and VHS in UK and on DVD in US

Vodka Cola, 1980, 53 min.

(prod./dir. Alan Clarke, researcher Nicholas Claxton, photography Noel
Smart)
ATV for ITV, Tx 22 July, 10.30pm

Play for Today: Beloved Enemy, 1981, 1 hr 15 min.

(w. David Leland, prod. Keith Williams, des. Don Giles, DoP Elmer Cossey,
Barry McCann)
Cast: Graham Crowden (Sir Peter), Tony Doyle (Blake), Steven Berkoff
(Kozlov), Oscar Quitak (Whitaker), Larry Hoodekoff (Boris), Eileen Helsby
(Maggie), Wendy Gifford (Barbara), Richard Bebb (Robbie), Glenn
Williams (Waters), Jerry Harte (Kettner), Malcolm Ingram (Clive), Edward
Dentith (Bob), Czeslaw Grocholski (Vasin), George Pravda (Pervitsky), Jiri
Stanislav (Russian interpreter), Philippa Jarvis (English interpreter)
Tx: BBC1, 10 February, 9.25pm

Play for Today: Psy-Warriors, 1981, 1 hr 13 min.

(w. David Leland, prod. June Roberts, des. Marjorie Pratt)
Cast: Rosalind Ayres (Turner), Anthony Bate (Warren), Colin Blakely
(Northey), Warren Clarke (Stevens), Julian Curry (Hooper), John Duttine
(Stone), Derrick O'Connor (Richards), Laurence Payne (Weaver), Bill
Stewart (Doctor), Roger Evans, Terry Forrestal, David McGaw, Paul
Vaughan-Teague (Guards)
Tx: BBC1, 12 May, 10.15pm

Classic Play: Baal, 1982, 1 hr 3 min.

(BBC documentation states *Classic Play*, but was referred to as *David Bowie in Baal* on-screen and in publicity)
(w. Bertolt Brecht, adapted for television by John Willett and Alan Clarke, translated by John Willett, prod. Louis Marks, des. Tony Abbott)
Cast: David Bowie (Baal), Robert Austin (Mech), Russell Wootton (Piller), Julian Wadham (Johannes), Juliet Hammond-Hill (Emilie), Jonathan Kent (Eckhart), Wally Thomas (First cab driver), Roy Evans (Second cab driver), Michael Miller (Hargreaves), Sylvia Brayshay (Louise), Tracey Childs (Johanna), Paola Dionisotti (Porter's wife), Zoe Wanamaker (Sophie), Polly James (Soubrette), Hugh Walters (Pianist), Leon Lissek (Mjurk), Julian Littman (Lupu), James Duggan (First policeman), Bill Stewart (Second policeman), Brian Coburn (First woodcutter), P. J. Davidson (Second woodcutter), Michael Hughes (Third woodcutter), Trevor Cooper (Fourth woodcutter)
Tx: BBC1, 2 March, 9.25pm

Brief Encounters, 1983

(prod. Marshall Marinker, edited by John Holloway, Video Presentations)
MSD Foundation

Tales Out of School: Made in Britain, 1983, 1 hr 13 min.

(w. David Leland, prod. Margaret Matheson, art director Jamie Leonard, DoP. Chris Menges)
Cast: Tim Roth (Trevor), Terry Richards (Errol), Bill Stewart (Peter Clive), Eric Richard (Harry Parker), Geoffrey Hutchings (Superintendent), Sean Chapman (Barry Giller), John Bleasdale (Policeman), Noel Diacomo (Solicitor), Maurice Quick (Magistrate), Sharon Courtney (House Parent), Stephen Sweeney (Job Centre Youth), Kim Benson, Catherine Clarke (Job Centre Girls), Jean Marlow (Job Centre Woman), Jim Dunk (Chef), Vass Anderson (Canteen Manager), David Baldwin (Leroy), Allister Bain (Hopkins), Richard Bremmer (Policeman), Brian Hayes, Jiri Stanislav (Men on stairs), Frankie Cosgrove (Viv Parker), Christopher Fulford (PC Anson), Eric Kent, Joan Ware, Madelenine Athansi, Virginia Frol, Hyacinth Malcolm, Cathy Murphy, Gary Patrick, Ava Hrela
Central for ITV, Tx: 10 July, 10.30pm
* Available on DVD and VHS in UK and on DVD in US

The British Desk, 1984, 52 min.

(prod. Nicholas Claxton, editor Paul Cleary)
Central for ITV, Tx: 8 May, 10.30pm

Stars of the Roller State Disco, 1984, 1 hr 12 min.

(w. Michael Hastings, prod. Michael Wearing, des. David Hitchcock)
Cast: Perry Benson (Carly), Cathy Murphy (Paulette), Christina Greatrex
(Voicespeak), Paul McKenzie (Burt), Bernice Rowe (Deborah), Gary Beadle
(Derek), Suzette Llewellyn (Sharon), Kate Hardie (Margaret), Catherine
Clarke (Janice), David Sibley (Doctor), Christine Ozanne (Carly's mum),
Gary Hailes (Barry), Sam Smart (Jason), Steve Fletcher, Graham Fletcher
Cook (Hooligans), Pete Lee Wilson (Charles), Chris Lang (Desmond),
Gillian Taylforth (Kiosk typist), Lilian Rostkowska, Kamilla Blanche,
Beverley Martin, Nula Conwell (Typists), Ashley George (Marvis), Jason
Cunliffe ('Livver Boy'), Jem Ahmet (Fat boy), Dennis Savage (Weightlifter),
Richard Bremmer (Security guard), Charles Rayford (Night security guard),
John Blundell, Veronique Choolhum, Danny Schiller, Sarah Doyle, Debbie
Lennon, Miles Ross, David Chandler (Video training staff)
Tx: BBC1, 4 December, 9.25pm

Screen Two: Contact, 1985, 1 hr 6 min.

(w. A. F. N. Clarke, prod. Terry Coles, des. Michael Young, DoP Philip
Bonham-Carter)
Cast: Sean Chapman (Platoon commander), John Blundell (Corporal),
Ozzie Stevens (Lance Corporal), Jem Ahmet, Jason Cunliffe, Steve Fletcher,
Graham Fletcher Cook, Gary Hailes, Chris Lee, Dennis Savage, Sam Smart,
Steve Sweeney (Men), James Matthews (Farmer)
Tx: BBC2, Sunday 6 January, 10.10pm.

Billy the Kid and the Green Baize Vampire, 1986, 1 hr 30 min.

(w. Trevor Preston, lyrics by Trevor Preston/music by George Fenton, prod.
Simon Mallin, production designer Jamie Leonard, DoP Clive Tickner)
Cast: Phil Daniels (Billy Kid), Alun Armstrong (Maxwell Randall), Bruce
Payne (TO), Louise Gold (Miss Sullivan), Eve Ferret (Mrs Randall), Richard
Riding (Egypt), Don Henderson (The Wednesday Man), Neil McCaul (Big
Jack Jay), Zoot Money (Supersonic Sam), David Foxxe (The Spook), Johnny
Dennis (Referee), Trevor Laird (Floyd), Daniel Webb (TV Director), Ben
Cole, Peter Cooke, Trevor Cooper, Chrissie Cotterill, Sarah Crowden, Ricky

Diamond, Teresa Garraway, Peter Geeves, Glyn Grimstead, Tracie Hart, Sam Howard, Gareth Kirkland, Edwina Lawrie, Claire Lewis, Kevin Lloyd, Sarah London, Christian Mathews, Liz Morton, Paul Mulrannan, Clive Panto, Robert Pereno, Caroline Quentin, Nick Revell, George Rossi, Liza Sadovy, Roger Tebb, Claire Toeman, Tim Whitnall, Justin Case, Tony Chinn, Joe Fordham, Lisa Hart, Johnny Irving, Arnold Lee, Lyndsay Neil, Joan Rhodes, Fiona Sloman, Gillian de Terville
Film released by Zenith Productions with ITC Entertainment, GB
First tx: Channel Four, 2 April 1987

Rita, Sue and Bob Too, 1987, 1 hr 29 min.

(w. Andrea Dunbar, prod. Sandy Lieberson, co-prod. Patsy Pollock, executive prod. Oscar Levenstein, production designer Len Huntingford, DoP David Jackson, Steve Saunderson)
Cast: Siobhan Finneran (Rita), Michelle Holmes (Sue), George Costigan (Bob), Lesley Sharp (Michelle), Willie Ross (Sue's Father), Patti Nichols (Sue's Mother), Kulvinder Ghir (Aslam)
Film released by Umbrella Entertainment Productions for British Screen and Channel Four
First tx: Channel Four, 10 May 1990
* Available on DVD and VHS in UK

Screenplay: Christine, 1987, 51 min.

(w. Arthur Ellis, Alan Clarke, prod. Brenda Reid, des. John Coleman, DoP David Jackson, Steve Saunderson)
Cast: Vicky Murdock (Christine), Kelly George (Eddie), Joanne Mapp (Jessie), Mark Harvey (Ben), Anthony Smith (Eric)
Tx: BBC2, 23 September, 9.25pm

Screenplay: Road, 1987, 1 hr 2 min.

(w. Jim Cartwright, prod. Andree Molyneux, David M. Thompson, des. Stuart Walker, DoP John Ward, John Goodyear)
Cast: Jane Horrocks (Louise), Mossie Smith (Carol), Neil Dudgeon (Brink), William Armstrong (Eddie), Susan Brown (Helen), David Thewlis (Joey), Moya Brady (Clare), Alan David (Jerry), Lesley Sharp (Valerie), Barbara Keogh (Brenda), Tim Dantay (Soldier), Andrew Wilde (Brother), Willie Ross (Dad)
Tx: BBC2, 7 October, 9.25pm

Elephant, 1989, 37 min.

(w. no credit [BBC records attribute copyright to Alan Clarke, Bill Morrison, Chris Ryder], prod. Danny Boyle, des. Paul Clarke, DoP Philip Dawson, John Ward)
Cast: Gary Walker, Bill Hamilton, Michael Foyle, Danny Small, Robert Taylor, Joe Cauley, Noel McGee, Patrick Condren, Andrew Downs, Terence Doyle, Michael Liebmann, Gavin Bloomer, Barry Brent, Paul Nemeer, Sam Doyle, Burt Murray, Tim Loane, Kenny Harris, Paddy Rocks, Ken McIlroy, Hamish Fyfe, Trevor Moore, William Walker, Brian Giffen, Billy Dee, Michael Fieldhouse, William McAllister, Alan Craig, Stephen Potter, David McDade, Mark O'Donnell, James Moore, Mike Maxwell, Michael Magee, Nigel Craig, Liam Hefferon, B. J. Hogg, Bobby Stinton, Dave Bustard, Brian McGabhann, David Smith, Niall McLean
BBC Northern Ireland, Tx: BBC2, 25 January, 9.50pm
* Available on DVD in US

Screen Two: *The Firm*, 1989, 1 hr 7 min.

(w. Al Hunter, prod. David M. Thompson, des. Chris Robilliard, DoP John Ward, with Richard Philpott, Ben Philpott)
Cast: Gary Oldman (Bex), Lesley Manville (Sue), Philip Davis (Yeti), Andrew Wilde (Oboe), Charles Lawson (Trigg), William Vanderpuye (Aitch), Jay Simpson (Dominic), Patrick Murray (Nunk), Robbie Gee (Snowy), Terry Sue Patt (Yusef), Nick Dunning (Simon), Nicholas Hewetson (Beef), Steve McFadden (Billy), Steve Sweeney (JT), Hepburn Graham (Stu), Dan Hildebrand (Sully), Kevin Allen (Lomax), Roderick Smith (Cliffie), Martin Barrass (Alan), Stephen Petcher (Mark), Herbert Noville (Joe), William Hayes (Phil), Dave Atkins (Bill), Kim Durham (Hospital PC), Stefan Escreet (Travel agent), Robert Hamilton (Pullen), Phillip Joseph (Sociologist), Debbie Killingback (Gill), Mark Monero (Wesley), Cassie Stuart (Siobhan), Mandy Vickerman (Strippergram), Jo Warne (Ethel), James Woolley (Housebuyer), Albert Bentall (Sammy)
Tx: BBC2, 26 February, 10.10pm
* Available on DVD and VHS in UK and on DVD in US

Bibliography

Written sources

Ackroyd, P. (1983), 'House of cards', *The Times*, 4 July, 16.

Afton, R. (1978), 'Why must *we* pay for the BBC's £120,000 clanger?', *Daily News*, 26 January.

Althusser, L. (1971), *Lenin and Philosophy*, London, New Left Books.

Anonymous (1966), 'A *Macbeth* of violent contrasts', *Thames Valley Times*, 9 November.

—— (1967), 'Good scripts mean *Half Hour Story* is extended', *Stage and Television Today*, 8 June, 9.

—— (1968), 'Best director of the year Alan Clarke', *Questopics*, February.

—— (1969), 'Keeping faith with the viewer', *Radio Times*, 16 January, 4.

—— (1972), 'Out of the air', *Listener*, 13 April, 485.

—— (1975), 'The single play – a means of preserving and nurturing the creative talent among writers', *Stage and Television Today*, 9 October, 14.

—— (1976a), 'The attraction and scope of the original serial', *Stage and Television Today*, 18 March, 12.

—— (1976b), 'Richard Bates leaves *Love for Lydia*', *Stage and Television Today*, 20 May, 13.

—— (1976c), 'ADP challenges Bates "dismissal"', *Stage and Television Today*, 17 June, 12.

—— (1976d), advertisement for *Plays for Britain*, *Stage and Television Today*, 1 April, 23.

—— (1976e), 'Thames come back to the single play', *Stage and Television Today*, 1 April, 24.

—— (1977a), 'Viewers' reaction to BBC drama and comedy', *Stage and Television Today*, 7 April, 13.

—— (1977b), 'Tackling public subjects in plays that stand alone', *Stage and Television Today*, 1 September, 14.

—— (1977c), 'Looking for a booking', *The Times*, 29 June, 16.

—— (1978a), untitled article, *Daily Telegraph*, 28 January.

—— (1978b), 'Play for another day', *Times Educational Supplement*, 27 January, 2.

—— (1978c), '*Scum* decision commended', *The Times*, 10 February, 4.

—— (1978d), 'Milne talk – it's just routine', *Stage and Television Today*, 16 February, 13.

—— (1978e), 'DG and price paid for *Scum*', *Stage and Television Today*, 23 February, 13.

—— (1978f), 'Closer scrutiny needed before problems arise', *Stage and Television Today*, 26 January, 14.

—— (1978g), '"Play" intro opinion not fact – BBC', *Stage and Television Today*, 24 August, 15.

—— (1979), 'Scum to the top?', *Evening Standard*, 30 August.

—— (1981), 'Is it all fair, when we ask the questions?', *Radio Times*, 9–15 May, 5.

—— (1982a), 'Lack of incentive that has filtered through drama', *Stage and Television Today*, 17 June, 18–19.

—— (1982b), 'BBC plays – compiling a mix, advancing techniques', *Stage and Television Today*, 16 September, 14–15.

—— (1983), 'Storm in a teacup', *Broadcast*, 18 July, 15.

—— (1984), 'IBA error over referral of Borstal film', *The Times*, 14 April, 30.

—— (1985), 'A welcome decision that might turn tide', 'IBA's duty under Act' and 'Criticism of John Whitney was misplaced', *Stage and Television Today*, 11 April.

—— (1989a), 'Violence explored', *Times Educational Supplement*, 10 March, 20.

—— (1989b), 'Fear and loathing on the terraces', *Today*, 2 March, 9.

—— (1994), 'Alun Owen', *The Times*, 6 December.

—— (1996), 'Tony Parker', *The Times*, 11 October.

—— (1998), 'The 50 greatest TV moments of all time', *Cult TV*, June, 20.

Ansorge, P. (2003), 'Singled out: who killed the single play?', *ScriptWriter* 8.

Armstrong, G. (1998), *Football Hooligans: Knowing the Score*, Oxford, Berg.

Banks-Smith, N. (1972), '*A Life Is Forever*', *Guardian*, 17 October.

—— (1974), '*Penda's Fen*', *Guardian*, 22 March.

—— (1981), 'Bognor', *Guardian*, 11 February, 10.

—— (1985), 'Silent night, holding tight', *Guardian*, 7 January, 11.

Barker, S. (1983), 'The Leland films', *Independent Broadcasting*, 36, 3–6.

Barr, C. (1969), '*Au hasard, Balthazar*', in I. Cameron (ed.), *The Films of Robert Bresson*, London, Studio Vista, 106–14.

Barrett, H. (2002), 'Britain on the brink: Alan Clarke the lost provocateur', *Metro*, 131/132, 226–32.

Barron, C. (1975), 'Fine acting not enough for incest play that changed its style', *Stage and Television Today*, 17 July, 13.

Bazin, A. (1967), 'An aesthetic of reality: neo-realism', *What is Cinema?* Volume 1, Berkeley, University of California Press, 16–40.

—— (1969) '*Le Journal d'un cure de campagne*', in I. Cameron (ed.), *The Films of Robert Bresson*, London, Studio Vista, 51–67.

—— (1971a), 'De Sica: metteur en scène', *What is Cinema?* Volume 2, Berkeley, University of California Press, 61–78.

—— (1971b), '*Bicycle Thief*', *What is Cinema?* Volume 2, Berkeley, University of California Press, 47–60.

BBC (1972), *Violence on Television*, London, BBC.

BBC WAC (BBC Written Archives Centre files), *To Encourage the Others* R134/538/2: Camera script with major alterations, 22 March 1972; *To Encourage the Others* T47/220/1: Robin Scott Memo to The Solicitor, 2 November 1972; Daphne Shortman Memo to Head of Scenic Design Television, 16 June 1972; various Memos between the Solicitor, Christopher Morahan and Mark Shivas between October 1972 and January 1973.

Behr, M. (1972), untitled article, *Guardian*, 28 March.

Bell, J. (1989), 'Yob rule', *Daily Mirror*, 25 February, 13.

Benedictus, D. (1975), 'We've woken up to a grey dawn', *Stage and Television Today*, 4 September, 14.

Bennett, C. (1976), 'Richard Bates dismissal', *Stage and Television Today*, 8 July, 13.

Bentley, I. with P. Dening (1995), *Let Him Have Justice*, London, Sidgwick and Jackson.

Bermange, B. (1969), *No Quarter and The Interview*, London, Methuen.

Bignell, J., S. Lacey and M. Macmurraugh-Kavanagh (eds) (2000), *British Television Drama: Past, Present and Future*, Basingstoke, Palgrave.

Billington, M. (1968), 'An expert of the half-hour play', *The Times*, 20 June, 9.

Billy the Kid and the Green Baize Vampire (1986): press book and publicity material viewed at British Film Institute Library.

Black, P. (1972), *A Life Is For Ever* review, 17 October.

Bloch, E., G. Lukács, B. Brecht, W. Benjamin and T. Adorno (1977), *Aesthetics and Politics*, translated by Ronald Taylor, London, New Left Books.

Bordwell, D. (1982), 'Happily ever after, part two', *The Velvet Light Trap*, 19.

Bowen, J. (1972), 'Chickens', *New Statesman*, 7 April, 467.

Boumelha, P. (1987), 'George Eliot and the end of realism', in S. Roe (ed.), *Women Reading Women's Writing*, Brighton, Harvester.

Bowley, M. (1991), 'Let's make a theatre', *Guardian*, 23 January, 39.

Bragg, M. and T. Cash (1979), 'Criticism & self-criticism', *Encounter*, 53:4, 85–8.

Branigan, E. (1992), *Narrative Comprehension and Film*, London, Routledge.

Braun, E. (2000), '"What truth is there in this story?" The Dramatisation of Northern Ireland', in J. Bignell, S. Lacey and M. Macmurraugh-Kavanagh (eds), *British Television Drama: Past, Present and Future*, Basingstoke, Palgrave, 110–21.

Bream, P. (1972), 'Spreading wings at Kestrel', *Films and Filming*, 18:6, 36–40.

Brecht, B. (1978), quoted in J. Willett (ed.), *Brecht on Theatre: The Development of an Aesthetic*, London, Methuen Drama.

Bresson, R. (1997), *Notes on the Cinematographer*, translated by Jonathan Griffin, Copenhagen, Green Integer.

Bright, M. (1994), '*In the Name of the Father*', *Sight and Sound*, 4:3, 41–2.

Brooks, R. (1989), 'TV that's too near the knuckle', *Observer*, 5 March, 51.

Buckman, P. (1978), 'Broadcasting and the arts: money matters', *Listener*, 2 February, 149–50.

Burn, G. (1970), 'I've got to reach the people I've moved away from', *Radio Times*, 10 December, 9.

Buscombe, E. (1973), 'Ideas of authorship', *Screen*, 14:3, 75–85.

Bushell, G. (1988), 'Storm as BBC plan soccer yob TV shocker', *Sun*, 26 May, 32.

Campbell, P. (1972), 'The quiet revolution in BBC drama', *Stage and Television Today*, 10 February, 10.

—— (1973), '*The Love-Girl and the Innocent*', *Stage and Television Today*, 20 September, 16.

—— (1977), 'The writer overplayed his hand', *Stage and Television Today*, 24 November, 22.

Capsuto, S. (2003), '*Penda's Fen*', www.alternatechannels.org, accessed 7 April.

Carmody, R. (2001), '*Penda's Fen*', www.elidor.freeserve.co.uk/pendasfen. htm, 25 August. Accessed 7 April 2003.

Carpenter, H. (1998), *Dennis Potter: The Authorised Biography*, London, Faber and Faber.

Cartwright, J. (1986), *Road*, London, Samuel French.

Casey, B., N. Casey, B. Calvert, L. French and J. Lewis (2002), *Television Studies: The Key Concepts*, London, Routledge.

Cassidy, C. (1979), 'Men behind *Scum*', *Irish Times*, 1 August.

Caughie, J. (1980), 'Progressive television and documentary drama', *Screen*, 21:3, 9–35.

—— (2000a), *Television Drama: Realism, Modernism and British Culture*, Oxford, Oxford University Press.

—— (2000b), 'What do actors do when they act?', in J. Bignell, S. Lacey and M. Macmurraugh-Kavanagh (eds), *British Television Drama: Past, Present and Future*, Basingstoke, Palgrave, 162–74.

Chilcott, R. (2001), 'Alan Clarke', in Y. Allon, D. Cullen and H. Patterson (eds), *Contemporary British and Irish Film Directors*, London, Wallflower Press, 56–9.

Church, M. (1978), '... And a play you may not see', *The Times*, 23 January, 9.

Ciment, M. (1985), *Conversations with Losey*, London, Methuen.

Clarke, A. (1966), '*Macbeth* – Play of the Month: "Striking – Original"? "Wait and see" says Alan Clarke', *Questopics*, November.

Clarke, G. (1972), '*To Encourage the Others*', *Stage and Television Today*, 6 April, 9.

Clifford, A. (1991), 'The *Scum* manifesto', *Guardian*, 16 July, 30.

Cohen, S. (1980), *Folk Devils and Moral Panics*, Oxford, Martin Robertson.

Cook, J. R. (1998), *Dennis Potter: A Life on Screen*, Manchester, Manchester University Press.

Cooke, L. (2003), *British Television Drama: A History*, London, BFI.

Copeland, S. (1969), 'Fellows & birds', *Sunday Times*, 30 March.

Coren, A. (1989), 'A double-barrel blast at censors', *Mail on Sunday*, 5 March, 35.

Cornell, P, M. Day and K. Topping (1996), 'Alan Clarke', *Guinness Book of Classic British TV*, Enfield, Guinness, 390.

Corner, J. (1996), *The Art of Record: A Critical Introduction to Documentary*, Manchester, Manchester University Press.

Cotton, B. (2000), *Double Bill: 80 Years of Entertainment*, London, Fourth Estate.

Cropper, M. (1989), 'Thuggery and skulduggery', *The Times*, 27 February, 16.

Curtis, L. (1984), *Ireland: The Propaganda War*, London, Pluto.

Cushman, R. (1976), 'Dennis Potter: the values of a television playwright', *Radio Times*, 3–9 April 1976, 61–5.

Danaher, G. and T. Schirato, J. Webb (2000), *Understanding Foucault*, London, Sage.

Davalle, P. (1983), 'Weekend choice', *The Times*, 2 July, 7.

Davis, A. (1967), 'For me – drama without padding', *TV Times* Southern region, 13–19 May, 8.

Dawson, J. (1979), '*Scum*', *Monthly Film Bulletin*, 46:548, 201–2.

Day-Lewis, S. (1972), *A Life Is For Ever* review, *Daily Telegraph*, 17 October.

Dickens, C. (1874), *Oliver Twist*, London, Chapman and Hall.

Dickson, A. (1989), 'BBC breaking its own guidelines, says Whitehouse', *Sunday Telegraph*, 5 March, 5.

Dugdale, J. (1989), 'Watching week', *Listener*, 23 February, 41.

Dunbar, A. (2000), *Rita, Sue and Bob Too*, London, Methuen.

Edmands, R. and N. Hewitt (1968), 'Just a face looking', *Torchlight*, 15 November, 9.

Eyre, R. and N. Wright (2001), *Changing Stages: A View of the British Theatre in the Twentieth Century*, London, Bloomsbury.

Fenwick, H. (1978), 'Exiles', *Radio Times*, 14–20 October, 4–5.

—— (1982), 'The man who fell for Brecht', *Radio Times*, 27 February–5 March, 6–7.

Fiddick, P. (1977), 'You will be shocked ...', *Guardian*, 9 November, 10.

—— (1978), 'A brutal truth barred from the screens', *Guardian*, 23 January, 8.

—— (1991), 'Out of the bunker, into the light', *Guardian*, 22 July, 21.

Forwood, M. (1983), 'Rape horror to be shown on 4', *Sun*, 4 June.

Foucault, M. (1980), *Power/Knowledge: Selected Interviews and Other Writings 1972–1977*, translated by C. Gordon, Brighton, Harvester Press.

—— (1981), 'What is an author? (extract)', in J. Caughie (ed.), *Theories of Authorship*, London, Routledge & Kegan Paul/BFI, 282–91.

—— (1984), *The Foucault Reader*, P. Rabinow (ed.), London, Penguin.

—— (1991), *Discipline and Punish: The Birth of the Prison*, translated by A. Sheridan, Harmondsworth, Penguin.

—— (1997), *Ethics: Essential Works of Foucault 1954–1984, Vol. 1*, P. Rabinow (ed.), London, Penguin.

Frick, N. A. (1967), 'Many good moments in Owen play', *Stage and Television Today*, 25 May, 12.

Fuller, G. (ed.) (1998), *Loach on Loach*, London, Faber and Faber.

Garnett, T. (2000), 'Contexts', in J. Bignell, S. Lacey and M. Macmurraugh-Kavanagh (eds), *British Television Drama: Past, Present, Future*, Basingstoke, Palgrave, 11–23.

——, J. Allen, R. Battersby, C. Goodwin, K. Loach, J. MacTaggart, R. Smith and K. Trodd (1969), 'Keeping faith with the viewer: a letter to the editor', *Radio Times*, 13 February, 2.

Gilbert, W. S. (1978), 'The case for *Scum*', *Observer*, 29 January.

—— (1980), 'The television play: outside the consensus', *Screen Education*, 35.

—— (1981), 'Off-air', *Broadcast*, 25 May, 12.

—— (1989), 'Briefing', *Independent*, 25 January, 29.

—— (1990), 'Alan Clarke', *Guardian*, 26 July, 13.

—— (1995), *Fight & Kick & Bite: The Life and Work of Dennis Potter*, London, Hodder & Stoughton.

Gillman, P. (1972), '"Let him have it!" – did Bentley say it?', *Radio Times*, 23 March, 6–7.

Gitlin, T. (1994), *Inside Prime Time*, London, Routledge.

Gore Langton, R. (1986), '*Road*', *Plays and Players*, 395, 25.

Gow, G. (1979), '*Scum*', *Films and Filming*, 25:11, 31–2.

Gramsci, A. (1971), *Selection from Prison Notebooks*, London, Lawrence & Wishart.

Greenfield, S. and G. Osborn (1996), 'Pulped fiction? Cinematic parables of (in)justice', *University of San Francisco Law Review*, 30:4, 1181–98.

Greengrass, P. (2002), 'My hero: Alan Clarke', *Guardian* G2, 1 February, 8.

Greenslade, R. (2000), 'Editors as censors: the British press and films about Ireland', *Journal of Popular British Cinema*, 3, 77–92.

Hall, S. (1988), *The Hard Road to Renewal: Thatcherism and the Crisis of the Left*, London, Verso.

Hansard (1970), Cransley Onslow and Ian Gilmour, Defence: Oral answers to questions, House of Commons, 29 October, in *Hansard* (Parliamentary Debates), Fifth Series Volume 805, Session 1970–71, column 20.

—— (1972), Russell Kerr and Reginald Maudling, Written Answers, House of Commons, 25 May, in *Hansard* (Parliamentary Debates), Fifth Series Volume 837, Session 1971–72, columns 435–7.

Hardy, P. (1970), *Samuel Fuller*, London, Studio Vista.

Hare, D. (1990), 'A camera for the people', *Guardian*, 27 July, 35.

—— (2002), 'Theatre's great malcontent', *Guardian* Review, 8 June, 4–6.

Hattenstone, S. (1998), 'Hitting where it hurt', *Guardian* Review, 1 August, 4.

Hayward, S. (1993), *French National Cinema*, London, Routledge.

Hebert, H. (1989), 'Bloodless coup', *Guardian*, 27 February, 38.

—— (1994), 'A man of many parts', *Guardian*, 20 September, 6.

Hewson, D. (1984), 'TV victory for Whitehouse as judges rebuke IBA on *Scum*', *The Times*, 14 April, 4.

Hiley, J. (1984), 'Going round in circles', *Radio Times*, 1–7 December, 94.

—— (1985), 'Other highlights', *Listener*, 3 January, 31.

Hill, D. (1976), 'Where he went wrong was having a big tea before the fight', *TV Times* Yorkshire region, 1–7 May, 8–9.

Hill, J. (1986), *Sex, Class and Realism: British Cinema 1956–1963*, London, BFI.

—— (1997a), 'Interview with Ken Loach', in G. McKnight (ed.), *Agent of Challenge and Defiance: The Films of Ken Loach*, Trowbridge, Flicks Books, 160–76.

—— (1997b), 'Finding a form: politics and aesthetics in *Fatherland*, *Hidden Agenda* and *Riff-Raff*', in McKnight, *Agent of Challenge and Defiance*, 125–43.

—— (1999), *British Cinema in the 1980s: Issues and Themes*, Oxford, Clarendon Press.

—— (2000), 'From the New Wave to "Brit-grit": continuity and difference in working-class realism', in J. Ashby and A. Higson (eds), *British Cinema, Past and Present*, London, Routledge, 249–66.

—— and M. McLoone (eds) (1996), *Big Picture, Small Screen: The Relations between Film and Television*, Luton, University of Luton Press.

Hoggart, R. (1957), *The Uses of Literacy*, London, Chatto & Windus.

—— (1980), 'Ulster: a "switch-off" TV subject?', *Listener*, 2 February, 261–2.

Hollingsworth, M. and R. Norton-Taylor (1988), *Blacklist*, Basingstoke, Macmillan.

Honigsbaum, M. (2001), 'Coke and the reel thing', *Guardian* Guide, 20 January, 5.

Hooligan '96, video accompanying the staging of the European Championships in England in 1996.

Hopkins, D. (2000), *After Modern Art: 1945–2000*, Oxford, Oxford University Press.

Houston, P. (1984), Introduction to 'British cinema: life before death on television', *Sight and Sound*, 53:2, 115–16.

Hunt, A. (1981), *The Language of Television: Uses and Abuses*, London, Eyre Methuen.

Hutchinson, M. (1987), 'Grim and gritty reflections of life's estate', *Hampstead and Highgate Express*, 28 August, 20.

Isaacs, J. (1989), *Storm Over 4: A Personal Account*, London, Weidenfeld and Nicolson.

Jacobs, J. (2000), *The Intimate Screen: Early British Television Drama*, Oxford, Clarendon Press.

Jessop, B. and K. Bonnett, S. Bromley, T. Ling (1988), *Thatcherism: A Tale of Two Nations*, Cambridge, Polity Press.

Jobson, R. (2004), 'The ten best gang movies', *Independent*, 23 July, 12.

Karpf, A. (1989), 'Blanket protest', *Listener*, 9 March, 8–9.

Kelly, R. (1998), *Alan Clarke*, London, Faber and Faber.

—— (2002a), National Film Theatre: Alan Clarke season notes, February, 14–17.

—— (2002b), National Film Theatre: Alan Clarke season notes, March, 8–11.

Kennedy Martin, T. (1964), 'Nats go home: first statement of a new drama for television', *Encore*, 48, 21–33.

King, F. (1968), 'The screening of Aida', *Listener*, 15 February, 219–20.

Knight, D. (1997), 'Naturalism, narration and critical perspective: Ken Loach and the experimental method', in G. McKnight (ed.), *Agent of Challenge and Defiance: The Films of Ken Loach*, Trowbridge, Flicks Books, 60–81.

Knowles, S. (1977), 'Lydia goes skating – and four men fall for her', *TV Times* Yorkshire region, 3–9 September, 8–11.

Kolker, R. (1998), 'The film text and film form', in J. Hill and P. Church Gibson (eds), *The Oxford Guide to Film Studies*, Oxford, Oxford University Press, 11–23.

Last, R. (1978), 'Author of banned play accuses BBC', *Daily Telegraph*, 21 January.

—— (1989), 'Depraved and corrupt', *Daily Telegraph*, 27 February 1989, 13.

Lawrence, J. (1970), 'Environment somehow did not ring true', *Stage and Television Today*, 23 December, 9.

Lawrenson, E. (2004), 'The Football Factory', *Sight and Sound*, 14:6, 56–7.

Lawson, M. (1989), 'The Irish way of death', *Independent*, 26 January, 14.

Lawson, P. (1974), *Penda's Fen* review, *Sunday Times*, 24 March.

Leapman, M. (1987), *The Last Days of the Beeb*, London, Coronet.

Leland, D. (1986), *Tales Out of School: Made in Britain*, Cambridge, Cambridge University Press.

Lennon, P. (1989a), 'The smell of corruption', *Listener*, 2 February, 36–7.

—— (1989b), 'Terrorists of the terrace', *Listener*, 2 March, 46.

Limmer, K. (2003), '*Rita, Sue and Bob Too*: investigating the authority of the literary text in critical debate', conference paper presented at Reading Screens: from text to film, TV and new media, Oxford University.

Lowe, S. (1972), 'Veracious', *Morning Star*, 21 October.

Lucas, T. (2004), 'Secret weapon', *Sight and Sound*, 14:11, November, 75.

Lukács, G. (1973), *Marxism and Human Liberation*, New York, Delta.

McArthur, C. (1975/6), '*Days of Hope*', *Screen*, 16:4, 139–44.

—— (1981), 'Historical drama', in T. Bennett, S. Boyd-Bowman, C. Mercer and J. Woollacott (eds), *Popular Television and Film*, London, BFI, 288–301.

MacCabe, C. (1974), 'Realism and the cinema: notes on some Brechtian theses', *Screen*, 15:2, 7–27.

—— (1976), '*Days of Hope*: a response to Colin McArthur', *Screen*, 17:1, 98–101.

McGrath, J. (1977), 'TV drama: the case against naturalism', *Sight and Sound*, 46:2, 100–5.

McIlroy, B. (2001), *Shooting to Kill: Filmmaking and the 'Troubles' in Northern Ireland*, Richmond, Steveston Press.

Malcolm, D. (1987), 'Nowt but truth', *Guardian*, 3 September, 15.

Malone, M. (1974), 'The "magic" box earns its keep', *Daily Mirror*, 22 March.

Mansfield, M. (1994), 'Writer's block: Jurassic justice', *Sight and Sound*, 4:3, 7.

Markham, D. (1978), 'The banning of *Scum*', *The Times*, 30 January, 13.

Martin, M. (1990), 'Moving image of the hooligans', *Sunday Telegraph*, 11 February, 42.

Miller, R. (1973), 'The writer out in the cold', *Radio Times*, 13 September, 66–71.

Millington, B. (1984), 'Making *Boys from the Blackstuff*: a production perspective', in R. Paterson (ed.), *BFI Dossier 20: Boys from the Blackstuff*, London, BFI, 4–20.

—— and R. Nelson (1986), *Boys from the Blackstuff: Making a TV Drama*, London, Comedia.

Minton, R. (1979), *Scum*, London, Hutchinson.

Morace, R. A. (2001), *Irvine Welsh's Trainspotting*, New York, Continuum.

Moreton, A. (1967), 'Ian Hendry at his cryptic best', *Stage and Television Today*, 7 December, 12.

—— (1968), 'What was the author driving at?', *Stage and Television Today*, 12 December, 12.

Morgan, J. (1980), *Report of the Seminar 'The Television Play and Contemporary Society'*, London, University of London Goldsmith's College.

Munro, C. R. (1979), *Television, Censorship and the Law*, London, Saxon House.

Murphy, P., J. Williams and E. Dunning (1990), *Football on Trial: Spectator Violence and Development in the Football World*, London, Routledge.

Murphy, S. (2003), 'The representation of violence in Northern Irish culture', unpublished seminar paper presented at The University of Hull, 24 March.

Murray, J. (1974), 'Teenager in nightmare world of grown-ups', *Daily Express*, 22 March.

—— (1978), 'TV shocker', *Daily Express*, 21 January.

—— (1979), 'Borstal', *Daily Express*, 28 January.

Naipaul, S. (1975), 'Madness and their methods', *Radio Times*, 20 February, 14–15.

Nichols, B. (1991), *Representing Reality: Issues and Concepts in Documentary*, Bloomington, Indiana University Press.

Nightingale, B. (1981), 'Nasty business', *Radio Times*, 7–13 February, 14–15.

Norman, B. (1989), 'Talking pictures', *Radio Times*, 25 February–3 March, 16.

Nowell-Smith, G. (1981), 'A note on history/discourse', in J. Caughie (ed.), *Theories of Authorship*, London, Routledge & Kegan Paul/BFI, 232–41.

Oppenheimer, P. (1996), *Evil and the Demonic: A New Theory of Monstrous Behaviour*, New York, New York University Press.

Orr, J. (2000), *The Art and Politics of Film*, Edinburgh, Edinburgh University Press.

—— (2002), 'Traducing realisms: *Naked* and *Nil By Mouth*', *Journal of Popular British Cinema*, 5, 104–13.

Orwell, G. (1949), *Nineteen Eighty-Four*, London, Martin Secker & Warburg.

—— (1968), *The Collected Essays, Journalism and Letters 2*, London, Secker & Warburg.

Owen, A. (1968), *Thief*, unpublished camera script viewed at British Film Institute Library.

Paget, D. (1998a), *No Other Way to Tell It: Dramadoc/Docudrama on Television*, Manchester, Manchester University Press.

—— (1998b), '*Road*: from Royal Court to BBC – Mass Observation/minority culture', in J. Ridgman (ed.), *Boxed Sets: Television Representations of Theatre*, Luton, University of Luton Press, 107–27.

Palmer, M. (1970), 'Coaxing the writer out of his garret', *Radio Times*, 12 November, 5.

Parker, T. (1970), *The Frying-Pan: A Prison and Its Prisoners*, London, Hutchinson.

—— (1972), *A Life Is For Ever*, unpublished script viewed at the British Film Institute Library.

—— (1973), *A Man Inside: An Anthology of Writing and Conversational Comment by Men in Prison*, London, Michael Joseph.

Parkinson, M. (1978), 'Mike Parkinson', *Daily Express*, 28 January.

Paterson, P. (1989), 'On very unfirm ground!', *Daily Mail*, 27 February, 23.

Penfold, P. (1994), 'Truth or friction', *Yorkshire on Sunday*, 6 February, 62.

Pennant, C. (2002), *Congratulations You Have Just Met The ICF*, London, John Blake Publishing.

Perkins, V. F. (1972), *Film as Film: Understanding and Judging Movies*, London, Pelican.

Petit, C. (1989), 'Violence rules, OK!', *The Times*, 25 February, 38–9.

Petley, J. (1985), 'The upright houses & the romantic Englishwoman: a guide to the political theatre of David Hare', *Monthly Film Bulletin*, 52:614, 71–2.

Phillips, J. L. (1968), 'How the medium is now creating its own style', *Stage and Television Today*, 5 September, 10.

Philpott, T. (1969), 'More compelling than fiction', *Radio Times*, 20 February, 33.

Pilger, J. (1999), *Hidden Agendas*, London, Vintage.

Potter, D. (1974), 'Boy in a landscape', *New Statesman*, 29 March, 459.

—— (1975), 'Switch back', *New Statesman*, 7 March, 319.

—— (1994), *Seeing the Blossom*, London, Faber and Faber.

—— (1996), *Karaoke and Cold Lazarus*, London, Faber and Faber.

Preziosi, A. (1995), 'Tre film e tanti TV-play – Alan Clarke', *Segnocinema*, 15:75, 79.

Questors Theatre: listing of productions, production details, reviews, access to photographs, and pieces from *Questopics* listed separately.

Rabey, D. I. (1994), 'Rudkin, (James) David', in M. Hawkins-Dady (ed.), *International Dictionary of Theatre – 2, Playwrights*, Detroit, St James Press, 825–6.

—— (1997), *David Rudkin: Sacred Disobedience – An Expository Study of his Drama 1959–96*, Amsterdam, Harwood Academic.

Raynor, H. (1967a), 'Simplified history of opera', *The Times*, 20 May, 7.

—— (1967b), 'Radio play for television', *The Times*, 31 August, 5.

—— (1968), 'Tactful play on sex', *The Times*, 25 July, 6.

Reader, K. (2000), *Robert Bresson*, Manchester, Manchester University Press.

Road, A. (1979), '*Scum* for the big screen', *Observer Magazine*, 15 April.

Robertson, G. (1985), 'Censorship could be less than IBA now imposes', *Stage and Television Today*, 8 August, 19.

Robinson, K. (1978), 'Out of the air: *Scum* spiked', *Listener*, 2 February, 143.

Rotha, P. (1949), *The Film Till Now*, London, Vision Press.

Rothman, W. (1988), *The 'I' of the Camera: Essays on Film Criticism, History and Aesthetics*, Cambridge, Cambridge University Press.

Rudkin, D. (1974), 'I wanted to write something that grew out of the landscape', *Radio Times*, 14 March, 12.

—— (1975), *Penda's Fen*, London, Davis-Poynter.

—— (2003), '*Penda's Fen*', www.davidrudkin.com/html/penda.html, accessed 7 April.

Rumley, S. (1999), 'Call sheet: *Scum*', *Film Review*, 588, 76–81.

Ryerson Institute of Technology: Programmes of studies in Radio and Television Arts 1958–59, 1959–60, 1960–61; 1959 Ryersonia article on the soccer team and Clarke's 1961 graduation entry.

Sarris, A. (1968), *The American Cinema*, New York, Dutton.

Sartain, D. (1971), '*Play for Today: Everybody Say Cheese*', *Stage and Television Today*, 10 June, 11.

Saunders, J. (1968), *Neighbours and Other Plays*, London, Heinemann.

Sawicki, J. (1992), *Disciplining Foucault*, London, Routledge.

Saynor, J. (1992), 'Writers' television', *Sight and Sound*, 2:7, 28–31.

Schlesinger, P. and G. Murdock, P. Elliott (1983), *Televising 'Terrorism': Political Violence in Popular Culture*, London, Comedia.

Schuman, H. (1998), 'Alan Clarke: in it for life', *Sight and Sound*, 8:9, 18–22.

Scovell, B. (1989), 'Palace fury over BBC play', *Daily Mail*, 28 February, 39.

Selway, J. (1979), 'Terms of confinement', *Time Out*, 21 September.

Sexton, J. (2003), '"Televerite" hits Britain: documentary, drama and the growth of 16mm filmmaking in British television', *Screen*, 44:4, 429–44.

Shaw, D. (1970), '*Sovereign's Company*', *Stage and Television Today*, 12 November, 14.

Shepherd, S. (1994), 'Pauses of mutual agitation', in J. Barron, J. Cook and C. Gledhill (eds), *Melodrama: Stage, Picture, Screen*, London, BFI, 25–37.

Shivas, M. (1990), postscript to D. Hare, 'A camera for the people'.

Shubik, I. (2000), *Play for Today: The Evolution of Television Drama*, Manchester, Manchester University Press.

Singer, A. (1978), 'A film on Mr Bukovsky', *The Times*, 2 February, 15.

Smurthwaite, N. (1987), '*Road*', *Stage and Television Today*, 8 October, 21.

Solzhenitsyn, A. (1969), *The Love-Girl and the Innocent*, London, The Bodley Head.

—— (1974), *The Gulag Archipelago*, London, Fontana.

Sweeting, A. (1989), 'Anatomy of a lout', *Guardian*, 24 February, 34.

Taubin, A. (1994), 'Small screen giant', *Village Voice*, 20 September, 60–2.

Tessé, J. (2003), 'De l'origine d'une espèce', *Cahiers du Cinéma*, October, 15.

Thatcher, M. (1989), *The Revival of Britain: Speeches on Home and European Affairs*, London, Aurum.

Thomas, A. (1987a), 'Goodchild takes a risk on a trial run', *Stage and Television Today*, 16 July, 18.

—— (1987b), 'Going for sex, drugs and rock 'n' roll', *Stage and Television Today*, 14 May, 16.

Thompson, K. and D. Bordwell (1994), *Film History: An Introduction*, New York, McGraw-Hill.

Thomson, D. (1993), 'Walkers in the world: Alan Clarke', *Film Comment*, 29:3, 78–83.

—— (1995), 'Alan Clarke', *Biographical Dictionary of Film*, London, André Deutsch, 131–3.

—— (2002), 'Film studies: They don't make 'em like him anymore', *Independent on Sunday* Arts Etc., 3 February, 9.

Todorov, T. (1977), *The Poetics of Prose*, Oxford, Basil Blackwell.

Tordoff, S. (2002), *City Psychos: from the Monte Carlo Mob to the Silver Cod Squad*, Bury: Milo Books.

Towler, J. (1970), 'The character I remember most', *Stage and Television Today*, 19 February, 12.

Tribe, K. (1977/8), 'History and the production of memories', *Screen*, 18:4, 9–22.

Trodd, K. (1983), 'Introduction to Trodd Index', in J. Pilling, K. Canham (eds.), *The Screen on the Tube: Filmed TV Drama*, Norwich, Cinema City.

Trow, M. J. (1990), *Let Him Have It, Chris*, London, Constable.

Truss, L. (1991), 'Walking-shots run on the wild side', *The Times*, 10 August, 19.

Tulloch, J. (1990), *Television Drama: Agency, Audience and Myth*, London, Routledge.

Usher, S. (1978), '"Pirate" showing for a banned TV play', *Daily Mail*, 21 January.

Venner, M. (2001), 'I'm the Daddy now! Or how great British realist Alan Clarke can be father of NYC cool', *Film Ireland*, 83, 20–3.

Walker, A. (1985), *National Heroes: British Cinema in the Seventies and Eighties*, London, Harrap.

Walsh, M. (2000), 'Thinking the unthinkable: coming to terms with Northern Ireland in the 1980s and 1990s', in J. Ashby and A. Higson (eds), *British Cinema, Past and Present*, London, Routledge, 288–98.

Ward, C. (1996), 'Tony Parker', *Independent*, 11 October.

Warner, M. (1994), *Managing Monsters: Six Myths of Our Time*, London, Vintage.

Welland, C. (1970), *The Hallelujah Handshake*, unpublished script viewed at British Film Institute Library.

White, H. (1981), 'The value of narrativity in the representation of reality', in W. J. T. Mitchell (ed.), *On Narrative*, Chicago, University of Chicago Press, 1–23.

—— (1996), 'The modernist event', in V. Sobchack (ed.), *The Persistence of History: Cinema, Television, and the Modern Event*, New York, Routledge, 17–38.

—— (1998), 'The historical text as literary artifact', in B. Fay, P. Pomper, R. T. Vann (eds), *History and Theory*, Oxford, Blackwell, 15–33.

Whitehead, P. (1972), 'Television: minorities', *Listener*, 30 March, 432–3.

Willett, J. (1998), *Brecht in Context*, London, Methuen.

Williams, P. (1978), 'Milne to meet BBC drama department to air censoring questions', *Broadcast*, 20 February.

Williams, R. (1971), *Orwell*, Glasgow, Fontana/Collins.

—— (1976), *Keywords*, London, Fontana.

—— (1977a), 'A lecture on realism', *Screen*, 18:1, 61–74.

—— (1977b), 'Realism, naturalism and the alternatives', *Cine-Tracts*, 1:3.

—— (1979), *Politics and Letters*, London, New Left Books.

Wootton, A. (1987), '*Rita, Sue and Bob Too*', *Monthly Film Bulletin*, 54:644, 282.

Yallop, D. (1971), *To Encourage the Others*, London, W. H. Allen.

—— (1972), *To Encourage the Others*, camera script viewed at BBC WAC.

Yeats, W. B. (1990), 'Easter 1916', *W. B. Yeats Collected Poetry*, London, Pan, 93–5.

Zavattini, C. (1978), 'A thesis on neo-realism', in D. Overbey (ed.), *Springtime in Italy: A Reader on Neo-Realism*, London, Talisman Books, 67–78.

Zola, E. (1964), *The Experimental Novel & Other Essays*, translated by Belle M. Sherman, New York, Haskell House.

Television and radio: selected appearances and tribute broadcasts, in chronological order

Late Night Line-Up (BBC2, 22 April 1970), discussion of *Sovereign's Company* with Don Shaw.

Late Night Line-Up (BBC2, 20 March 1972), discussion of *Under the Age* with E. A. Whitehead.

Real Time (BBC2, 21 March 1974), discussion of *Penda's Fen* with David Rudkin.

Tonight (BBC1, 23 January 1978), discussion of *Scum* with Alasdair Milne and Peter Fiddick.

The South Bank Show (LWT/ITV, 28 January 1978), short segment on banning of *Scum* with a statement by Roy Minton.

Arena: 'When is a play not a play?' (BBC2, 17 April 1978), includes brief location interview with Clarke on the banning of *Scum*.

The South Bank Show (LWT/ITV, 17 June 1979), Segment on *Scum* film, featuring behind-the-scenes footage and a studio discussion chaired by Melvyn Bragg with Clarke, former Borstal inmate Alan Leader and former deputy governor Mike Whitlam. *Scum* section postponed from 3 June.

Did You See ...? (BBC2, March 1982), discussion of *Baal*.

Independent Local Radio (1983), phone-ins on *Made in Britain* (see Chapter 3).

Did You See ...? (BBC2, 13 January 1985), discussion of *Contact*.

Open Air (BBC1, 8 October 1987), discussion of *Road*.

Open Air (BBC1, 21 January 1989), discussion of *Elephant*.

The Late Show (BBC2, 25 January 1989), features recorded statement from Los Angeles by Clarke on *Elephant*.

Right to Reply (C4, 26 January 1989), discussion of *Elephant* with Danny Boyle.

The Late Show (BBC2, 27 February 1989), interview with Clarke.

Film 4 Today (C4, 22 July 1990), David Rudkin introduction to repeat broadcast of *Penda's Fen*.

Director – Alan Clarke (BBC2, 12 July 1991), Corin Campbell-Hill's posthumous tribute featured interviews with collaborators and critics. Shown as part of the Alan Clarke Season (see below). Released as part of *The Alan Clarke Collection* (2004) (see below).

Alan Clarke Season (BBC2, 12 July to 10 August 1991), David Leland introductions to repeat broadcasts of *To Encourage the Others* (12 July), *Made in Britain* (13 July), *Contact* (20 July), the first transmission of *Scum* (27 July), and repeats of *Road* (3 August) and *The Firm* (10 August).

Scum (1999), DVD featured interviews with Roy Minton and Clive Parsons.

Alan Clarke: 'His Own Man' (Film Four, 18 September 2000), Andy Kimpton-Nye's posthumous tribute featuring interviews with collaborators and family.

Memories of Elephant (Film Four, September 2000), Andy Kimpton-Nye's brief featurette on *Elephant* featured interviews recorded for *Own Man*, some not previously shown.

The Big Picture (BBC Radio London, 9 February 2002), preview of NFT season featured interview with Richard Kelly and Vicky Murdoch.

Tim Roth: Made in Britain (Film Four, 8 April 2002), Andy Kimpton-Nye's brief featurette on *Made in Britain* featured interview recorded for *Own Man*, some not previously shown, first shown at National Film Theatre in March 2002.

Happy Birthday BBC Two (BBC2, 20 April 2004), brief segment from *Elephant*.

The Alan Clarke Collection (2004), DVD in US which included commentaries on both versions of *Scum*, *Made in Britain* and *Elephant*.

Scum (2005), DVD featured both versions, with commentaries.

Index